The Christian Faith

For Oliver

The Christian Faith

An Introduction to Christian Doctrine

Colin E. Gunton

King's College, London

BT
75.3
.G86
2002

Copyright © Colin E. Gunton 2002

The moral right of Colin E. Gunton to be identified as author of this work has been asserted in accordance with the Copyright, Designs and Patents Act 1988.

First published 2002

2 4 6 8 10 9 7 5 3 1

Blackwell Publishers Ltd
108 Cowley Road
Oxford OX4 1JF
UK

Blackwell Publishers Inc.
350 Main Street
Malden, Massachusetts 02148
USA

British Library Cataloguing in Publication Data

A CIP catalogue record for this book is available from the British Library.

Library of Congress Cataloging-in-Publication Data

Gunton, Colin E.
    The Christian faith: an introduction to Christian doctrine / Colin E. Gunton.
    p. cm.
    Includes bibliographical references and indexes.
    ISBN 0–631–21181–0 (alk. paper)—ISBN 0–631–21182–9 (pbk. : alk. paper)
    1. Theology, Doctrinal. I. Title.
    BT75.3 .G86 2002
    230—dc21

                                                                    2001001139

Typeset in 10.5/13pt Bembo
by Kolam Information Services Pvt. Ltd, Pondicherry, India
Printed in Great Britain by MPG Books Ltd, Bodmin, Cornwall

This book is printed on acid-free paper.

Contents

Preface

'Faith' is much in vogue; any faith, it would seem, is good so long as it is faith. (The embarrassing fact that the totalitarian and terrorist political creeds of our time also involve what can only be called faith does not always exercise the enthusiasts for 'inclusiveness'). The stress on faith as a universal subjective dimension of the human being has a long history, and took its most influential form in the theology of Friedrich Schleiermacher at the beginning of the nineteenth century. However, that is not the only way to speak of faith, for when we use an expression like 'the faith', we should realize that there is an objective dimension which can be stressed over against this. It refers to the content of faith, that which is believed in contrast to the faculty by which we believe it. It is this which will be the main focus of this book, despite the fact that the title is the same as that by which Schleiermacher's *Glaubenslehre* is translated into English, and despite the fact that it moves to its conclusion in a manner similar to that of Schleiermacher's great book.

The reason for the approach taken in this book is that Christianity is a faith which – among other things – claims certain things to be true: about God, the world and our human species. In recent times a number of strategies have been devised which attempt to bypass or evade Christianity's claim to be true, but they will not finally work – except to bring about the contempt in which evasions of the faith's offensive truth claims are justly held. This claim for truth is made first of all by a community of belief known as the church, and takes the form of articulation in creeds and confessions. Over the course of history, there has been – at least until the era we call 'modern' – a general and remarkable unanimity about the content and centrality of those creeds. It is when theologians begin to articulate the details that the real disagreements begin. In fact it could be said that such credal agreement as has been achieved came about largely as the result of the labours, including the major disagreements, of theologians. The salutary feature of the process is that it teaches us that truth in all spheres, and especially this one, can be achieved, and then only precariously, by the most rigorous public debate and testing.

As part of the process, there have developed schools and movements in theology, and it also remains the case that theologians are like musicians and writers in that each one has his or her own distinctive emphases, style and preoccupations. The latter tend particularly to be shaped by the kind of debates that go on at the time of writing. Theology is a part of a broader human culture, and it not only uses the language of that culture, however much it may wish to adapt that language, but is also exercised by the questions which dominate its time. Today, a theologian cannot fail to be affected by science, by ecological concerns, by movements such as feminism and the range of phenomena called postmodernism, and so on. Particular theologians who seek to be as loyal as possible to the church's credal tradition none the less engage with it in a particular world, and as particular people. They also, after centuries of debate, reveal a consciousness of where they believe theology to have gone wrong, in encouraging, perhaps, forms of thought and behaviour that are not appropriate to the Christian gospel and which therefore diminish rather than enhance the life of the world.

The reference to recent movements and trends also requires some explanation about the method of approach taken in the book. It is common, especially in the modern era, for theologians to devote the opening pages, or even chapters, of their books to a justification and description of the practice in which they are engaging. The very possibility of theology has been called into question in recent centuries, and appears to be in need of defence. Thus theologians begin with proofs of God, an account of the universality of religion or a defence of the authority of scripture and/or the Christian tradition. More recent trends may appear to demand even more, for they call into question not merely theology, but all claims from any source for objective truth. The assumption or belief of such 'postmodern' approaches is that all foundations are now in question, and must therefore be reviewed in some way or other.

I myself believe that they are right to suggest that the foundations of our culture have been shaken, but not in identifying what they are. It is essentially a crisis of belief in the reality of creation. There is a crisis because, and only because, confidence has waned in the teaching that God has so set the world on its foundations that it is a proper place for the various human enterprises we know as culture, including those whose quest is for truth. The right theological response to this is to reaffirm the doctrine of creation, not as an act of irrational assertion, but in such a way as to demonstrate its rational viability. That is to say, it is to set out the doctrines of creation and providence as together constituting one way of seeing the world, a way which in its turn illuminates our human condition as we live it out in time. When all other foundations have failed there is a case not so much for repeating an old one which appears to have failed, but for an attempted reformulation which takes into account some of the reasons for its failure. That is the reason for the shape that this book takes, laying first a theological foundation in a doctrine of creation and providence, and then proceeding to other aspects of the whole.

This book represents one man's attempt to articulate the heart of the Christian faith's claim to be true. That it is a man's, and indeed a white westerner's, enterprise may in the eyes of some disqualify it from achieving what it sets out to do. That, in my view, is just silly, for all human beings have advantages and disadvantages inherent in their particular situation, and their faithfulness is judged not by where they begin, but by where they go on its basis. Christianity, for all its communal and credal form, is a religion of particularities, centrally those of Israel and the Jewish Jesus of Nazareth, and at its best has always encouraged by its communal form the development of the individuality of its members. I have written what appears in this book because I believe it to be true; otherwise, I hope, I would not have written so. Others will recognize in it things that are at best one-sided, at worst errors and distortions. That is the nature of all human enterprises, and especially the theological one.

When a first draft of this book was completed, I had a conversation with my colleague John Webster about whether one can say that there is a single leading idea in scripture. If there is, then 'life' – that indefinable word which is so central to our habitation of our world – has some claim to be it. In the beginning, God gives life; in the middle, he raises Jesus Christ from the dead, itself a promise of new life now and at the end, when God will be all in all. It seems to me, on looking back on the book after it has been written, that something like that emphasis appears in its pages, perhaps in part between its lines, and I shall await with interest the responses of readers and critics to see whether they recognize something of the same.

The book has been organized in a way that achieves a balance between two polar concerns. The primary division, into chapters, represents the different topics which must be treated in any account of the Christian faith that hopes to be reasonably complete. The creeds tend to divide the subject matter into three or four, roughly corresponding first to creation, second to the person and work of Christ and finally to the work of the Spirit in the realizing and completing of what are called the benefits of salvation in ecclesiology and eschatology. Each of the three parts, and each of the 10 chapters, could on its own comfortably be the subject of a book, indeed of a lifetime's work. The part and chapter divisions are therefore, as that description implies, divisive, in dividing up the subject matter. Creation is not christology, justification is not sanctification. And yet if any of the divisions is to be understood, it must be understood in relation to the others and to the whole of which it forms a part. The continuous numbering which runs from the beginning through to the end is designed to indicate this aspect of things, to be both cumulative and systematic in showing how things belong together. This is not the same as attempting to arrange things into a system – for the Christian faith cannot without falsification be systematized – but to show one way in which they can be arranged cumulatively, in order that something may be understood of how beginning, middle and end belong together. It would be possible to arrange things in other ways, without necessary detriment to the subject matter, though it does not follow that any arrangement would do. If ever the work is developed into an extended work, it is likely – for example – that the first part and the conclusion would together form the basis of a study of God and creation. But that alteration of order would immediately necessitate some reorganizations of the material, with a different way of referring forward to material that is not yet treated. As for the form of that project, much depends on the response which this book receives. Already there has been some.

In the course of writing this book, and, more important, of preparing for it over many years, I have been taught in many kinds of ways by many people, some of them neither male nor western – nor, indeed, believers – in the growing range of family relationships and friendships with which I am blessed as I grow older. Members of the Research Institute in Systematic Theology met in seminar to discuss the book chapter by chapter, and I am grateful to Steve Holmes who chaired the sessions and contributed characteristically probing questions. Of the student members, I am particularly grateful to my friend Shirley Martin who subsequently read the whole of the typescript, and made many helpful comments – in places saving me from a near Pelagianism in the accounts of human freedom. Others who have read all or part of the typescript and contributed in different ways are my wife Jenny, my daughter Sarah and my friend Anne Gourlay. I am grateful to my other daughter, Carolyn, for meticulous index compilation. The book is dedicated to her and Peter's son Oliver.

Chapters 4–6, the christological section of the book, were delivered in revised form as the 2000 Shenfield Lectures, at St Mary's Church, Shenfield, Essex. I am grateful to the Rector, the Reverend Canon Paul Brett, for the invitation, and to members of the audience whose questions and comments have helped me to clarify what is probably the most complex of the three main divisions of the work.

Most quotations from scripture are taken from the New International Version of the Bible. Where I have been discontented with that, I have either drawn from elsewhere or translated myself.

Colin Gunton

King's College, London
February, 2001

Part 1

Foundations: 'Maker of Heaven and Earth'

Chapter 1

Establishing: The Doctrine of Creation

§1. The Mediation of Creation

To create is to establish, to bring into being something previously without existence. This holds whether we are speaking of a piece of disposable art in the modern fashion, something as changing as a garden, or the 'possession for all time' intended, with remarkable success, by the Greek historian Thucydides and achieved by the greatest artists and musicians. Many of the biblical characterizations of God's creating action speak of it in this straightforward way. Yet they do it in such a way as to suggest that there is only one to whom the act of creation in its full sense can properly be attributed. The indescribable act which they seek to describe, at once ordinary and extraordinary, has its counterpart in the language they use, for in their accounts of the world's creation the writers drew on myths current in their time, and yet they used them in such a way as to bring out the exceptional character of the action to which they sought to refer. Neither feature should surprise us, for they had only the human resources that lay to hand – as we do when we attempt to write a poem or paint a picture, however 'original' we hope to be; and yet Hebrew thought about creation is also absolutely unique.

A second introductory point follows. All eras are not only marked by their times and places but also share in a common human culture, in which a recognizable set of questions and concerns recurs again and again: not necessarily all of the topics all of the time, but some of them all of the time and all of them some of the time. Perennial among the questions is the notion of creation, in the broad sense of the bringing into being of the world in which we work out our lives. We may think that the modern quest for the first infinitesimal moment after the 'big bang' is unique, but it is so only in the respect of being the particular form that a universal quest takes in a world dominated by science. In other respects it is the same quest as that of the ancient myth-maker, the early Greek cosmologist and the Buddha: not only to ask the traditional question, 'Why is there something rather than nothing?', but also to discover what makes the world the setting for the human life that we wish to inhabit as meaningfully as possible. The unique achievement of the biblical writers was that the common and inherited stock of language was drawn upon in the interest of a notion of creation as personal divine action. Noting the salient features of this will enable us to approach the question of what is distinctive about Christian claims for the meaning of the universe, because the biblical account was only in a limited respect yet another version of the universal human curiosity to plumb the meaning of things. They put something much more disturbing and unexpected in face of the human quest to understand: a characterization of a God strangely remote from the objects of normal religious quests, as if they were impatient to replace their neighbours' religious enterprises with something far more mysterious and transcendent. This takes two forms, as follows.

In the first place, God's establishing action according to biblical re-presentation is uniquely free and sovereign. Whether we consider the myths of the surrounding cultures or the emerging philosophies of the early Greek cosmologists, we find notions of a struggle with essentially intractable material. In these cases, divine agency in some way mirrors human limit-ations, typified as they are by a perpetual struggle against opposition and finally death. In complete contrast, in some easily recognizable but not so easily describable way, the Bible's God is above all that. He is indisputably the Lord. That does not make belief in him any easier; in fact the reverse. It reinforces the difficulty of believing that the universe is in the hands of someone good and powerful rather than something simply indifferent – the fashionable modern belief – or actively hostile. The more powerful the god, the more perplexing becomes his apparent refusal to overcome suffering and death. This worry, if that is what it is, will be with us to the end of this book. Yet the overall biblical teaching, from Genesis to Job and Hebrews to Revelation, maintains this absolute divine sovereignty. Without the funda-mental presupposition of God's sovereign disposing we shall understand neither the Bible's God nor the faith that derives from his revelation; nor, I believe, the world in which we live.

In the second place, the biblical writers employ a varied, but overall consistent, pattern of understanding the processes of creation – of what is called the mediation of the divine action. This appeal to mediation in some respects simplifies but in others complicates all that we shall have to say about God's relation to the world. Mediation denotes the way we understand one form of action – God's action – to take shape in and in relation to that which is not God; the way, that is, by which the actions of one who is creator take form in a world that is of an entirely different order from God because he made it to be so. It is similar to the way in which we understand human actions to take shape in the world: for example, how the intention to make a pot is realized in the relation between the potter's hands and the clay which takes shape through them, or in the way the poet's feeling, ideas and experience take shape in words on a page. Again and again we find Jewish and Christian writers likening God to one who executes his intention by a mere word of command: he spoke, and it came to be. 'And God said, "Let there be light," and there was light' (Gen. 1.3). The notion of creation by word is particularly strong in one of the three religious traditions which stand in some relation to the Old Testament, Islam, where God simply orders the world into being: 'Be'.

However, the model of creation by commanding or calling into being by word requires some qualification in Christian theology. This is indeed free and sovereign action, but is in some mysterious way also action that accommodates itself to the nature of that which it brings about. It is noticeable that in the Genesis account God does not say: 'Be', but 'let there be'. This is distinctive in maintaining a balance between the command and the being of that which is established. There is a greater stress on what we might call the giving of space to be to a reality that is other than God. The world is not simply a function of God's action, though that remains in the centre, but that action creates something that has its own unique and particular freedom to be. As Francis Watson has pointed out, there is in Genesis a more varied pattern of mediation than simply creation by word.[1] First, God's creating action involves the *forming* of that which has been created. This is particularly applicable to the human creation, for example in

[1] Francis Watson, *Text, Church and World. Biblical Interpretation in Theological Perspective* (Edinburgh: T. & T. Clark, 1994), pp. 142–3.

both Genesis 2 and Psalm 139: 'For you created my inmost being; you knit
me together in my mother's womb. I praise you, for I am fearfully and
wonderfully made' (Ps. 139. 13–14). A similar pattern of craftsmanship is to
be found in chapters 38–9 of the Book of Job, applying the same notion of
formation to the wonders of the natural world: 'The earth takes shape like
clay under a seal; its features stand out like those of a garment' (Job 38. 14).
We should not be afraid of the personal language, as if it were somehow
inappropriate to the divine mystery. There is, as we shall see when we come
to give an account of human being, nothing higher than the personal, for to
be human is to be made in the divine image, and that centrally means to be
personal. For our purposes, however, the point is that the spacious movement of Genesis 1's story of the days of creation indicates that God 'takes his
time', in the sense of conforming his action to that which he makes, as a
great playwright allows a play to conform to the immanent or intrinsic
development of character and plot. Barth sometimes calls this form of action
God's patience. 'God's patience [is] his will... to allow to another... space
and time for the development of its own existence, thus conceding to its
existence a reality side by side with His own...'[2] We shall learn more of
this characteristic of the Bible's God as the book proceeds.

At this place, however, we must pause to say something more about the
language of Genesis, and especially its ordering of God's action into a
pattern of days. It may be that the writer did believe that God created in
six days of 24 hours, although that would not be my own judgement. But
anxiously for that reason to attempt to adapt the pattern to, for example, eras
of evolution, in order to make it conform to modern structures of understanding, is to wrench the writing out of its context. It is both to tear it out
of the hands of its author, who said what he said for good theological
reasons, and to divorce it from the broader context of biblical conviction
about creation, which takes a variety of forms while continuing to express
the same basic belief. To treat this as 'primitive science', as some rationalist
critics have done, is to misunderstand it, and to overprivilege the modern
way of understanding. What is significant is that, as Basil of Caesarea
(c. AD 330–379) said, the pattern of days serves to establish the world's
relation to eternity.[3] We have seen already that the pattern of mediation in

---

[2] Karl Barth, *Church Dogmatics*, translation edited by G. W. Bromiley and T. F.
Torrance (Edinburgh: T. & T. Clark, 1957–75), vol. 2/1, p. 410.

[3] Basil of Caesarea, *Hexaemeron*, 2. 8.

Genesis enables us to develop a notion of the patient creator who takes his time, and so gives the creation its own way of being. The often quoted graffito that 'Time is God's way of preventing everything from happening at once' has here its own profound wisdom, especially in face of our modern world's frantic attempt to force the pace of time. Shakespeare's saying shows us a better way, including as it does a reference to the dynamic of time: 'How many things by season seasoned are/to their right praise and true perfection.'[4] The biblical notion of time as that which God gives to things for their right development is further elaborated in Genesis' depiction of God's resting on the seventh day. This appears to be a naive way of speaking until we realize that it allows the time of creation to point forward to its fulfilment according to the purposes of God. The creation is not a static and timeless lump of matter, but – and we have already compared God to a playwright – something with a direction and destiny. Creation is God's project, the block of marble which he and those to whom the creation is entrusted are, enabled by him, to shape into things of beauty, truth and goodness. That is why New Testament symbolism sometimes suggests that on Easter Sunday the eighth day of creation begins, the resurrection of Jesus being the beginning of the creation's reorientation to its proper end, its being placed again into its right direction.[5]

However that may be, and we shall not be able to avoid constant recurrence to it, our task here is to continue to explore the theology of mediation. We have seen that creation by personal word and creation in terms of craftsmanship are together ways of giving time and space to that which God creates. A third notion of mediation is that according to which God enables the created world to operate, as some of the mediaeval theologians of creation put it, 'ministerially'. This means that parts of the world are empowered to serve as mediators of God's creation of other parts. So God says, 'Let the earth bring forth . . .' (Gen. 1.11, 20 – this time the sea – and 24), as a mother brings forth a child from her womb. The juxtaposition of 'Let the earth bring forth living creatures' (v. 24) and 'God made the beasts . . .' (v. 25) shows that we are still in the realm of God's action, which is not surrendered to the earth. We truly are encountered by an account of

[4] William Shakespeare, *The Merchant of Venice*, 5. i. 108–9
[5] Douglas B. Farrow, *Ascension and Ecclesia. On the Significance of the Doctrine of the Ascension for Ecclesiology and Christian Cosmology* (Edinburgh: T. & T. Clark, 1999), p. 7, note 23.

creation in which a sovereign God enables the world to be itself. Worldly agencies are enabled by divine action to achieve their own 'subcreating', not in the absolute way that God creates, but relatively, as creation from what already is. There, as we shall learn, is the basis for human creativity in art, science and ethics: in a word, for wisdom, that neglected and difficult way of speaking of the best features of the human habitation of the world. However, if we are to go on, as we shall, to highlight the unique capabilities and responsibilities of the human race in the realm of what we call culture, this notion of men and women as the chief ministers of creation must not blind us to the fact that the difference between human and non-human creatures is relative, not absolute. God grants to the lesser creatures their own capacity to generate beauty and truth. The garden needs to be tended, but the gardener does not make the plants grow, merely provides some of the conditions for their growth. If this side of things had not been as neglected as it has in the history of theology, the theory of evolution might not have proved the stumbling block to belief that it has in recent times.

The way in which the Old Testament lays the groundwork for the New Testament's more explicitly Christian conception of the mediation of creation is to be read both in Genesis' varied patterns and in other Old Testament conceptions of mediation, for example, 'By the word of the Lord the heavens were made, and all their host by the breath of his mouth' (Ps. 33.6). To be sure, the psalmist is not here being explicitly trinitarian, for he is in effect saying the same – or a very similar – thing twice in two parallel metaphors for sovereign divine action. But it is none the less a conception of mediation that is subsequently to be filled out in the New Testament in the light of Jesus Christ. Similarly, in some later Old Testament writings the conception of God's wisdom is employed in the service of mediation, as a way of expressing the way by which God interacts concretely with the material world, for example, 'I [wisdom] was there when he set the heavens in place, when he marked out the horizon on the face of the deep ... Then I was the craftsman at his side ...' (Prov. 8.27,30). There is also a varied tradition of speech about God's Spirit, beginning with the obscure notion of the Spirit of God 'hovering over the face of the deep' in Genesis 1.2. The translation of this as 'the wind of God', briefly fashionable for a time, seems not to be convincing, but the fact that the same Hebrew word is used for wind, breath and spirit, recalls the fact that we are not here concerned with something opposed or hostile to matter and embodiment, as in some

modern notions of spirit or spirituality, but with a Spirit in positive relationship to all the creation, the 'material' and 'spiritual' alike. So, God breathes
into Adam the breath of life (Gen. 2.7) and in a great psalm of creation it
is the material living world over which God's Spirit presides. '[W]hen
you take away their breath, they die and return to the dust. When you
send your Spirit, they are created, and you renew the face of the earth'
(Ps. 104.30,31).

The Spirit is shown to be the mediator not only of God's creation, but
also of his recreating and transforming action, as in Ezekiel's great vision of
the valley of bones, which is, as we shall see, an important passage for our
understanding of the resurrection of Jesus. The prophet puns on the three
meanings of the Hebrew *ruach*: 'Come from the four winds, O breath [or
Spirit!], and breathe into these slain, that they may live' (Ez. 37.9). Here the
Spirit is God's free and unpredictable power of life and renewal in action.
The Spirit is not the Spirit of the 'spiritual' or 'religious' part of the human
person, but of life in all its dimensions. 'So I prophesied as I was commanded, and breath entered them; they came to life . . . ' (v.10). The Spirit's
relation to life was picked up in the early church's confession of 'the Lord
and giver of life', and it is above all with life – that indefinable characteristic
of some forms of being in our world, what we call the animal and the
vegetable – that this also indefinable 'Spirit' is concerned. This has in turn
led some writers to see 'life' as peculiarly the Lord's realm, his special
territory, so to speak.[6]

It did not take the New Testament writers long to identify God's creating
Word with Jesus Christ, who is that Word become part of the created order.
The opening affirmations of John's Gospel, that without the Word nothing
was made that was made, have their antecedents in some of the earliest
writings of the New Testament. 1 Corinthians 8.6 – 'one Lord Jesus Christ,
through whom are all things and through whom we exist' – is probably the
earliest literary association of Christ with creation, and may be quoting an

---

[6] All meals are intrinsically religious occasions, indeed sacrifices, and were so
understood especially in Israel. For all life belongs intimately to God, so that the
killing involved in eating – which we do not at all avoid by eating vegetables – is an
intrusion into his domain . . . . Sharing a meal is therefore always a communal act of
worship and establishes fellowship precisely before the Lord. (Robert W. Jenson,
Systematic Theology, vol. 2, *The Works of God* (New York and Oxford: Oxford
University Press, 1999), p. 185.)

already widely used credal affirmation. Numerous other New Testament writings make the same kind of point.[7] In the theology of creation, therefore, language of mediation by God's Word enables us to speak both of God's free involvement within his creation and, ultimately, in Christ, of his equally free and sovereign identification with a part of it. The theology of the creating Word indicates that God can become 'worldly' while remaining truly God. Correspondingly, the Spirit's action is characterized by freedom both over against and in relation with the creation. This gains sharp focus in one place above all. Some theologians have argued, on the basis of texts such as Romans 8.11 – 'the Spirit of him who raised Jesus from the dead' – and 1 Peter 3.18 – 'put to death in the body but made alive by the Spirit' – that it is by his Spirit that God raised Jesus from the dead, and this enables us to make a general, although not absolute, distinction between the Son's and the Spirit's ways of mediating. Simply put, the incarnation of the eternal creating Word in the human being, Jesus of Nazareth, betokens God's freedom of action *within* the material world, while the Spirit's sovereign action is the mark of God's freedom toward or *over against* it – from outside, so to speak. Irenaeus of Lyons (fl. c. AD 180), the church's greatest theologian of creation, spoke here – far more sophisticatedly than may appear – of God the Father's 'two hands', the Son and the Spirit, who are the divine mediators of his action in and towards the world. 'For with Him were always present the Word and Wisdom, the Son and the Spirit, by whom and in whom, freely and spontaneously, He made all things . . .'[8]

§2.   The Meaning of the Doctrine of Creation

The theology of mediation sketched in the previous section was designed to show how it is that God is active both towards the world and within its structures. It enabled four points to be made about what is taught by the doctrine of creation. First, it establishes the fundamental and only distinction that has to be made in this realm: 'The first proposition [of a doctrine of

---

[7] See Colin Gunton, *The Triune Creator. A Historical and Systematic Study* (Edinburgh: Edinburgh University Press and Grand Rapids: Eerdmans, 1998), pp. 20–2 for a brief rehearsal of the evidence.

[8] Irenaeus, *Against the Heresies*, 4. 20. 1.

creation]: that God creates means that there is other reality than God and that it is really other than he.'[9] This means in turn that the only meaningful distinction between different kinds of being – in technical terms, ontological distinction – is between creator and creation. There are no intermediate forms that are half divine and half created, or which in some other way fill the intervening 'space' between creator and creature. God both maintains and crosses that space by means of the energies of his Son and Spirit, through them allowing and enabling the world to be itself. If angels do exist, they belong as truly in the created realm as the rest of the world.[10] However, this *duality* of God and the world is not a dualism of the kind that divides one sector of created reality from another – body from soul, mind from matter. There are two realities, God and the world he has made, each what they are in their own proper sphere. Looking forward, we can see that the basis for this duality-in-relation is to be found in the fact that in Jesus Christ the creator and the created meet without any subversion of the being of the other. Already, however, the author of Genesis has his own means of subverting the otherwise universal ancient view that some parts of the world are at least semi-divine. Not only is light created before the sun and the moon, but those 'heavenly beings', worshipped as divine in ancient cultures – and in modern astrology? – are almost contemptuously relegated to their place under God. The great and lesser lights – 'and the stars also', deities relegated to an afterthought – are simply hung up by God as lights, 'to mark seasons and days and years . . . and to give light to the earth' (Gen. 1.14–15). The whole universe – everything that is not God – is created to be truly itself, a realm other than the divine, because it is established by God's mediated and personal relation to that which he has made.

Second, we must hasten to add that rather than its being a slight to the world that it is not God, or even godlike, quite the reverse is implied. It is no discredit to the world to be worldly, because that is what it is graciously made to be; it is as such, in its own right, that it is good. Everything made by God is good, indeed very good, because it is made through, to, and for Jesus Christ. The problems this raises we shall have to meet in due course, but they scarcely need pointing. The world we encounter is very far from good, and seems to present us with a combination of good and evil, so that those

---

[9] Jenson, *Systematic Theology*, vol. 2, *The Works of God*, p. 5.

[10] See Revelation 19.10: Then I fell down at his [the angel's] feet to worship him, but he said . . . 'You must not do that! I am a fellow servant with you and your brethren . . .'.

religions which have speculated that there are both good and evil divine principles at work in the world have some of the evidence on their side. It is by no means self-evident that we live in a world presided over by a good creator. The repeated refrain in the liturgical progress of Genesis 1 leaves us in no doubt, however, that this was the judgement of the priestly writer who composed the final form of this document fairly late in Israel's history. The sixth day, on which we, the most problematic inhabitants of the earth – problematic to ourselves and to God – were created, ends with an even more emphatic version of the refrain: 'God saw everything that he had made, and it was very good' (Gen. 1.31).

The third point to be made with the help of our theology of mediation, and specifically the New Testament teaching that the creation was formed 'in Christ', is that it is created to be the realm of one who holds it together as a unity.[11] There is one universe, and it is not only a law-abiding universe, but one in which the same laws hold throughout its vast extent. Different conceptions of both its unity and its lawfulness are, however, available. Let us review some that have been proposed in recent centuries, for their differences reveal something of the importance of our topic. There have been pantheistic systems, like that of the philosopher Spinoza (1632–77), which have held that every part of the universe derives necessarily from the state of the whole. This whole is at the same time and in different respects both God and the universe, so that according to Spinoza the universe is so rigid a unity that plurality is effectively non-existent. The state of the whole determines everything, so that a thoroughly determinist conception of law prevails in a kind of cosmic totalitarianism. Everything within this thing known as God-or-nature has to be what it is, and a thing or event can no more be other than it is than a triangle can decide to have more than three angles totalling one hundred and eighty degrees. Similarly, there have been systems which conceive the world more on the analogy of a machine than of a geometrical theorem, with or without a creating deity, and they also have tended to see all variety and multiplicity as simply a function of the state of the whole. We shall meet this world and its clockmaker deity from time to time in this book, because it has had a dominating influence in our world, producing conceptions of natural law which have increasingly been

---

[11] What are we to make of the 'in' in Colossians 1. 16: 'For in him were created all things in heaven and on earth . . .'? For a discussion, see Gunton, *The Triune Creator*, pp. 140–3.

called into question since the nineteenth century, but which die hard. Only apparently at the other extreme there have been idealist systems, which have conceived the unity of things to be but a function of the human mind, but they, too, like the clockmaker deity, often subject the world ruthlessly to the unitary patterns the mind projects or decides.

Monistic systems of this kind are in different ways describable as 'modern' or 'modernist', and they contrast with recent tendencies to deny them in the name of plurality. Much recent thought has turned into a contest between exponents of the essential unity of things and those advocating a fundamental, even chaotic, plurality. Many currently fashionable schools and approaches claim or are given the label 'postmodernist', and they mostly live from their denial of the various forms of modernism on which they are parasitic. So cautious are they of any unifying concept or 'grand narrative' that they suggest, or sometimes dogmatically assert, that there is no single universe which can be understood in terms of the unity of being and truth, but that all is sheer, unrelated plurality. There is no single 'logos' or unity, because such conceptions are 'oppressive', imposing on the world – and often consequently on human beings – a 'totalizing' perspective which subjects reality to external constraints.

Against both of these tendencies, and this is our fourth point, the conception of mediation with which we are working establishes a fundamental unity to the world without prejudice to its variousness and diversity. Here also we come up against the problematic heritage of some influential early interpretations of Genesis 1 which held it to teach that God created a limited number of fixed forms or types of things as models for his creating work, rather as an architect draws a plan and then puts it into reality. Evolutionary theory's positing of an open multitude of developing forms threw this teaching into disrepute. Yet the text does not, or certainly need not, teach such a doctrine. It is far more concerned with the richness and variety of God's creative action. Karl Barth, commenting on the tendency of modern criticism also to miss the point of the mathematics of the writer, observes that 'although the author counts the days he does not count the works of God because they are innumerable . . .'[12] Genesis teaches an open world, full of the kind of rich possibilities for development that evolutionary theory teaches, although that is not to claim that it is consistent with all the varieties of Darwinist dogma, which are in any case often in competition with one another.

---

[12] Barth, *Church Dogmatics*, vol. 3/1, p. 144.

Against both ancient interpretation and modern distortion, an adequate notion of the mediation of creation enables us to hold together without strain the sheer multiplicity and variety of creation within the generous embrace of creation's God. All forms of reductionism are excluded, both those which would spiritualize the world – and here such ideologies as the so-called 'creation spirituality' are in view – and those which would seek to explain everything simply in terms of the configurations of brute matter – or brute genes. It is important here that the sheer variety of forms of being is kept in mind, as testimony to the richness of a universe that contains both living and non-living forms in miraculous diversity, interrelated and indeed interdependent, but all part of one world. Irenaeus, as usual in this connection, has something worth listening to carefully, although to make a similar point today we should need to make more of the varieties of natural species:

> [God] formed [all things] as he pleased, bestowing harmony on all things, and assigning them their own place . . . In this way he conferred on spiritual things a spiritual and invisible nature, on supercelestial things a supercelestial, on angels an angelical, on animals an animal . . . while he formed all things by his Word that never wearies.[13]

Corresponding to the variety of the forms of God's mediating action there is a richness of the forms which created being takes. It is, as we shall see, part of the concept of the human that there are beings who are not only alive but are endowed with that mysterious quality called spirit, received from God's Spirit. Our being spiritual, however, far from enclosing us in a merely spiritual world, enables us, like God but in our own embodied way, to transcend the apparent divisions within things: to engage creatively with the animal, vegetable and mineral worlds, and so further to enrich the diversity of being, through industry, horticulture and the manifold arts and sciences. The outcome is that the theology of mediation sketched here makes it possible to hold that while reference to Christ shows how we may hold the world together in unity, the Spirit is the principle of reality's variety and multiplicity, for it is the Spirit who enables all things to be what they are particularly created to be. We shall ever and again recur to God the Spirit's diversifying and particularizing action, because it is both important and neglected.

---

[13] Irenaeus, *Against the Heresies*, 2. 2. 4.

As something of an appendix to this section of the argument, something should be said about what can rather barbarously be called the 'degendering' of the creation relation. In the myths of antiquity, everywhere but in Israel, the world took its origins in sex and violence: either from the coupling of deities or from being founded on the corpse of a defeated rival (or, of course, a combination of both). We can refer here to the Greek myth of the coupling of earth and heaven, and its philosophical form in Plato's *Timaeus*, where the male 'father' and 'receptive' mother represent aspects of Plato's cosmic dualism. The biblical language of creation is free of any of the active male/passive female imagery that attends myth.[14] The world is created actively so that it may itself, under God, be 'active' in its own way, with the earth bringing forth its creatures, and the human race commanded to fill the earth and replenish it. The Old Testament distances its sovereign God from all such pagan associations, just as it does from any association of creation with violence.

§3.   Creator and Creation

This distancing of scripture's sovereign God from all the deities of the world around naturally leads into a treatment of God's attributes, those characteristics which mark out the distinctive features of his being. They have surfaced already from time to time, notably in two we have met, God's patience and his wisdom. Two more now come to our attention. The first is God's unknowability. This is a most difficult concept, because it can easily suggest that God is unknowable in every way. Christian belief contends that God is knowable, because he has made himself known, and especially in Jesus Christ, as an essentially personal and active deity. But we know him, as the writer of Genesis was enabled to know him, as one who sets the limits to our capacity to tie him down to the measures of the human mind. We can know him only as the one who cannot be subjected to the general criteria of human knowing, whether that knowing be ancient myth or modern philosophy and science. The doctrine of revelation, which we shall encounter briefly in chapter 3, is designed to give an account of God's unique

---

[14] New Testament practice is the same. Father and Son language is assimilated to the relation between Jesus and the one to whom he prayed, and so made to stand for a different kind of relationship altogether.

knowability, the knowability of one who gives himself to be known as the one that he is, and yet at the same time sets definite limits to human probing of that reality.

Another equally difficult attribute, God's omnipotence or all-powerfulness, requires somewhat more extended treatment in this context. The development of the notion is a peculiarly Christian one, although the way it has taken shape has not always redounded to the credit of its exponents. It is easy to formulate it in terms of an abstract contrast between awareness of our finite power and a supposedly infinitely powerful deity who can, according to a famous definition, will everything except a contradiction. This approach, however, will not do, because if God is simply power magnified to an infinite degree, then God is little distinguishable from a tyrant or the devil. It is better that we remember two things, only apparently in tension with one another. The first is that Paul centres his notion of divine power on the salvation achieved by Christ on the cross and the power of the proclamation of the gospel to reconcile lost sinners to their loving creator. To call Christ 'the power of God and the wisdom of God' (1 Cor. 1.24) privileges a certain way of exercising power. This must not, however, be sentimentalized, as it often is in an era which has become too conscious of excesses committed in the name of divine power. There is much talk of non-coercive love and power, and indeed, the cross is a sign that in one respect God indeed does not coerce. But that is not the whole story, for the resurrection of Jesus from the dead is an act of power of another kind and, although in no way to be divorced from the divine action on the cross, is coercive of reality in a strong sense. As John Donne's great sonnet celebrates, death the coercer is coerced.[15] These two central insights together entail that in some way or other we must hold together the power that is made real in the suffering of Jesus and that manifested, on the one hand, in his 'works of power' and, on the other, in his being raised from the dead. Both alike are grounded in the sovereign action of a creator whose will is that the creation be truly itself.

If we return to the doctrine of creation, we shall see that it is indeed the case that God is omnipotent. According to Greek thought, which formed the context for the development of Christian theology, the gods were not omnipotent, for there were certain things that they could not do. Homer's gods cannot alter the course of things determined by fate, and the abstract

---

[15] John Donne, 'Death be not Proud'.

world-principles devised by the philosophers to provide a rationalized alternative to the gods of mythology were equally impotent. Whatever they did, they did not create, for universally in Greek thought the universe is eternal in at least some respect, and the most that God or the divine principle can do is to shape it. The idea that a personal God should create everything that there is was simply not conceivable until the Christian gospel's theologians came along. Irenaeus was not the first to deny the eternity of the universe, but he was the first to direct a formidable array of arguments against those who would limit the power of the Bible's God. He makes appeal, so important for later theology, to the contrast between human and divine power: 'While men, indeed, cannot make anything out of nothing, but only out of matter already existing, yet God is in this point pre-eminently superior to men, that He Himself called into being the substance of his creation, when previously it had no existence.'[16] He similarly deploys the negative argument, that if anything other than God is eternal, as all of his opponents, philosophers and mythologizers alike, had held, then that performs the function of God, for it defines limits within which God is able to act.[17] Whatever constrains God's actions from without is effectively God. But, according to biblical witness, God was utterly sovereign, utterly unconstricted by anything other than being the kind of God that he is.

It is at this place that there is to be found the meaning of the Christian teaching that God creates out of nothing, that God is not to be likened, let us say, to a potter who makes a pot from the clay which is to hand; he is, rather, like one who makes both the clay and the pot. This teaching, which baffles understanding and is often rejected because there is no analogy to it in human experience, must be understood as an interpretation and summary of scripture's witness to God as a whole. There are a number of places in the Bible where it seems to be implied, but, as one commentator has observed, it is not a way of thinking that would occur to the Hebrew mind.[18] It is a distinctive piece of teaching, unique in the history of thought, and deriving from the challenge presented to the church by the culture of the world in which it lived. It has a number of implications, two of which concern us.

[16] Irenaeus, *Against the Heresies*, 2. 10. 4.
[17] Ibid., 2. 5. 4.
[18] Claus Westermann, *Genesis 1–11. A Commentary*, translated by J. J. Scullion (London: SPCK, 1984), p. 100.

The first is that our world has a beginning in time and a limit in space. 'Once' there was nothing; then there was a universe, because and only because God willed it. That this appears to be more supported by recent scientific theory than by its predecessors should encourage us, but not too much, because scientific theories, especially those speculative theories called cosmology, are like human beings in that they come and go, have their day and cease to be. Always we should remember that had theology been content to be limited to what was conceivable in its contemporary world, neither it nor indeed the natural science that is indirectly its child would have come into being.[19] The second important implication of the teaching is that we and the world do not come from God, from out of his being, but are what we are distinct from God and by virtue of his loving will. He wills that there be a reality other than himself, both for his own glory and for the sake of that world, and in that is to be found the very heart of our doctrine.

Unlike the definitions of the being of God and the person of Christ, the dogma of creation out of nothing was not made the subject of definition by an early church council, and appears to have been generally accepted, in theory if not always in clear practice, as the result of Irenaeus' decisive intellectual defeat of his opponents in the second century. It became the subject of a council's ruling only in the West, and as late as 1215, significantly in face of the threat presented by the newly fashionable philosophy of Aristotle, which taught the eternity of the world. But although its function is to exclude any rival universal powers, the doctrine takes its origin in a specific historical *context* which is decisive for shaping its *content*. Creation is not simply the outcome of God's will, of his sheer power, because we worship not power deified but the God and Father of our Lord Jesus Christ, a God whose power is exercised in the particular forms of mediation we have met. That God operates in the world by means of his 'two hands' both fills out and delimits our understanding of his power in creation. In his Son and by the power of his Spirit he identifies himself with a part of his world, demonstrating a capacity to interact freely and graciously with it, perfecting rather than constraining, or rather constraining its structures from within,

---

[19] All scientific theories purporting to demonstrate the eternity or infinity of the universe must remain no more than theory, for natural science is the discipline, or set of disciplines, that investigates the structure of *this* universe, as it is given to be understood. In principle, it is not qualified to move outside the universe in order to determine its limits and conditions.

according to their particular being. This is power as freedom, as the wise and patient freedom that is powerful enough to conform itself with the being and needs of its object both for the sake of that object and for the glory of its creator. God's action in Jesus Christ confirms, enlarges and perfects the pattern we met in our reference to the spacious movement of creation in Genesis 1. The resurrection is another kind of power, power eschatologically exercised, bringing into the present the promised redemption of all things, yet it too is power directed to the nature of the object, this time to its perfecting through time. As we have seen, this is a freedom over against the world, demonstrating the reality of the power of involvement, and further filling out what we mean by God's omnipotence. This is indeed complete power, but power ordered so that the world should become what it was created to be: truly the world, able in its own way, by being truly itself, to praise the one who made it.

We should not end this first foundational chapter without making a final essential point. Creation is very good: perfect. But perfect is not here a static concept. There are two senses in which we can use the word. We might say that a newborn baby is 'perfect', but it is there to become something else; not something else that is no longer itself – it is not to be turned into a pig – but a mature human being who is to be made perfect through time. Human beings are created to be perfected, and so in a different way is the whole creation – partly, as we shall see, by the activity of human agents. There is therefore no creation 'in the beginning' without an eschatological orientation. From the beginning, it has a destiny, a purpose. Creation is 'out of nothing' in that it is made both to be and to become something, not something else but something perfected, able to praise and give glory to God for what it has been enabled by him to become. It is therefore 'established' and cannot be annihilated unless God himself returns it to nothing, as he has contracted not to do. It is established, however, not as a timeless mechanism or cosmos, but to form the basis for a history whose meaning, through time, takes shape in its relation to its creator. We must then say that God has two purposes in creation, and they are precisely coincident: to make something that is valuable in itself, and to make something that is valuable in itself because it is created to serve God's glory. It will be the purpose of the remainder of this book to show that such a theology is neither as paradoxical nor as objectionable as may at first sight appear.

Chapter 2

Providence

§4. The Historical Context: Modern

It is sometimes observed that should the sun, that giant celestial light bulb, suddenly blow out, life in the solar system would be extinguished instantaneously. So, according to Christian belief, would it be were God to withdraw his sustaining and providential action. That which is created is held in being from day to day, indeed, from instant to instant, by the one who is not only creator but also upholder of that which he has made. Like so many of the beliefs once almost unquestioningly held in our western world, this is no longer something that can be assumed. The reasons for its loss lie in part in the development of mechanistic science – now widely believed to be at least qualified, if not rendered obsolete by later developments – and more especially the philosophy that turned an early modern scientific metaphor into an ideology, with its suggestion, if not dogmatic assertion, that a clockwork universe simply runs under its own steam, needing no continuing impulse from a creator.

There are, however, many more aspects to a theology of providence than this. A mere conservation or upholding could be achieved by many other entities than the biblical God: Plato's forms, for example, Aristotle's unmoved movers, or Spinoza's God-or-nature. We must here recall the eschatological note sounded from time to time in the previous chapter. The 'very good' creation is made to go somewhere, to be perfected by divine and human action, and that requires more than a mere holding in being. Providence involves a claim even more radical than that of the previous chapter: that God does not merely uphold but actively directs and involves himself in the day to day life of his creatures. That teaching, too, has been undermined by its early modern critics, perhaps notable among them the great Scottish philosopher, David Hume (1711–76). The debate takes us back into the thought of two of his predecessors, English and Irish respectively.[1] John Locke (1632–1704) sought to provide a philosophical basis for the burgeoning Newtonian science with – among other things – a doctrine of real causes. When one thing is shown regularly to follow another, it is reasonable, he held, to attribute the succession to an unseen but none the less real entity called a cause. It seems to us a commonsense belief: the stone thrown at the window causes the glass to shatter, even though there is nothing called a 'cause' that we can observe, only the stone and the glass. Similarly, Locke defended Christian belief by appeal to miracle. Miracles were things directly *caused* by God outside the normal run of things to provide evidence of his existence.

George Berkeley (1685–1753) did not like the drift of the supposition of hidden causes. Suppose that is the case – we may summarize and simplify his argument – is it not to make God redundant? Does it not suggest, imply even, that God is not required to account for the day to day running of the world because the 'causes' are adequate to explain the way things are? Berkeley rightly held that this is far more than a matter of miracles. If God is not at the heart of everyday reality, then he is effectively redundant, and no amount of appeal to miracles can bring him back. Berkeley therefore sought to abolish the necessity for hidden causes, wanting to say that all that was needed to account for events was that God caused them all directly. In the process of his abolition of hidden causes, however, he used an argument which gave a hostage to fortune. He showed that when we see one thing happen after another, and say that the first caused the second, all we see is first the one thing, then the other, and that is all – apart from the ever-present providential action of God – that there is. Hume's question to this was whether, in that case, even God was required. All that we know, he argued, is that things happen regularly, for example that fire burns and ice freezes. Anything more – whether hidden cause or God – is simply attributed by this philosopher to the mind's tendency to assume that the second will happen when we experience the first. There is, we might say, no logical

---

[1] Yes, there really were an Englishman, an Irishman and a Scotsman . . . , and the Irishman was the finest theologian among them.

necessity for the sun to rise tomorrow; all that we can say is that because it has happened on every day of our life so far, we come to expect it to continue to happen. The question about God is therefore unanswerable, because it is not truly askable in the first place. Rather inconsistently Hume also argued that miracles could not happen either, because, it seems, he believed that things had to happen the way they did. Whatever the case with that particular belief, he effectively undermined, and knew that he undermined, the Christian belief in God's providential government of the universe. The world goes its own way, but it is simply pointless to enquire how and why it does so.

Hume's doctrine has proved widely influential, but the internal contradictions in his case and the questionable, and indeed increasingly questioned, assumptions on which it depends, give cause for disagreement. It is a strange philosophy that wishes to rule out of court the deepest questions that human beings have sought to explore, among them the enquiry as to why things happen in the way that they do. Even after centuries of scientific exploration of the order of things, it is not self-evident that the world is an order, a reliable place where things happen according to knowable regularities. To be sure, human beings have always relied upon the fact that fire heats and that water is necessary for life. But much of what we are now told about the order of things appears on reflection to be quite miraculous, especially perhaps the fact that, according to the latest theories,[2] the earliest expansion of the universe was so fine-tuned that it produced, apparently spontaneously – whatever that might mean – the conditions for the development of life. Slightly slower, and the thing would have collapsed back in upon itself; slightly faster, and it would have dispersed, unformed, into empty space. It is not that this demonstrates a divine hand; but that, given other reasons for believing in God, it looks very much as though we have here a process that was intended. As one recent popular science writer, no Christian apologist, has written, 'We are truly meant to be here.'[3]

The broader theological case for providence, however, is based on something rather more substantial than arguments about causality and miracles. Indeed, in the Bible miracles are not for the most part used as a proof for

[2] And, we must remember, most scientific theories are doomed to be rejected or radically revised.
[3] Paul Davies, *The Mind of God. Science and the Search for Ultimate Meaning* (London: Penguin Books, 1992), p. 232.

things that would not otherwise be believed. They are part of a wider set of beliefs about the way God is and the way he works in the world. And here we reach a profound difference of basic conviction, not decidable by argument alone, about what we consider to be at the heart of our understanding of our world. Neither Hume's claim that at best our minds can guess at the meaning of things nor the biblical belief that all things happen under the governance of the creator is self-evident. To find out what is at issue between them we must ask why, in the latter case, the biblical writers do appear to take it as read that their God is the one that they believe him to be. For whatever reasons, and there were many, they had a confidence in God's upholding of the order of things – often a very hard-won confidence – that we should take seriously, if only because they lived in a more threatening world than ours, with few of the devices with which we more or less successfully stave off starvation and death by heat or cold. Because it was in some ways more difficult for them than it is for us to believe in providence we should listen very carefully to their reasons for believing what they did.

§5.   The Historical Context: Ancient

The doctrine of providence in the early church, was, like that of creation, hammered out in conversation with, and in partial dependence on, the conceptions of providence then current in the world. Two encounters were crucial. The first was that between Irenaeus, Origen and the Gnostics. The Gnostics – or rather some of them, for what is generalized under the name 'Gnosticism' was, and remains, a varied set of phenomena – believed that if things were as orthodox Christianity claimed them to be, under the control of a creating and redeeming God, then that God was manifestly unfair in his apportionment of good and evil, happiness and suffering. They therefore modified what was, according to Irenaeus, the universal teaching of the church, and held the material world, rather than human fault, to be the cause of evil. That world, they claimed, was the work not of the high God, but of a lesser divinity, often named the 'demiurge' or workman, whose incompetence was the reason for this patently inadequate world. Over against the bungling creator God of the Old Testament, they set the 'spiritual' God of the Christ, who had nothing to do with the material world, but, only apparently bodily himself, led those who were 'spiritual' into a higher, non-material redemption. This 'god's' providential action consisted in taking the enlightened ones out of the lower merely material world into a higher, 'spiritual' realm.

Theology had two strategies against this teaching, both of which involved its rejection, but which are in the end incompatible. Origen of Alexandria (c. AD 185–c.254), whose influence still remains, conceded part of the Gnostic case. He acknowledged that some human beings do receive in this world a worse deal than others, and therefore attributed the diversity of human fates in this world to the better and worse choices made by souls in a world created *before* this one. Correspondingly, he located God's providence in his provision of opportunity for a better, and ultimately redemptive, exercise of freedom in this world. Because, however, this appeared to imply that a return to wholeness might require a number of worlds after this one, and so a relative lack of control by God over the course of history, Origen's conception did not meet with approval. But its deepest weaknesses are to be seen in two other features. In his account, the fall took place before our world of time was created, with the result that the creation of this material world in which the writer of Genesis had so gloried became essentially a repair job, contingent on there having been a fall. It is a second-best resort. And because the creation of the world is conceived as instrumental to the greater good of human salvation, there is always a danger of 'spiritualizing'; of producing a merely 'religious' notion of salvation divorced from its setting in the world. The outcome is that providence is oriented to a return to a purely spiritual order outside and beyond this one, with the result that the importance of this life, this life as the particular embodied persons that we each are, becomes minimized, subordinated as it is to a higher end. And the second flaw – in the light of the forward movement of creation proposed in chapter 1 – is to be found in the fact that Origen's eschatology is one of return, a movement back to the beginning rather than forward to perfection. Accordingly, the destiny of human souls is to return to the timeless perfection of the beginning. Origen's doctrine of providence, therefore, takes the form of divine educative action by which the return to an original and spiritual starting point is realized. It therefore tends to orient human life out of this world to a higher realm beyond it at the expense of, rather than in the interests of, the perfection of the created world as a whole.

Irenaeus, by contrast, by virtue of his robust doctrine of the incarnation of the Son of God in the flesh, was able more resolutely to affirm the goodness of this world, which is for him, as it is created, the object of God's providential concern. His doctrine of recapitulation, which we shall meet in a later chapter, sees Jesus as achieving not the redemption of spiritual beings created before the material world, but the completion through redemption of material-spiritual, flesh and blood men and women. Jesus is, like them, a fully human being who, as the incarnate Son of God, relives the story of Adam and Eve. This time, however, he does not fall captive to sin, death and the devil, but overcomes them by his faithfulness and human integrity. Irenaeus' eschatology is not therefore one of return, *back* to spiritual conditions which prevailed before the world was created, but is a movement *forward* to the perfection of all things intended by the creator. God's providence has, therefore, a direct concern with the destiny of this world, whose structures – represented in the material realities bread and wine – are inextricably bound up with those who bear the image of their creator. God provides, that is to say, not for a *spatial* ascent out of the material world, but for a *temporal* movement in and with it, in eschatological perspective.

The second crucial encounter of theology with the world about it was with Stoicism, and took place in quite another way. Stoics were more or less pantheists in holding that the world itself was the divine being, and therefore created itself. They were also determinists, effectively denying human freedom and so giving rise to the popular use of the word 'stoical' as referring to the stiff upper lip that accepts unchangeable fate ('What will be, will be'). Just as Origen's theology of providence raises the questions of the relative weight given to spirit and matter in God's shaping of the way the world goes, Stoicism introduces the question of the relation of the human being to the cosmos, to what we might call the material world as a whole. How far are we free over against the world, for example the genes that shape our bodies and personalities? It is not surprising that early modern critics of the Christian doctrine of providence lighted upon this question. The metaphor of the world as a machine, applied to the world and sometimes to the human being too, suggested that human agents had no choice but to obey the laws of impersonal logic. In the hands of the Stoics' greatest modern successors, Spinoza and Kant, two opposing conceptions of providence emerged. Spinoza, as we have seen, was a fairly straightforward determinist, who held that our actions are without remainder predetermined. His successors are with us

---

[4] A readable discussion of the arguments about modern genetic determinism is Keith Ward, *God, Chance and Necessity* (Oxford: Oneworld, 1996).

today, mainly in biology, with their doctrines that our genetic make-up determines everything about who and what we are.[4]

At this stage, two remarks must be made. The first is that Darwin's own theory for the most part makes far more modest claims than this, being essentially an attempt to show how species emerge in a way similar to that in which human breeders develop desirable characteristics in the animals they domesticate or farm. Whether or not simply to disarm criticism, Darwin accepted that it would be possible for God to shape things in this way, or to create a world, as later Christian apologists were to argue, so wonderful that it was able to create itself, something we met in the discussion of ministerial creation in chapter 1.[5] What finally undermined Darwin's faith was not evolution as such, but the traditional problem of evil: that the process, involving so much apparent waste and suffering, was not good evidence of a providential deity. Although it did not take a theory of evolution to show that, it does suggest that any adequate doctrine of providence must be able, if not to 'explain' evil, at least to indicate something of the way in which its overcoming is begun and promised. The second remark to be made about evolution is that, theologically considered, the theory of evolution often does appear to provide an alternative to the biblical teaching of providence. Not God but the world provides all the reasons we need for why things are as they are, so that providence becomes a kind of inner-worldly mechanism or agency and thus a rival account to the theological. But that simply raises again our recurring question: what is to count as evidence, and for what kind of conception of providence?

We return, therefore, to our main argument. We have seen that the first modern alternatives to providence we have considered are monistic in that they attribute the direction of things to only one thing or only one kind of thing, whether the state of the universal machine or the state of the genes. Ranged in modern thought against the monism of providence is a far more dualistic concept. Owing much to the philosophers Descartes (1596–1650) and Kant (1724–1804), it makes a strong distinction between the outer, physical part of our being – its material shell – and our inner reason, will, existentiality (or whatever), which can generally be likened to the spiritual

---

[5] A celebrated author and divine has written to me that 'he has gradually learned to see that it is just as noble a conception of the Deity to believe that He created a few original forms capable of self-development...as to believe that He required a fresh act of creation to supply the voids caused by the action of His laws'. Charles Darwin, *The Origin of Species*, edited by Gillian Beer (Oxford: Oxford University Press, 1996), p. 388.

inner being posited by the Gnostics. While we may be mechanically determined from without, this approach holds, there is an inner core which is free; in some modern theories, absolutely free. According to this, or at least to its outcome in the modern doctrine of progress, the providential ordering of things is in the hands of the human race, who will by its knowledge and power bring about ever-improving states of things. Despite the mounting evidence – to put it at its mildest – against it, the myth of progress dies hard, surviving, as a colleague recently commented, now mainly in the realms of biological and medical science, and even in the latter scepticism is setting in.[6]

It will be apparent that truly theological questions are here at issue. The chief one is that of 'god', as referring to the being or force who or which accounts for the way things are and the way they are going. The first modern alternative to the traditional theology – what I term monistic providence – is to all intents and purposes identical with the old Stoic, essentially cosmological, conception, whose origins themselves are to be found in the earlier Greek conception of fate. It is the state of the world as a whole which is conceived to determine the state of the parts, and in essential respects neo-Darwinian determinism carries on the old Stoic tradition. Impersonal forces determine everything, and so are in effect the deity. It requires, however, as the more clear-sighted cosmologists have observed, a considerable act of faith to trust that these purposes are benevolent, or lead 'upwards' in the sense of producing any outcome other than universal death. The second modern conception, which places the direction of things in human hands, requires an even greater measure of faith, for trust is placed in human freedom, power and benevolence, three characteristics for which there is certainly some evidence, but not enough, as a glance at last century's grisly and murderous history will demonstrate. According to this conception, man[7]

---

[6] Shall we necessarily go on living longer and longer, healthier and healthier lives? To read some popular literature, one might suppose so. The instability of the modern view is shown by the fact that in the same newspapers one can read of ever longer life spans supposedly in prospect and the 'evolution' of organisms resistant to antibiotics, as well as the resurgence of diseases like tuberculosis.

[7] I believe that there is a case to be made that the word 'man' is, if not irreplaceable, at least virtually so for those contexts in which a word is needed to suggest both particular and universal reference. Its indispensability is suggested by its continuing appearance in popular speech and writing, and I shall continue to follow this custom despite recent academic fashion.

has replaced God as the engineer of providence, and has so far appeared to make somewhat worse a job of it. At least, it seems to me, there is a case, when the modern gods have manifestly failed, to examine whether proper trial was made of the biblical doctrine of providence before it was so summarily displaced.

§6.   Biblical Considerations

Therefore, the question insisting to be asked is: given the world as we experience it, what is it about the state of the whole that accounts for the way things happen within it? If we are to discover what is truly at stake, we must consider the situation in broad biblical perspective. There we shall find that providence is by no means limited to the maintenance and upholding of that which has been made. That is indeed part of the overall scheme. Yet it is also the case that God the creator is not one to make a world only to leave it to its own devices, but actively involves himself in the direction the world takes. That is the starting point for our explorations, and we move on from there by observing that God's continuing relation to the world has been characterized with the aid of a number of concepts, all of which bring out different aspects of the situation. Conservation, or preservation, the one we have tended to consider in the recent discussion of the modern problem, is but one, and implies that God continues to hold in being that which was established in the first place. Barth has rightly objected to this view that it is not forward-looking enough, so that with him we shall prefer the word 'providence', as will be illustrated below. But the moments of truth in the concepts must also be noted. That which is created out of nothing remains essentially fragile and, given the fall, is always in danger of returning to the nothingness from which it came. It is part of the continuing care of God for the world that he protects it from its self-induced fate.

That is, however, only part of a broader picture, and to view it we shall introduce some evidence that has not always been thought to be central. We shall begin with Genesis, a wonderful resource for our topic because it sets the scene for all treatments of providence thereafter. The first human creatures live within a providential order, although not one without labour, despite what some accounts of Eden as paradise might suggest. The world of Genesis 1 and 2 is a place of labour, though not yet laborious labour. It is not 'paradise'. We are presented rather with an empty earth, whose order is in need of completion ('subdue' of Genesis 1.28 presupposes that even here there is a disturbing lack of habitable space), while similarly Adam and Eve are called to till the ground. More especially is God's providence instanced in the strange but profound story of the creation of Eve. The first man is incomplete as he is, for none of the beasts is the kind of equal that can give him true companionship. 'It is not good for the man to be alone. I will make a helper suitable for him' (Gen. 2.18). In both cases, providence is bound up with God's promise: the good world waits for its human inhabitants to make it more able truly to praise its creator. But, as we shall explore later, the ordering under promise is disrupted by what has been called the Fall: a rebellion against God's gracious promise which brings in its train disaster both moral and material.

Hereafter, providence takes shape in a fallen world which God purposes both to continue to uphold, and, indeed, to perfect, so that providence takes the form both of conservation and of a movement towards redemption. The moral disorder is typified by Cain, the first murderer. He is expelled from the land, to wander restlessly without home. And yet even in his punishment of exile, he is within the providential order: 'and the Lord put a mark upon Cain, so that no-one who found him would kill him' (Gen. 4.15). When the forces of chaos have been let loose, providence consists in God's preventing their consequences from exacting their full toll, so that even the murderer, the greatest of sinners, is protected from further punishment. The story of the flood, another tale with parallels in other ancient literature, is similarly given a unique twist as a vehicle of promise. It is at this place that we begin to see the relation between providence and God's eschatological purposes. Following the flood, representing as it does the breaking of the forces of chaos into God's good order, and reminding us again of the threat of a return to nothingness hanging over the fragile creation, there comes, once again, the promise: 'Never again will all life be cut off by the waters of the flood; never again will there be a flood to destroy the earth' (Gen. 9–11). The story of Noah represents both the low point of human history, when God apparently repents of creating this recalcitrant being, and alongside it the renewed promise that the forces of chaos will not again be let loose in final destructiveness.

The discussion with which this chapter opened, and particularly that with the exponents of mechanistic science, runs the risk of making it appear that doctrines of providence are mostly concerned with finding gaps for divine action in an otherwise seamless web of causality. I have treated it that way in order to set the historical scene, but also to highlight the contrast with biblical conceptions which are radically different from both modern conceptions and the Greek world views from which they take their direction. We cannot evade the challenge of the philosophical and scientific, because if God is as he was claimed to be in the previous chapter, he is Lord of all creation, and his action cannot be restricted to a merely 'religious' or historical realm. Yet we must explore the universal dimensions of providence in the light of God's history with his people. History is determinative for the way we must understand providence, because the God whose action is mediated by his two hands is a God who works through particulars, and because his eschatological purposes for his creation involve time as well as space for their outworking. We shall therefore approach the topic from a different direction.

Again taking our cue from Genesis, we shall find election to be a seminal notion. At a crucial stage in the progress of the book, after the cataclysm of Babel comes the choice and call of Abraham, to be the one in whom all peoples of the earth – those scattered abroad after Babel – will be blessed. God's providing for the fulfilment of his purposes first takes concrete form in this remarkable act of simply calling a man to leave home and go somewhere else. Never is it more important than in this context to distinguish election from determinism. We have seen that according to the Stoics, the two are one and the same: providence means that everything that happens is determined, has to be what it is. According to scripture, God's providing takes the form of his calling particular people and groups in order to bring about his promised salvation. The first of them is Abraham. Until him, there is a continuing chain of disasters leavened only by God's merciful refusal to allow chaos to break in. With Abraham comes the first step in a story of salvation, a story which must be the primary, though not sole, focus for a theology of providence. And after Abraham come the Patriarchs, chosen not for their goodness – there was rarely a greater rogue than Jacob – but because in God's mysterious providing they happen to be the vehicles of his will. And then comes the centre of the action, Israel, chosen once again not arbitrarily but for God's own reason – 'not because you were more numerous than other peoples... [b]ut because the Lord loved you....' (Dt. 7.7). We have met already God's wisdom, power and patience. We here encounter another attribute, his mercy, which is a mode of his providential care especially of those who offend against God, man and the earth. We found

God's mercy restraining the severities of human justice and revenge in the tale of Cain. In the case of Noah God's mercy similarly predominates over other forms of his action, notably the well-earned judgement that rampant wickedness might appear to have merited. Now, with this new initiative, God's merciful care for his world takes concrete form in election, especially the election of those we might least expect.

For Christian theology – and that is where it parts company with what we now know as Judaism – the meaning of that election of Israel, which is in no way abolished by it, is found in Jesus of Nazareth. In him, God's providence becomes particular in a decisive and personal way. The offices of the prophets, priests and kings of Israel, those through whom God variously called and held Israel to her vocation, are concentrated in him, so that he is the one in whom providence now finds its primary focus. Barth points out that in Genesis 22.8 – 'God will provide a lamb' – we find evidence to support the view that providence does not mean foreseeing, but making provision for. It is an active conception.[8] And the use made of this notion by the New Testament, seeing, as it does, Jesus as the lamb who fulfils this and other anticipatory divine saving acts, provides an example of how we can understand the Old Testament conception to be concentrated in Jesus Christ. He is the concrete realization in person of God's providential dealings with his people and so reveals the shape of the preparatory history.

The Letter to the Ephesians sees in Jesus, as he brings together in one all the scattered people of God, Jew and Gentile alike, the vehicle of God's eschatological purposes. However, those providential purposes have been misunderstood in the history of Christianity, which has tended to make two grievous mistakes. The first is often to have taken them as excluding the Jewish people, and the outcome has been a history of anti-semitism whose bitter fruit the last century above all tasted. Only relatively recently has Christian theology begun the exercise in repentance which acknowledging that history requires. And the second mistake, which is the other side of the same story, is to treat election as more concerned with the other-worldly destiny of a limited number of human beings than with the destiny, in and through time, of the whole world. Only in its brutal explicitness is the *Westminster Confession*, one of the major influences on

---

[8] Karl Barth, *Church Dogmatics*, translation edited by G. W. Bromiley and T. F. Torrance (Edinburgh: T. & T. Clark, 1957–75), vol. 3/3, pp. 3–4.

modern British Protestantism, any different from the universal teaching of the western church from Augustine until recent centuries: 'By the decree of God, for the manifestation of his glory, some men and angels are predestinated unto everlasting life, and others foreordained to everlasting death.'[9] Against any narrowing of the doctrine Ephesians is emphatic, speaking of: 'the mystery of his will...to be put into effect when the times will have reached their fulfilment – to bring all things in heaven and on earth together under one head, even Christ' (Eph. 1. 9–10). According to this vision, providence is that form of divine action whereby a universal and reconciling design is achieved through time and by the agency of particular people, Abraham, Israel, Jesus and the community called to order its life through him.

In sum so far: a treatment of providence in the light of the doctrine of God's creation as encompassing all of reality suggests that although God's providing takes shape historically, its outworking embraces not only the human world, but also all creation. It is not merely cosmic, like the theories of the Stoics and the philosophy of mechanism; nor merely historical, like theologies based only on 'salvation history', or those who would attempt to turn all reality into history. It is a history rather which embraces all the creator's world, destined as it is to work out its destiny in and through time. Nowhere is this better illustrated than in the ministry of Jesus as it is recorded in the gospels. Here is a flesh and blood human being, the outcome not of an immaculate but of a miraculous conception by which the tired and soiled matter of the earth is by the Spirit made the bearer of the life of the Son of God. We shall come to that in its own place. Correspondingly, there is no dualism of spiritual and material in Jesus' life and teaching: healing leads to the forgiveness of sins, and the forgiveness of sins leads to healing, variously, because human life and needs are all particular, but holistically also because human beings are – as we shall see in more detail – matter and spirit together, not matter in which a soul or mind is precariously and temporarily lodged. Jesus' healings of those described as in the grip of the demonic illustrate this vividly, as does his apparent lordship of the elements: 'Who then is this, that even the wind and the sea obey him...?' (Mk. 4. 41). For him, the human being is at the centre, the one whose needs and plight cry out for mercy and healing; but, in some way or other, that centre is inextricable from the periphery, so that the natural world is

---

[9]   *Westminster Confession of Faith* (1646), III, iii.

mysteriously incorporated in the restoration of human beings to their proper destiny and end.

§7. The Content of the Doctrine of Providence

In this chapter so far I have juxtaposed the ideology of recent philosophy and the view of providence that appears to reign in the Bible. Theology, however, is inevitably affected by the former, and cannot simply assert its position over against whatever ideology happens to be ruling at the time, but must engage with it critically, as Irenaeus and Origen engaged in their different ways with Gnosticism. A still more important point is that it is part of the gospel's claim to be true not merely theoretically, indeed not mainly so, but only as bearing upon the world in which our life is worked out from birth to death. The search for evidence is a dangerous one because it may involve seeking too hard for the agreement of 'the world' where none should be sought. And yet if God is the universal creator, confirmatory signs may surely be sought in the world that is upheld by his 'Word that never tires' (Irenaeus) and is moved forwards by his Spirit. And here we must say that the evidence is mounting that Hume and the mechanists are simply wrong. The recent history of natural science, the dominant cultural force of the day, includes an increasing realization, accepted everywhere but by those still blindly beholden to the view of a war between science and theology, that the biblical view of creation is among the determining factors in the development of natural science. Its affirmation that the material world is good worked, finally albeit slowly, against the view deriving from philosophy that only mind is really significant. Indeed, it was a precondition for the emergence of experimental science. That the child later found it expedient to bite the hand of its parent is a long and complicated story, on which there is now much good literature.[10] But that is not our chief concern here. Rather, we shall cautiously call in evidence two developments in late modern science that give encouragement to those who would defend a doctrine of God's providential upholding of the order of things.

The first is an increasing realization, accepted everywhere but in the last outposts of biological fundamentalism, of the fact that our knowledge of the

[10] John Hedley Brooke, *Science and Religion. Some Historical Perspectives* (Cambridge, UK: Cambridge University Press, 1991).

workings of the world is limited in principle. Reductionist claims that this or that science, or science as a whole, will ever be able to explain everything are simply arrogant and untenable. The second is that much modern science suggests that far from being the closed system of mechanistic physics, the universe is open in ways that do not preclude God's interaction with it, not only at the 'spiritual' level, but in all kinds of ways. If it is the case, as increasingly appears, that what we call matter and mind are different forms of the organization of a common and universal energy, it follows that classic Christian conceptions of providence, especially that found in one modern form in Barth, are by no means as inconsistent with the best modern knowledge of the workings of the world as is often still supposed. We can therefore approach the world of science with two theological doctrines in mind. The first is that the doctrine of creation founds a world that is knowable, reliable and law-abiding because it is the product of a good and reliable creator. It is noteworthy that Michael Faraday, who is as important a nineteenth century figure for the development of later science as Charles Darwin, believed that the truth of the first chapter of Genesis was what gave him reason to be a scientist.[11] And the second doctrine is that the regularities which God has provided for our habitation of his creation take their shape and meaning within a broader eschatological purpose, which from time to time supervenes upon the regularities to make provision for the overall destiny of things. According to this view, God's providence is his action both within and alongside the structures of the world he has created so as to both uphold and shape the direction of things according to their proper season. Karl Barth summarizes this in terms of preserving, accompanying and ruling.[12]

The weakness of all pantheistic and mechanistic conceptions of providence is that they turn the richness of the created order into a homogeneity: there is only one form of causal regularity, and all must conform to it. But neither theology nor experience confirms this procrustean enterprise. Modern physics was compelled to break out of Newtonian homogenizing, and it can similarly be argued that light will finally dawn on the proponents of genetic determinism. Can Bach and Mozart, Shakespeare and Goethe, sensibly be understood to be merely the product of their genes? Scientific

[11] Geoffrey Cantor, *Michael Faraday: Sandemanian and Scientist. A Study of Science and Religion in the Nineteenth Century* (London: Macmillan, 1991).
[12] Barth, *Church Dogmatics*, vol. 3/3, pp. 58–238.

and philosophical reductionism do not begin to plumb the richness and variety of our world, which is increasingly being revealed to be a compound of vastly varied patterns of energies, corresponding both to the variety of the creator's mediations through Son and Spirit and to the richly various world of Genesis 1. Even the miraculous need not be outside this patterning, nor subvert the lawful behaviour of the world. If all patterns of energy flow from the gracious giving of the divine energy expressed in the way that we have seen, who is to rule out surges of energy which anticipate the eschatological perfection of the creation in a way which usual patterns of causality cannot achieve?

To repeat the rather schematic characterization made in the previous chapter, we can sum up the theology of this one by recalling again the distinct but interrelated mediation of the two hands of God. All things hold together in Christ: there is the basis of the wonderful order and unity revealed in the miraculous world of the scientist. But all things are particularized, each in its own way, by the Spirit, who relates them through Christ to God the Father. This is a particularizing, not a compelling, because the Spirit is the one whose function it is to enable things to realize that for which they were made. Miracle is, to be sure, a kind of divine compelling, but it takes place in order to overcome creation's bondage, not to force its normal reality out of place. That is why the standard philosophical definition of miracle as a violation of the laws of nature simply will not do. 'Normal' reality is the creation doing and being that which it was made to do and be, and in so far as the Spirit is sent to achieve that, the miraculous is a violation only of the rule of evil. In chapter 4 we shall give more detailed attention to the problem of human evil at least. In the meantime, we must take account of the fact that providence can be understood in our world only in respect of the fact that its present shape is now distorted, so that within God's providing are embraced acts devoted at once to *maintaining* the direction of the universe to its perfecting; and to *redirecting* its movement away from dissolution to its proper destiny. Both the ministry and cross of Jesus presuppose a world so at loggerheads with its destiny that only the personal and active presence of the creation's mediator can effect its redemption.

But why so long, why the apparently unprovidential direction of so much? God cannot here be let off the hook: as omnipotent creator, he is ultimately responsible for everything ('I am the Lord, and there is no other. I form light, and create darkness. I bring prosperity and create disaster.' Is. 45.

6–7). This and other direct engagement with God's apparent active permission of evil – see, for example, the opening of the seals in Revelation 6 by the Lamb himself – is a way of showing that sometimes the wicked are abandoned to the consequences of their actions. That, too, can be attributed to God's mercy, which allows time for the wicked to repent; but only, apparently, at the cost, sometimes the grievous cost, of those who suffer from the wickedness of the wicked. In that regard, the point of the miraculous and the unusual is to represent God's merciful and always particular anticipation of the reconciliation of all things. They are not therefore violations of the laws of nature but anticipations of final redemption. They have their own law, and it is eschatological, in that they enable God's project to move forward, particularly at crucial junctures, the Exodus, the threat of Israel's apostasy and, concentrating them all, both what was done with Jesus – his death and resurrection above all – and what he did.

Thus, like all the doctrines of the Christian faith, providence must be understood eschatologically, from the end. In that light, we can encapsulate the meaning of providence by saying that it is conservation in eschatological perspective. God's providential purposes are realized only eschatologically, and that means, first of all, only through time; the creation needs time to be and become itself. Yet because eschatological time bears now upon created time, the purposes of the creator are ever and again realized, in advance, so far as we are concerned, as people and things are enabled to be that which they were made to be. In that regard, we should not be reluctant to see human beings as the primary objects of God's providential caring. They are the ones whom he wishes to reconcile to himself, in completion of his will to have alongside him a personal creature who is made to praise and worship him. It does not follow that we have to be 'anthropocentric' in the pejorative modern sense, raping and polluting nature for short-term and greedy purposes. That the human comes first does not involve a downgrading of the remainder of the creation, which is created in order to be made perfect with and partly through human agency. The balance is expressed in the saying of Jesus, 'If that is how God clothes the grass of the field, which is here today and tomorrow is thrown into the fire, will he not much more clothe you, O you of little faith?' (Mt. 6.30). In our next chapter we shall examine some of the ways in which the human creature is at the centre of God's creation, but first let me conclude by saying something about the relation of the first two chapters.

At the beginning of this one, the point was made that conceptions of providence which construe it merely in terms of God's upholding of an essentially timeless universe fall well short of the active and forward-looking biblical conception. That is why we need to distinguish between the establishing of a world and what is made of that world, both alike by divine disposing. The doctrine of creation affirms that 'in the beginning' a reality other than God was established as truly itself by triune divine action. The doctrine of providence presupposes that, but adds that the kind of God with whom we have to do is also actively concerned for the continuing life of that world. The best concrete illustration of the double relationship is provided by Genesis' depiction of God's rest on the seventh day. This is not crude anthropomorphism, but, as Barth says, indicates at once that something is by now complete, and that the creator must be distinguished from a mere 'world-principle developing in an infinite series of productions . . . To this extent, the seventh day implies a break between the work of creation and all the divine work which follows . . .'[13] John's Gospel shows that the divine work which follows has its climax in the human career of Jesus and makes direct allusion to the theme in a much quoted verse: 'My Father is working still, and I am working' (Jn. 5.17). Here, in what this man does in obedience to the Father and in what the Spirit makes actual through him, is providence not only in action, but in constitutive and definitive action.

[13] Barth, *Church Dogmatics*, volume 3/3, p. 7.

Chapter 3

Man and Woman

§8. Matter and Spirit

Most religions and most philosophies suppose some continuity between the divine and the human – those, that is, that are not touched by the Bible's decisive rejection of such a continuity. In the West, both classical and modern philosophy have often assumed or taught that the continuity lies in the mind or the will: that there is an inner core, different in being from the outer material body, which, if correctly deployed, relates us directly to the divine, even, in the modern version, turns our deeds into 'the works of God'.[1] The Bible is decisively different, and although it is often assumed that Paul's distinction between flesh and spirit is the equivalent of the traditional philosophical distinction between body and mind, that is not the case. Paul's division is not ontological but eschatological: not between different kinds of being temporarily put together, but between the fallen and the redeemed human person. In order, therefore, to avoid misunderstanding, we shall begin our account of the being of man, created male and female together, with the Old Testament, which is in this respect far less liable to misunderstanding.

The apparently more 'primitive' of Genesis' two complementary accounts of the creation of this most problematic creature[2] makes it clear that the

---

[1] An excellent account of the modern version of this almost universal teaching is Edward Craig, *The Mind of God and the Works of Man* (Oxford: Clarendon Press, 1987).

[2] 'Man has always been his own most vexing problem. How shall he think of himself?' So run the opening words of one classic of twentieth century theological anthropology, Reinhold Niebuhr, *The Nature and Destiny of Man* (London: Nesbit, 1941), p. 1.

human creature's continuity is not with God, but with the earth. In that regard, theology has nothing at all to fear from Darwin and his successors. Adam is created from the dust, and Eve from his side, signifying, as is sometimes commented, complementarity rather than inferiority or super- iority, because not from his head or feet. And these creatures are made distinctively what they are not by virtue of the fact that an immaterial soul is inserted into their bodies, but because God breathes into them the breath of life. Note that breath is a far more material image than mind or soul. That this is not to be understood as simply a primitive version of later and more sophisticated philosophical distinctions between body and mind or soul is evident from the fact that the remainder of the Old Testament is similarly holistic. Here I need do no more than review some of the themes of Hans- Walter Wolff's study of biblical anthropology.[3] Wolff devotes a chapter each to three Hebrew words with which the Old Testament writers characterize the human condition. *Nepes*, often translated as 'soul' means first of all throat – as in 'He satisfies the hungry throat' (Ps. 107.9) – and so refers to 'needy man', the creature in need of sustenance from God. At another level, *basar* meaning, materially, flesh – 'eating *basar* and drinking wine' (Is. 22.13) – can refer to the human body as a whole, as in the famous description of marriage, where man and woman become 'one flesh' (Gen. 2.24). More generally, it refers to 'man in his infirmity', both physical and ethical, characterized as he is by being dependent at once on physical and divine support. '*Basar* is really man as a being who is weak and incapable . . .'. But the story is not yet complete. The third word, *ruach*, which we have met already as wind, breath and spirit, refers in our context to 'man as he is empowered'. It expresses not a permanent piece of equipment, like the Greek soul, but something that can be given and taken away, something always in the gift of the creator. This is the climax of our cumulative description, for, as Wolff says, 'Most of the texts that deal with the *ruach* of God or man show God and man in a dynamic relationship. That a man as *ruach* is living, desires the good and acts as authorized being – none of this proceeds from man himself'.[4] The picture, in sum, is of a spiritual-material unity, a psychophysical person whose created reality depends at every turn on being upheld and empowered by the Spirit of God. Only after this

[3] H.-W. Wolff, *The Anthropology of the Old Testament*, translated by Margaret Kohl (London: SCM Press, 1973), chapters 2–4.
[4] Wolff, *The Anthropology of the Old Testament*, p. 39.

beginning should we turn to that useful but dangerous concept, the image of God.

In the two previous chapters an account was given of two forms of relationship of the creation to its creator. The world is what it is because it is in a particular twofold relationship to the one who made and upholds it: those according to which the world stands to God as its creator and provider. Both creation and providence are universal relations, relations of the whole of created reality to God. We now come to a third form of relationship, the specifically personal, where we cannot avoid particularities; indeed, if we do, all is lost. We have not been able to avoid anticipation of such matters. Especially in respect of the fact that the doctrine of providence is rooted in history, it is grounded in the personal relationship into which God enters with the particular human beings indicated most prominently by the names of Abraham, Israel and Jesus. According to Christian faith – as, indeed, according to most religions and philosophies – the human creature has a particular centrality, for good and ill; did not Pascal call man the glory and refuse of the universe? According to scripture, that centrality derives from a relationship of the kind that has come to be called personal. We encounter here not a relationship between personal God and impersonal world, but between personal God and also personal creature. According to rather few texts from the Bible, which may appear to have exercised a disproportionate influence in later theology, this distinctiveness is described in terms of the image of God. The first and classic expression of it must be cited in full:

> Then God said, 'Let us make man in our image, in our likeness, and let them rule over the fish of the sea and the birds of the air, over the livestock, over all the earth, and over all the creatures that move upon the ground.' So God created man in his own image, in the image of God created he him; male and female he created them (Gen. 1.26–7).

Noteworthy is the emphatic repetition of the word 'image', and also, once again, the polemical intent of the writer. For other cultures, it was – indeed still is, as those who remember the dismantling in recent years of statues of former communist rulers will know – the king who was the image of God, and his image – his statue – reinforced in lands under his sway the message that he was God's representative on earth. For Israel, it was man, as male and female together, to which that status can be ascribed. All people are made in the image of God; indeed, as the gloss in the first cited verse suggests, are *like*

God. In that respect, at least, though definitely not in others, God is, according to the modern metaphor, democratic. If there is a sacramental reality, something in the creation uniquely or especially fitted to mirror the divine, it is the human race.

What, however, does it mean? Traditionally, it has been held, with the aid of Greek theories of human being, that the image refers to the human capacity to reason. This, however, is but another version of the overphilosophizing of the God–world relation that we have already met. In any case, it is now very widely agreed that this cannot be right so long as our conception depends upon scripture. The teaching in some way incorporates the whole human person, body included, as Irenaeus taught.[5] But in what does the image consist? It is sometimes claimed that it does not refer to a human structural likeness to God, but has to do with a capacity to be addressed by God, or a moral responsibility of some kind. That both are additionally the case, however, does not mean that they are adequate descriptions of what the writer means, and what his meaning can be taken to be in the light of the whole biblical witness. It is clear that some special form of relation to God is primary in all that we have examined so far, and our text continues the emphasis. To be created in the image of God is to be differently related to God from the way in which all other creatures are. The image is therefore 'structural' in the respect that it is an intrinsic part of human createdness to be in a special relation to God that is unbreakable except by his act.

Particular ways of being and acting are indeed also involved, and in this respect two other forms of relation are clearly identified as central. To be created in the image of God places us first in relation to human beings, especially to the 'other' that man and woman are created to be; and second to the rest of the created order. In the former case, at least if Genesis 2 is read alongside our text, a clear reciprocity is in view; whatever has happened in some later theology, there is no hierarchy of man and woman. In the latter relation, however, there is a hierarchy: under God, the created order cannot be fully itself without us. That the possibilities for its corruption and pollution are equally great follows from this, for it remains an indisputable principle of all life that the very worst derives from the corruption of the very best, as we shall need to explore later in the book.[6] But our sensitivities

---

[5] Irenaeus, *Against the Heresies*, 5. 6. 1.

[6] And as the use of technological power in the twentieth century only too well demonstrates.

about what has now come to be called 'ecology' should not blind us to the responsibility that is implied by the text. Here, also, we may recall Barth's comment on the words, 'fill the earth and subdue it', that we must allow the text its particularity. It is a command given when the earth was still under-populated and not yet a home for the human race.[7] The way it has some-times been employed may well have contributed to ecological devastation, but only if it is taken out of its theological context, which is of obedience to God. It does not, further, in any way disparage the non-human creation. As we have seen, God glories in everything that he has made; it is *all* very good. And yet the human being has a special responsibility and authority which we cannot object to on ecological grounds, for it is a fact. In our hands, nature is either cherished and enabled to be itself, or plundered and pol-luted. As Pannenberg has pointed out, the biblical mandate did not cause the ecological crisis; it is only when modern culture began to ignore its religious context, and simply treated the world as a mine or a machine, that the real trouble developed.[8]

In sum, then, the heart of the human derives from the forms of relation that we have sketched: to be in the image of God is to be related to God in the way that other creatures are not, and so related to the other creatures differently from the way in which they are related to one another. As we have already seen this does not, emphatically does not, mean that there is a fundamental difference in being between the human and the animal, as Greek thought has always been tempted to argue: that the mind or the soul is in some direct relation to God while the remainder of the human being and the animals are not. What makes a difference is not that, but the mysterious reality of spirit, which in the Bible is not opposed to matter, but in some way represents a qualification of matter. The beasts are indeed not outside the care of God's Spirit, as we have already seen in chapter 1 in reference to Psalm 104. But the fact that men and women have spirit means that theirs is an openness to God and the creature denied to the other creation, an openness which yet remains in the gift of God.[9] We do not

[7] Karl Barth, *Church Dogmatics*, translation edited by G. W. Bromiley and T. F. Torrance (Edinburgh: T. & T. Clark, 1957–75), vol. 2/2, p. 673.

[8] Wolfhart Pannenberg, *Systematic Theology*, translated by G. W. Bromiley (Edinburgh: T. & T. Clark, 1994), p. 204.

[9] Such a conception is not liable to the same challenges from evolutionary theory as some others, because it could be argued that in the process of time, there was created by

need to deny that such faculties as reason, will and consciousness characterize this openness, only that they determine it.

§9.   Personal Being

It follows that the key to the doctrine of the image of God is the notion of
the personal, that which both God and man are, albeit at their different
levels. 'Person' is not easy to define; indeed, like all the most basic of our
categories, it is one which can only be indicated indirectly, for it is that in
terms of which other things are to be understood. The roots of the notion
lie in trinitarian theology, as we shall see when the course of this book is
almost run. Here, I shall simply say something of what I believe to be
implied by it for our topic. To be a person is to be distinct from other
persons, and yet inextricably bound up with them: to be 'other' only in
'relation'. Just as God is who he is in the inextricable fellowship of Father,
Son and Spirit, so for us to be personal is to be what we are in relation to
other persons. We have already seen that this involves being in special
relation to God our creator, but it also means that relations with other
people are crucial. We are what we each particularly and uniquely are in
large measure by virtue of our particular connections with the people who
have made and continue to make us what we are. Parents, children, lovers
and friends contribute to shaping our being, in all kinds of ways and for
both good and ill. This shared way of being is congruous with the stress
already laid on our continuity with the whole material creation. We are
variously, like all other living creatures, shaped by our genetic make-up, as
that is handed on to us by our parents, and by what we eat and drink. But
it does not follow that nothing else constitutes us, for our specific personal
uniqueness is derived from a combination of this and of what is made of it
in what we call nurture and in our continuing personal relations. The
shaping power of these hugely various patterns of connection can be
illustrated in many different ways: a tendency to disease can be passed on
genetically, while, at the other end of the scale, a betrayal can embitter

God, in continuity, and so from out of the common stock of the created world, a
creature which was for the first time given a nature different from all the others. That is
not to deny that aggressively naturalistic forms of evolutionary ideology are a problem
for any theological account.

someone for life in such a way that his or her personal being is shaped, or rather misshapen, by it.[10]

It follows also from the personal character of human being that of central significance in our theology of the image of God are two slippery and often misused concepts, love and freedom. If God is eternally love in the mystery of his tripersonal being, then to be personal in his image is to be made to love: it is to be created to be *from* and *for* the other. Scripture's model for this is the relation between man and woman, as its first book makes manifest. Corresponding to Adam's ecstatic welcome of Eve – 'This is now bone of my bones and flesh of my flesh' – is the amazing evocation of what can only be called romantic love in the story of Jacob: 'So Jacob served seven years for Rachel, and they seemed to him but a few days because of the love he had for her' (Gen. 29.20). But it by no means follows from this that we should subscribe to the debased modern reduction of 'love' to sexual relations, however central they may be to making us the kind of people that we are. There are many other forms of love, none more important than love of our enemies, which, we must insist, does not mean liking, but treating them also as human beings made in the image of God. That is, I think, why murder and slander – assassination of body or character – are two of the moral prohibitions directly linked to the doctrine of the image of God in Genesis 9.6 and James 3.9. More positively, love receives its basis in the actual love of God for his alienated creature: 'God demonstrates his own love for us in this: While we were still sinners, Christ died for us' (Rom. 5.8, compare 'God's enemies', v. 10).

Human persons are, then, created to love, and that involves a spectrum of relations to others, from marriage to treating even those who mistreat us with the respect due to one made in the same image. The second essential concept, also subject to misunderstanding and distortion, is freedom. To be a person is to be free in a way that other creatures are not. That does not imply the kind of absolute freedom sometimes implied in modern discourse, that we are absolutely free, in some existential decision, for example, to choose the kind of people that we wish to become. We are not God, and, as Calvin perceptively pointed out, there is a sense in which even God is not absolutely free: '[F]rom his boundless goodness comes

---

[10] That is why the concept of reconciliation, however much trivialized and misused in modern parlance, is so central to our being. Where there is no forgiveness, bitterness spreads and grows, and the development of a person is stunted.

God's inability to do evil. Therefore...that he must do good does not hinder God's free will in doing good...'[11] An equivalent, and indeed, greater, limitation is true in the case of human freedom, and we shall therefore understand what it is to be free only if in the light of this we return to the notion of personal particularity. Everything that exists is particular. In the immortal words of Bishop Butler, 'Everything is what it is and not another thing.' It may or may not be the case that no two blades of grass are identical, but it is certainly the case that no two persons are.[12] Even the cloning of human beings, supposing that such an offence against the image of God came to be committed, would not produce identical humans, for differences of relationships with others and within the world would shape them differently, in however minor a way. The fact is that in one sense I am not free to be other than I am, because I am the product of particular shaping through genetic inheritance, nutrition, nurture and social interaction. It does not follow that what I do now, or tomorrow, is in no way free, merely that my freedom can consist only in what I make of the particular inheritance that I have received. And even here the use of 'I' is dangerous, for freedom also is a relational concept. My freedom, such as it is, derives from my relation to God and to others. We shall examine the relation to God in future chapters, but it is an inescapable feature of our human situation that we are freed or enslaved by the way others love or hate us, thus enabling us to become or preventing us from becoming the people we were created to be.

And that leads to a further important point. Irenaeus' famous analogy, that Adam and Eve when first created were like children called to grow to maturity, indicates that person is an eschatological concept. Like the world created very good, human beings are called to become perfect. The saying of Jesus that, 'You are to be perfect as your heavenly Father is perfect' (Mt. 5.48), is one of the most difficult and offensive of sayings, at its worst encouraging people to strive, destructively, to become perfect by the exertion of effort. While, however, effort is part of human perfecting, it is

[11] John Calvin, *Institutes of the Christian Religion*, edited by J. T. McNeill, translated and indexed by F. L. Battles (Philadelphia: Westminster Press, 1960), 2 vols., Library of Christian Classics 20 and 21, II. iii. 5.

[12] This is, I think, a trinitarian principle. The uniqueness of every human person is an implication of the facts that the Father is not the Son, etc., and that the love of the three persons of the Trinity is that which establishes them each in their particular being.

neither the beginning nor the end, and the text is as much promise as it is demand. As best understood, the saying maintains in creative tension past creation, present striving and final redemption. The beginning and basis is that God creates and maintains us as persons, in unique personal relationship to him, the 'three personed God'.[13] Whatever we are and do, we are as those in his image and likeness upheld in relationship to our creator, by the agency of his 'two hands'. It may be that we must say of the unutterably evil people with whom history presents us, of those who have become so hardened in wickedness that they can without conscience consign millions to death, that this is all that remains; yet created in the image even they remain.[14] In any case, our eschatological perspective recalls to mind the warning in the Letter to the Hebrews that we do not yet see all things under the promised human dominion, 'But we do see Jesus...' (Heb. 2.9). Only there, as we shall have cause to explain in more detail in a later chapter, does there live and act one truly exercising the promised human authority over the creatures. With the human race as a whole, only in hope, and all too rarely – but truly, none the less – in anticipation, do things happen as they should. To put it more positively, the heart of the doctrine of the image of God is to be found in the promise that those who put their trust in God's love and mercy, and in that alone, may be presented by the two hands of God the Father faultless before the throne of grace, and so made perfect. In that light, the human being is one who is both created a person and placed on earth to become a person through giving and receiving love, in different ways to and variously from family, friends, acquaintances, enemies. In a word we are placed on earth to join in mutually loving relations with those whom God gives us to be loved by and to love through the finite time he grants.

It is at this place that we encounter the decisive difference between the divine and the human person. God is spirit without remainder, eternal and ever-living. Human persons are fleshly and material, and these imply finitude, limits in time and space through which we are not able to break, though we can in different ways transcend them. As Reinhold Niebuhr recognized, what we make of our humanity derives in part from what we

---

[13] The expression is John Donne's: 'Batter my heart, three personed God...', the opening line of *Holy Sonnets*, XIV.

[14] Whether God ultimately gives up on any of those made in his image is a question we shall have to face in a later chapter.

make at once of our limits and of our transcending of them.[15] Limitation in
space is inescapable for human beings, for although there is speculation
about travel in space, practical possibilities and the finite nature of resources
entail that for most if not all of the human race living anywhere but on earth
is out of the question. However, time is a different matter, for human
religion and philosophy have found it remarkably difficult to come to
terms with death, some form of immortality or 'survival' of a spiritual part
of the person being the majority opinion. Against this, however, as against
the dualistic anthropology it assumes, scripture places a large question mark.
Death is, for the Old Testament, almost universally the end of relationship
with God, and therefore the end of life in anything like a full sense. A long
tradition, taking its cue from a particular interpretation of Genesis 2.17
('You must not eat from the tree of the knowledge of good and evil, for
when you eat of it, you will surely die') has argued that Adam and Eve were
created naturally immortal, and died only because they offended. The
overall view of scripture, however, suggests that man, like the other creatures, has a limited life span ('three score years and ten') which is brought to
an end when God withdraws his life-giving Spirit. For the New Testament,
as is shown beyond all peradventure by Jesus' fearful expectation of his
execution, the same holds, except that there is a qualification. Death
represents a cessation of relationship, including relationship with God,
apart from divine action which re-establishes relationships at another level. Only a
new and recreative act of God through his Spirit, one involving a promise of
life at another level, can end the relentless passage to the dissolution of the
body and so the end of life. We shall have to engage with death in its two
senses later, but for the moment the point is clear: to be created means to be
finite, to have strict limits set in both time and space, limits at which we can
make only futile and self-defeating resistance.

§10.   The Blessings of Finitude

Accordingly, the perfecting of the person of which we have spoken is a
finite task, and must not involve tilting at infinity. It is, or should be,
liberating to know that we are able, and are indeed intended, to achieve

---

[15] Modern culture's failure to recognize human limits is one of its most alarming
features, as Niebuhr has shown throughout *The Nature and Destiny of Man.*

only so much in one short life. (It is also the case, as we shall see, that it is an ineluctable part of the human condition as we experience it that all of us in some way or other fail in what we are set or set ourselves to achieve.) The active human response to our creation is inseparable from the doctrine of the image of God, because that involves reference to God's creating and providing action. God's action shapes our action according to its limits, to the effect that human action in the world takes two distinct though related forms: in relation first to other people and second to the non-human world. As we have seen, the prohibition of murder shows that the doctrine of the image has implications for the moral life. But the command which is part of the teaching of Genesis 1.26–7 is a more broadly cultural mandate. We move on, then, to some brief remarks about ethics, including that immense range of activities summarized under the description of 'culture', a brief definition of which will be attempted below.

As we have seen, interaction with other men and women is more crucial than and for other relationships with the world apart from them. There is no direct instruction for human relations in Genesis 1–2, though much is implied by the centrality of man and woman in both chapters. However, ethics in a more problematic sense emerges thereafter, because the sorry tale of chapters 1–11 reveals the need for explicit moral teaching. That is the point of Paul's saying that the law is only necessary because of sin. The difficulty and ambiguity of ethics are that it derives from two features of our situation: first that finite beings require a measure of structuring for their lives, and second that we do not treat each other aright without both internal and external restraint. An adumbration is found in Genesis 9.1–7, a passage of great importance for later treatment of divine law, for it lays down a framework for the behaviour of the whole human race, especially toward the life, both human and animal, which is God's especial sphere. It is noteworthy that here for the first time is permission given to kill and eat animals, the diet in Genesis 1 being vegetarian. Food regulations, however, imply that even when used for food, the life of animals must be respected. Specific teaching for Israel is given in the Ten Commandments in Exodus and others of the first five books of the Bible, and this also has a bearing on how we are to understand ethics in general. Here, as in Genesis, the teaching is not what has since come to be called ethics, straightforwardly. *Torah*, the word translated 'law', has a far broader meaning than what we tend to denote by our narrow concept of morality, for it embraces the whole framework of human life under God. Its basis is one of grace and gratitude: not demand and restraint simply, but response to God's unmerited goodness with the whole of life. Torah thus embraces those things expected both generally of any human being and more specifically and in detail of the group which was saved out of Egypt and made a people for God's glory.

We are at this place concerned chiefly with an ethic of creation, with the form of action consequent on the creation of man. And the main point can be made quite simply. Creation consists in this respect of a giving of time and space in which men and women may grow into the maturity for which they are made. Ethics, accordingly, is directed to the right habitation of that time and space. For beings who are not God, a structure[16] is required, and this is given in what are called the two tables of the law. It is significant that what is called the first table of the law concerns Israel's relation to God, and only second come the regulations for her social order. And the first thing that is forbidden is worshipping anything other than the one God of Israel. This is the heart of an ethic of our createdness. That God is the creator and all other things are his creatures entails that nothing but God may be given the value of divinity. This is a God who excludes all rivals, both for his own sake and for that of the creature. Robert Jenson says of the God of Israel that among his attributes is that he is jealous, tolerant of no rivals.[17] While that cannot be denied, it seems better to bring out a similar point by concentrating rather on God's holiness, a less misleading way of making a similar point. God's holiness is his otherness, his sheer difference from everything else. It expresses itself negatively in a rejection of all that is unworthy to come into his presence, more positively in his establishing of the goodness of the creature that is other than he. It is that which puts the second table, those things which regulate human social relations, into their context. As its treatment in the book of Leviticus implies, God's holiness requires of the creature a range of forms of action, embracing at once personal integrity, just social order, and a respect for the land and its creatures.

The reference to the earth and its creatures indicates that this brief outline of ethics is already broadening into what we call culture. This is part of ethics because it incorporates reference to human responsibility for the

[16] The structure reflects the fact that even God's being is *structured* by the way in which the persons of the Godhead are to and from each other in love.

[17] 'In the Scriptures . . . it is first among the Lord's attributes that he is "a *jealous* God".' Robert W. Jenson, *Systematic Theology*, vol. 1, *The Triune God* (New York and Oxford: Oxford University Press, 1997), p. 47.

world as well as for other men and women. We are not here engaged in the characteristically modern disputes about culture: for example, whether there is a universal culture, or whether different cultures are sealed off from one another, or what is the relation of church and culture. Culture simply means those human activities, including but by no means exclusively the linguistic, by which men and women engage, both together and individually, with the world presented to their experience. It is distinct from nature in that it orders or changes the things that happen simply by virtue of natural laws. It turns wildernesses into gardens, empty land into housing, forests into deserts. Human beings shape their world, and Genesis appears not only to approve this, but to encourage it: indeed, Genesis 2 makes horti*culture* the primary task that Adam and Eve perform in the place in which they are set.

What is the purpose of culture? Let me attempt an answer in the eschatological perspective in which the creation is here being considered. First, in the light of chapter 1, we can say that culture is engaged in the perfecting of that which was created very good; completing, we might say, God's work of art – his drama or symphony, remembering always that these are metaphors which describe only partially. We are not to aspire – indeed, we are free not to aspire – to achieving more than is within our reach, as so much modern human activity impotently seems to attempt. Our responsibility is to the particular sectors of the world with which we have to do and for which we have the capacity. This point is reinforced by a second point, that in the light of chapter 2, which ended with a stress on the Holy Spirit's particularizing action, we may say that true culture is the achievement of particular instances of the good, the true and the beautiful in anticipation of the eschatological completion of all things. Here, divine and human action must be held in proper relation. If God the Spirit is God the Father's way of enabling truth, beauty and goodness to be realized in his creation, then culture is a matter of human agents being enabled by God to shape the creation towards what it is made to be.

Two things need to be said in clarification. First, to speak of the good, the true and the beautiful is an inclusive way of speaking of the whole gamut of right human action. It is not meant, for example, to exclude the useful – a piece of pottery may be beautiful, but it is a failure if it is designed to hold liquid and leaks – but to include all those things which serve for the enhancement rather than the corruption of the world and its inhabitants. And that leads to the second point, which is that all acts either enhance or degrade. No action is purely neutral, for all actions bring about alterations in the overall being of the universe. If a chance event on the other side of the universe can alter the behaviour of gases on this side, how can it not be that every human action has some effect or other, and must either anticipate or impede the movement of things to their perfecting?

All right culture, by whomever formed, is the gift of God the Spirit through Christ, and so the gift of God's perfecting action. It is surely no accident that the word 'inspiration' – breathed by the Spirit – is used in both secular and religious contexts, for we hear it used quite unselfconsciously of all kinds of events – for example, even that a stroke in a game of cricket was 'inspired', as some indeed appear to be. It has been used particularly of the arts, where human experience has often attributed an insight to a mysterious gift from without, even though in terms of empirical observation it is conceivable that it might also be reduced to a particular movement of electrodes in the brain. But that is part of the point. The Spirit's work in this respect is as much to do with ordering the material things of this world as with suggesting a realm beyond them. It is *this* creation which is the place where truth, goodness and beauty are to be realized, the Spirit enabling acts which may sometimes appear to be out of the ordinary, even miraculous, but which are even as such not foreign to the mysterious capacities of the creation.[18]

§11.   Scripture and Theology

All culture, then, is dependent upon God's gift, for there is none that does not depend on his creating goodness. It is for that reason that we are not entering an entirely different world when we come to treat of the specifically 'religious' side of the matter and speak of such things as scripture and

---

[18] We could also here speak similarly, although in rather more restricted perspective, of revelation, without which nothing could be known of other people, and perhaps of the world also. This is manifestly the case with human knowledge. Unless you reveal to me those things that touch your life the most deeply, I shall not be able to know who you are, while it is of the essence of love and friendship that we do entrust our bodies and souls to the tender mercy – an expression used, significantly, both positively and ironically – of others. But it is in a different way true of all being. It is arguable that the scientist would know nothing of the structures of the physical world if it were not the case that the world is created in such a way as to be able to give up its secrets to the enquiring mind. All these things are dependent on the gift of the creator Spirit.

theology. These too are ways in which culture takes shape in the world. The point has already been made that when the author of Genesis put together his accounts of creation he drew upon a common stock of language and imagery. Yet it has also been claimed that he made something absolutely unique of his material, so that both revelation and inspiration are necessary concepts for theology in a more radical sense than elsewhere. Why more radical? The first reason is that we are here concerned with the knowledge of God, who is not part of the material world, for he is its creator. Corresponding to the privacy that is part of the meaning of being a human person there is what theology calls the hiddenness of God, which means at least that he cannot be known unless he makes himself known. The second reason, discussion of which we shall postpone to its proper place, is that human sin and evil require that if he is to be known God should break through the barrier that man has erected against his love. Here, however, we are limiting ourselves to sketching an account of what our knowledge of the creator might entail for our understanding of revelation and inspiration with reference to scripture.

Scripture's unique inspiration – its distinct cultural character – derives from the fact that its writers participated in the events in which God made himself known as the God of Israel and the Father of Jesus. In explaining this we must avoid two equal and opposite errors. One is of supposing that these books are merely the products of a religious culture, and therefore equivalent to any other such products of human culture. The Bible's own claim for uniqueness is parallel to and indeed derived from the claim of its God to reject all rivals. It is based in a history, a series of events, culminating in the life, death and resurrection of Jesus, on whose uniqueness is based the affirmation of the priority of scripture over all other cultural products. The opposite error is to claim for scripture the kind of truth that denies its character as the product of human culture. As the one who perfects the creation, the Spirit is the one who awakes the capacities of those he inspires and perfects their work despite and through their errors and weaknesses. To propagate any doctrine of scripture that involves that the Spirit takes away the minds and personality of the writers – to claim, as has been claimed, that the words are not the authors' words but directly dictated by the Spirit – is to deny that the Spirit can work by enabling human capacities to speak of God and his works. This does not mean that the writers speak in their own strength, but that their strengths are enhanced and their weaknesses transcended in the interests of divine truth.

What we call divine revelation is accordingly God's making himself known by coming into personal relation with particular human beings in particular historical contexts, and definitively in Jesus, who is divine revelation in person. Corresponding to this, the inspiration of scripture refers to the Spirit's enabling those recipients of divine speech and action to compose the books which are, in response to revelation, in their own human way divine revelation to those generations who come after. This scripture is therefore *both* a form of human culture which can be analysed in the same way as are other human products *and*, because it speaks of things which are beyond human capacity in general, a form of human culture which insists on transcending that analysis.

Just as scripture is at one remove from the direct divine speech which takes place in the history of Israel and Jesus, so theology is a form of human culture at one remove from scripture. Theology began as an enterprise which sought – among other things – to defend the Christian message against internal threats and external criticism in the first centuries of our era. We have already met one example in Irenaeus' and Origen's doctrines of providence. What theology generally aspires to is an exploration of the logic of faith, its intrinsic meaning, and in a number of directions. Perhaps centrally, it seeks to integrate those things that scripture has to say, but in a way appropriate to the conditions it meets. In a world not shaped by biblical faith, as was Israel's world and that of the very first Christians, a different kind of enterprise was called for, one specifically oriented to spelling out the meaning of the universal claims of the gospel. At the centre, as the word 'theology' suggests, is the doctrine of God, for while, as we have seen, the Bible's God brooks no rivals, the ancient world was full of them, from the myths of the mystery religions to the austere, and often pantheist, speculations of the philosophers. In addition, however, as we have seen, this is a God who makes himself known by entering into relation with his world, so that consequent upon the doctrine of God are various topics which correspond to the main features of God's activity. We have already sketched two forms of it, creation and providence, and we shall meet others. The promise of theology is that its exponents may be enabled to cast light on God's creating and saving love. Its perils lie in seeking too confidently to know too much. That is why eschatology is again important, for its constant reminder is that we shall one day know as we now are known, and that all we must expect are anticipations of that clearer insight. Yet those anticipations are what we need if our path through life is to be sufficiently illuminated. The limits of theology provide one reason why it is the cultural enterprise of a community of faith and action, and not of gifted individuals apart from that. As in all culture, so especially in this, we can achieve only what we are given to achieve and along with others also engaged in the task.

§12.   Conclusion to Part 1: God the Father

The first article of the creed affirms belief in 'God the Father, maker of heaven and earth'. These first three chapters have been devoted to exploring some of the central ramifications of the claim, taking much of their orientation from the book of Genesis, albeit that seen in the perspective of the New Testament. As the argument proceeded, indications have been given of the implications of the subject matter for our understanding of the being of God. And so far we can provisionally conclude that God the Father is the creator of all, omnipotently mediating his work through his two hands, the Son and the Spirit. The fact that he makes a world that is other than he shows, first, that God the Father is holy, and his holiness consists in his utter difference and distinction from all other beings, and involves jealousy, the rejection of all rivals. Yet he is primarily holy in his being for, not against, the creature, in loving the work of his two hands. God's holiness is indeed revealed in his concern for his glory, but it is a glory which serves the interests of the goodness of the creature, whose well-being and perfecting derive from giving glory not to itself, but praise, thanks and glory to God alone. This should not be interpreted as analogous to the way in which finite creatures seek glory for themselves, because, as we have seen, all God the Father's work is patient, wise and merciful. His patience allows things time to become themselves; his wisdom shapes them into their own most proper being; his mercy gives them time for repentance and amendment beyond their expectations and deserts.

The doctrine of creation shows us, second, the uniqueness of God's action: its utter sovereignty and freedom, constrained by no material or limit. The concept traditionally used for this is omnipotence, and we need to maintain it. Yet, the distinctive feature of that freedom and sovereignty is that God's creating work arises out of love, from the love that God is eternally, the love of Father, Son and Holy Spirit in the communion that is one God; and then that same love moving out of itself to make creatures which are valuable and good for their own sake. This sovereign, holy, and so unique love is shown particularly to those made in his image, the creatures granted the capacity to respond to his love and share in his work, but is by no means restricted to them. Indeed, as God loves his whole creation, so the creatures made to love God and one another in freedom are in turn to love his world in response. Nevertheless, God the Father's omnipotence is revealed chiefly in his power to create creatures which are personal like himself.

The doctrine of creation shows us, third, the eternity of God, which Barth significantly paired with his glory.[1] There is a long tradition of arguing that God's eternity means his utter timelessness, and, to the extent that as creator God is not subject to the constraints of time, it is justified. As the creator of time, God is utterly other than the order which he creates. Yet the negative overtones of the word 'timelessness' mean that it is not the best way to construe this concept. Our knowledge of God's eternity comes not from a denial of the features of our time, but from God's free interaction with that which he creates and for which he provides. As we have seen, it is not wrong, indeed it is required by our doctrine to say that God takes his time, patiently and mercifully giving the creature space and time to be itself. God's absolute otherness from the creation is not therefore a threat to its integrity and value, but the reverse. God's eternity means that, being secure in his own being, he is able to confer on the creation its own security and integrity as his creation, the world he loves in and through time. Beyond that we need not speculate. It does not follow, however, that we have completed our account of what we can claim to have been shown of God's being, and we shall enrich the discussion as the book proceeds. Indeed, the true historical centre is still to be reached, except insofar as we have been able to speak of God's mercy, his patient refusal to allow the creature to destroy itself and so undo his work. That apart, the first three chapters have been devoted chiefly to summarizing what we have learned about God from his work as creator. There are wonders still to come, for our creator is also the one who loves us in still more miraculous ways; and to some of those we now proceed.

[1] Karl Barth, *Church Dogmatics*, translation edited by G. W. Bromiley and T. F. Torrance (Edinburgh: T. & T. Clark, 1957–75), vol. 2/1, pp. 608–77.

Part 2

'His Only Son, Our Lord'

Chapter 4

'Suffered Under Pontius Pilate':
A Theology of Salvation

§13. The Concept of Sin

Most religions are religions of salvation because they are based on beliefs
that something is wrong with human life – and indeed the whole world – in
its present condition, something which the religion proposes to mitigate or
heal. Their prescriptions for salvation depend in large measure on their
diagnosis of the ill. If with Socrates and the Gnostics it is held in different
ways that our imprisonment in a material body is a symptom of the disease,
then some form of escape from matter will be the solution. If, with some
forms of Buddhism, the diagnosis is that desire is the chief cause of our
discontents, then escape from it will be the path to be chosen. The same is
the case with the secular systems of salvation that so marked, many would
say disfigured, the history of the twentieth century. If the sickness is poverty
and religion, the cure will be economic revolution and the abolition of
religion. And so we could continue to multiply the variations. These
illustrations are simplified, and no doubt misleading, but they make the
point that diagnosis and proffered cure are correlative: the medicine corresponds to the disease.

Christian theology diagnoses the ill as the disruption or distortion of the
relation of personal beings with the personal creator God, a disruption that
in mysterious fashion incorporates the whole created world in its structures.
The technical term for this is sin, and I shall continue to use it although the
expectations often aroused by its use in the modern western world almost
inevitably create misunderstanding. Central to them is the tendency for it,

especially in the mind formed by the tabloid press, to be identified with sex. As we saw in the previous chapter, God affirms our sexual being, making the love of Adam and Eve central in its characterization of the human condition. And it is not merely the fault of the popular media, who, as is their wont, are simply distorting and amplifying something that is to be found in the tradition. One of the western theological tradition's chief weaknesses is to be found in its misreading of the story of Adam and Eve, so that it has come to appear that sin and the transmission of sin centre on sexual reproduction, rather than on a far broader range of human offence. In the story of Adam and Eve their sexuality becomes a problem only after they have eaten of the fruit of the forbidden tree, which is not in scripture described as an apple, but simply as a fruit. What they are offered by their tempter is the opportunity to grasp at being like God, aspiring to know everything rather than being like God in the love and freedom which are their defining attributes.[1]

The essence of sin is to attempt to be like God in ways other than that laid down for those who, because they are finite in time and space, are also limited in their capacity for knowledge and achievement. Sin is for the creature to think and act as if it were the creator. We are like God, but according to Paul's characterization of the way of Jesus Christ in Philippians 2, Jesus is godlike precisely in going the other way. He did not grasp at divinity, but made himself a slave, for the sake of those he loved. But there he is alone, for until him the case, rather, is that consequent upon the dislocation of the human relation to God is the whole gamut of disruption: murder, lying and all the other things so characteristic of our condition which we know to rupture our relations with one another and yet persist in. The story of the tower of Babel, which serves as a parody of Genesis 1, brings the sorry tale not to an end, but to a provisional closure, before God's call of Abraham and the beginning of the story of redemption. The repeated 'Let us' of the opening verses of Genesis 11, echoing the divine and sovereign 'Let us make' of Genesis 1, mockingly depicts the feeble attempt of the human race to make themselves equal to God: 'Let *us* make bricks...'; 'Come, let *us* build ourselves a city, with a tower that reaches

---

[1] The presence of the serpent in the garden implies that evil in some way predates the human fall. Where did it come from? We can but speculate, but because evil is by its nature irrational, in the sense that once explained it is no longer evil in the full sense, perhaps we should not.

to the heavens...' (Gen. 11.3–4). The essence of sin consists in wanting to be like God otherwise than in the way he invites and enables us to be like him. Repeatedly in scripture idolatry, both of the kind which actually bows down before images and the modern variety which worships things other than God while pretending not to do so, is diagnosed as the ill of which the gospel sets out to heal us. When we seek to displace the loving God from our lives, we replace him with an idol which, though inanimate, yet devours us.[2]

A review of two widely current misunderstandings of the doctrine of sin will enable us to expand these opening remarks. Individualistic conceptions of sin, encouraged by a certain kind of evangelistic strategy which seeks to impress upon individuals at almost any cost their need of salvation, underrate the fact that human evil takes essentially social form. To be sure, this must never be expressed in such a way as to absolve individuals from their fault and responsibility. We are individually responsible for what we do, unless so constrained physically or by sickness that our actions are no longer our own. The plight of the individual is that he or she – he *and* she, and all of the rest of us – adopt, inevitably but voluntarily, the inheritance that we have received. Sin is a social reality because that inheritance is mediated to us by our history and by the social setting in which our lives take shape. If the doctrine of original sin is taken to mean that sin is that which is transmitted by direct sexual begetting from the historical ancestors of the race to us today, the diagnosis is oversimplified. But it remains the case that our social being is the compost within which our historically transmitted fallenness is nourished and grows.

The objection to the individualist misunderstanding of the doctrine of sin leads into another point about the way the story has been told. We do not need to believe in a historical Adam, because the biblical story is itself too subtle to require such naive and literalist reading. But, whatever be the actual course of evolution – and, we must remember, all attempts to find a being truly intermediate between the animal and the human are purely speculative – there must have been a first couple or first social order, which was distinguished from all its predecessors by both the distinctiveness of its relation to God and the unique character of its relation to the world. In that respect, the person is absolutely different from the non-personal; one is

---

[2] Think of the power of money which, though increasingly but the movement of paper, or even less concrete than that, yet shapes so much of what happens in our world.

either personal or not, because one is either related to God and to others in the way persons are or one is not. Whether or not there was a primal catastrophe from which our characteristically fallen nature descends, it remains the case that human beings choose to go backwards to what the Bible sometimes calls death rather than forwards to the perfection that is the purpose of their creation. And that backwards movement is transmitted historically and socially. The situation can easily be illustrated by the fact that the abused so often − not automatically or universally, we must stress, for redemption does happen − become in turn the abusers. Similarly, the relation between necessity and freedom is illuminated by the fact that I − to bring the matter nearer home, so to speak − display some of the faults which I arrogantly trace back to my upbringing, and yet knowingly replicate. So that when it is debated between what are abstractly called left and right whether crime is the responsibility of the individual criminal or of society, the answer is, 'Both'. Our social world shapes us, and yet our freedom consists in what we make of our unique particularity.

The second misunderstanding of our doctrine derives from the fact that sin has sometimes been called 'total depravity'. If that is taken to mean that because of the fall there remains no good in human beings, it is clearly false: empirically false, because we see instances of goodness in all kinds of people, and theologically false, because it denies divine providence: his providential overruling of the full consequences of the fall and the consequent presence of all kinds of goodness, truth and beauty in his creation. The doctrine rather is that nothing escapes the corrupting effects of the disseminated poison that has been injected into the universe, and continues to be injected into both the personal and impersonal realms by the persistence of inherited patterns of behaviour. Even the most altruistic act is tinged with self-regard and self-seeking, even the most faithful marriage by some disloyalty and misdirected lust.

It scarcely needs to be pointed out today that human sins of greed and impatience pollute and endanger the life of the planet, and perhaps beyond, and this illustrates both the complexity and the reality of the historical and social effects of human endeavour. It may be that some form of what we call capitalism is inescapable for − fallen! − man, but its current manifestation, driven as it is by an insatiability that gives it a socially and ecologically destructive dynamic, well illustrates our theme. The suggestion that after the fall agriculture became burdensome toil (Gen. 3.17−19) again presents the situation pictorially and unsentimentally. We do not reap everything that we sow; that is again the message of God's providential love. And yet our acts do have effects, effects which mark the whole of the world we know, and indeed beyond. There is, we know, no simple correspondence between act and consequence. My sins affect others in all kinds of incalculable ways, and theirs mine, so that Schleiermacher is right to say of sin that it is at once individual and universal in its effects: 'in each the work of all and in all the work of each'.[3] We live in a world whose disseminated poison can be expelled, the alienation from each other and the world overcome, only by what is called salvation, and then only in a manner corresponding to its character, which, as we have seen, is everywhere and in everyone.

§14.   Creation and Salvation

The account of sin as both individual and social, both inherited and ever newly appropriated, leads to another important point. Because evil spreads its cancer throughout the body, embracing both its temporal and spatial dimensions, so salvation can take shape only over time and through space, social time and space especially, because it is with those who are made in the image of God that both the ill and its healing take shape. After that, it will not surprise the reader to be told that salvation is an eschatological concept, perhaps in that respect best rendered 'redemption', the final 'buying back' of the slave from bondage. It is something to be completed only from a 'beyond' which is the final and transformative gift of God. Corresponding to this insight, we must reject all merely psychological renderings of salvation, as feeling saved, and having an experience of forgiveness and release.[4] That may, indeed, be part of the matter, but it must be insisted that in eschatological perspective salvation means arriving safely at one's destination, and all other symptoms and manifestations are but greater or lesser stations upon the way. That is what we are made for, in Irenaeus' wonderful categorization:

---

[3] F. D. E. Schleiermacher, *The Christian Faith*, translation of 2nd edn. by H. R. Mackintosh and J. S. Stewart (Edinburgh: T. & T. Clark, 1925), p. 255.

[4] In answer to pietist type questions of when he was saved, Barth is reported to have replied, 'On Golgotha'.

that man should in the first instance be created; and having been created
should receive growth; and having been strengthened should abound; and
having abounded should recover; and having recovered should be glorified;
and being glorified should see his Lord.[5]

Salvation accordingly means the completion of that which was intended for
the human being. On account of sin, however, that final perfecting can
come about only through a buying back, a redemption, which takes account
both of the intended destiny of the creature and the way by which it fell
from its destiny.

The time frame in which we consider this matter makes much difference
to the way in which the relation between sin and salvation is understood. It
becomes even more complicated if we ask the question in relation to
eternity also, but for reasons of space that can be treated only briefly here.
It needs, however, to be mentioned in order to indicate the complexity of
the problems. God is eternal and the creator of time, and therefore not
subject to the constraints under which our created being takes its course. It
may then appear that, if we envisage God as an omnipotent eye, seeing the
whole course of history from outside, we must say that God foresaw the fall,
and therefore possibly even intended it. That is to speculate beyond the
evidence, and, although the image's moments of truth cannot be denied, it
is, as has already been suggested, better to understand God's relation to the
world rather as that of an author or playwright, whose pen does indeed
write the story, but in such a way as to allow the characters to develop
according to its and their intrinsic logic.

The purposed end of the story, as we have also seen, is the perfection of
the 'work of art' to the glory of its creator. Here we must hold two things in
tension. The first is the claim, widely acknowledged in the tradition, that
the salvation achieved in Jesus is such that it outshines even the glory of the
first creation. Does it then follow that the fall is a good thing, for Jesus
would not have come had evil not given him the opportunity? The second
thing to be held in mind, however, is that evil must not in any way be
justified or made to appear to be the cause of good. It may be the *occasion* for
good, as when an earthquake or rail disaster brings out human qualities of
compassion and enterprise, or when the execution of the Son of God
achieves human salvation, but that does not take away its quality as evil.

[5] Irenaeus, *Against the Heresies*, 4. 38. 3.

'The Son of Man goes as is written of him, but woe to the one by whom he is betrayed' (Mt. 26.24). As the vehicle of death – that which directs human life to failure and nothingness – evil can only be that which has to be overcome. That is why we just reject, for all its appeal, the famous Latin saying which, in translation, reads 'O happy fault, that merited such and so great a redeemer.' Nothing that constricts and confines human beings in misery and slavery can be 'happy', just as having an illness is not made the more pleasant because we shall appreciate the benefits of health so much more vividly when we recover.

However, to veer too far to the other side can also distort our understanding of the happening of salvation in time. If what is achieved by Jesus in his life, death, resurrection and ascension is not in some way within the divine intention from the outset, we obtain a strange notion of God's way with things. Is it really the case that God has one shot at his world called 'creation', and because that fails then has to send his Son to pick up the pieces? This doctrine, sometimes known as dishwater Protestantism, though a version of it also appears in Catholicism's classic theologian, Thomas Aquinas,[6] has the merit of stressing the absolute centrality of Christ and what he achieves. Yet it will not do, for a number of reasons. One is that it underemphasizes the fact that salvation begins with the call of Abraham and the election of Israel, which are to be treated not simply as background but as of constitutive significance. At least as seriously, this theology risks a divorce of creation from salvation, making salvation so radically different an enterprise that it may seem as though it involves salvation out of and away from the creation. The spotlight then falls on the salvation of souls not bodies, men and women out of, rather than as a part of, their material environment. Essential here is christology. If creation is in, through and for Christ, there is more of a continuity between it and salvation than is allowed by the theory which we are criticizing. The interrelation of the two was expressed by Athanasius early in the fourth century. Jesus Christ is the Son of God, the mediator of God's creation, returning to his own realm to reclaim it from threatened dissolution.[7]

We shall therefore require a more adequate model of the relation of salvation to creation if we are to do justice to both the unity and variety of the work of God. We shall find it only if we ask a prior question, one

[6] Thomas Aquinas, *Summa Theologiae* 3a. 1. 3. ad 2.
[7] Athanasius, *On the Incarnation of the Word*.

whose answer has already been anticipated in earlier chapters: what is God's purpose in creation? Of the two main answers that can be given, the first is one that has had enormous and enormously damaging effects in western Christianity. It tends to suppose that God's purposes are essentially other-worldly and spiritual in a narrow sense. God created and later saves a limited remnant of the human race in order that there shall be sufficient souls in heaven to make up for the spaces left by the departure of the fallen angels.[8] The means by which this end is achieved are the death of Jesus and the election of a finite number of those destined to be saved. There are, to be sure, variants of this view, only one particularly definite version of which here serves to illustrate the situation. Suffice it to say here that until the modern reaction against it, the teaching of the election of a limited number and the rejection in hell of the majority was the mainstream teaching of both mediaeval Catholicism and the Protestantism that reacted against it. To be sure, there were more generous versions of the doctrine in currency, particularly those which tended more to a view that God's will was that all should be saved. A flaw, however, remained even there, and this was the essentially other-worldly and overspiritualizing view of salvation which stressed the destiny of the soul in another world at the expense of the redemption of soul and body together within the structures of this one. We shall again encounter this matter in the chapters in which eschatology and the resurrection are treated.

One great and generous recent reaction against the theory of the pre-destination of the few to salvation is that of Karl Barth, which is worth a brief review because it turns the tradition on its head without quite taking it into the position advocated in this study. Barth maintains the centrality of the doctrine of election, and indeed makes it into the first of God's works, first in intention if not in execution. According to him, God's purpose in creating is that there shall be another personal creature to bring into fellow-ship with him: 'Of all words that can be said or heard it is the best: that God elects man; that God is for man too the One who loves in freedom.'[9] Far from something to be feared and hated, the doctrine of election says that God has chosen the human race, all of it, in Christ, to come into loving relationship with its creator. The world is therefore created in order that

---

[8] See Anselm, *Why the God-Man*, 16–18.
[9] Karl Barth, *Church Dogmatics*, translation edited by G. W. Bromiley and T. F. Torrance (Edinburgh: T. & T. Clark, 1957–75), vol. 2/2, p.3.

there be a theatre of God's love, a place where his gracious purposes of love for all can take shape. This is an immense improvement on its predecessors, and despite what is sometimes said does leave open the small possibility owed to human freedom that some will finally turn their back on it and choose rejection. But a niggle remains. Is the remainder of the creation there only for this purpose, in some way instrumental to human election rather than integral to the grand design? Perhaps not quite for Barth, but at least it must be said that he leaves room for suspicion.

And so we return to the position that God creates in order that the whole of what he creates should be perfected to his praise and glory. Central among the agents of this perfecting are to be the men and women created in his image, and called to special responsibility for and among the creatures. As we have seen, that responsibility is structured by means of an ethic, a design for living on earth involving both social and cultural realms. It is the failure of the salutary relation to the creator and the subsequent social, cultural and eco-logical disorder which require what is termed salvation. And it gives salvation its corresponding shape, which is essentially to be understood as that activity of God whereby the movement backwards into dissolution and nothingness is reversed, and creation's original movement to perfection restored.[10]

Christology is at the centre of this conception, for, as we have seen, it is Christ the mediator of creation who comes to his own world in order to re-create it. This means that we can adopt for ourselves the moments of truth in the 'happy fault' theology. The coming of the saviour does indeed achieve something greater even than that which was achieved in the original creation, so that it is not a mere repair job, so to speak, but the crown of that which was there begun. We shall come to that in more detail in the chapters devoted to the person of Christ, but would here point out that what is being adopted is what is sometimes called a Scotist christology. Would Christ have come even had there been no fall? Hypothetical questions are dangerous in theology, because it is concerned with what God has done, not what he might have done instead. But in this case the question enables us to bring out the point of what has happened. The ways of God for his creation involve Christ, the one through whom he created and continues to uphold the universe *in any case*, and therefore he would have come – even had sin not dictated the *form* of his coming. Sin and evil are, then, in Edward Irving's words, the *formal* cause of the incarnation, determining the shape

---

[10] We may call this 'original blessing', though not in the sense usually intended.

it takes, in the suffering and death of Jesus.[11] But the efficient cause, that which gives it its point, is the love of God for his creature, a love rooted in his being, and begun, continued and ended in Christ. Whatever else we are to say of salvation, therefore, and of the cross which is the hinge on which all salvation turns, it is rooted in the love of God, his merciful refusal to allow the creation to destroy itself. Calvin quotes Augustine, one father of western theology appealing to another, to make this point: 'For it is not after we were reconciled to him through the blood of his Son that he began to love us. Rather, he loved us before the world was created, that we also might be sons along with his only-begotten Son – before we became anything at all.'[12] The cross is not, therefore, primarily punitive, as some theologies may have suggested, even though some punitive overtones are unavoidable, just as there must be punishment even in the most liberal social order. In the remainder of this chapter we shall explore something of the shape of the historical realization of God's eternal purposes of love.

§15.   The People of the Promise

Although I have begun this chapter with an account of the alienation between the creator and the human creature which disrupts everything else, there seems to be little doubt that the Bible's writers recognize sin for what it is only in the light of what they know God to have done for its overcoming. Paul speaks of sin only in the light of the gospel of Jesus Christ, Genesis only as the prelude to the call of Abraham and his descendants. And it is with Abraham that we begin an account of how it is that the historical and social shape of redemption corresponds to that which it seeks to amend. The promise to Abraham, at least as that was understood by later interpreters like Paul, is a promise according to which one people – Abraham's descendants – would be the source of salvation for all the peoples of the earth. The universal end is brought about by particular means; in other words, by means that take time and are realized in (social) space.

---

[11] G. Carlyle (ed.), *The Collected Writings of Edward Irving in Five Volumes* (London: Alexander Strachan, 1865), vol. 5, p. 10.

[12] John Calvin, *Institutes of the Christian Religion*, edited by J. T. McNeill, translated and indexed by F. L. Battles, Library of Christian Classics (Philadelphia: Westminster Press, 1960), vols. 20 and 21, III. xvi. 4, citing Augustine, *John's Gospel*, cx. 8.

Abraham's call is neither the first nor the last of the series of promises or covenants by which God's merciful and saving action advances his purposes through time. We have heard something of the promise to Noah that the creation will retain its stability, but in Abraham for the first time we meet a blessing which goes beyond that made at the creation. And from Abraham we move, through Isaac and Jacob, through Joseph in Egypt, to a call through Moses to the whole people of Israel, who are made what they are through the Exodus and the giving of the law on Sinai. However, the way in which Israel both understood and worked out her calling presents both a messy and a complicated story. Especially in the years before the time of Jesus there appear to have been radical differences in Israel's understanding of the way in which the people should go, with conflict between narrower and more universal interpretations. Those Jewish writers who in the New Testament era first interpreted the meaning of Jesus appealed to the more universal strand, and especially to the prophesies collected in the book of Isaiah. The four 'Servant Songs' of Isaiah 40–55, whose actual historical reference may have been to a particular individual or to Israel as a whole, provided a frame for the picture which was painted of Jesus: 'It is too small a thing for you to be my servant to restore the tribes of Jacob . . . I will also make you to be a light for the Gentiles, that you may bring my salvation to the ends of the earth' (Is. 49.6). The claim of the New Testament is that in the true Israelite, Jesus of Nazareth, that promise is made concrete.

But we cannot leap directly to him, because there is more to be said about the process by which Israel was taught to order her life before God and in the world. Israel had a number of means – God-given institutions – by which she maintained her relation to her God and contained the social and moral effects of the evil that was let loose and continued by human transgression of the limits of createdness. Central was the Torah, which included both moral and social teaching as well as what we would wrongly tend to separate off as the merely religious. That is to say, laws for society's well-being and regulations for the cult are presented alongside one another in mutual dependence and significance. Like all societies, Israel had religious, moral and political dimensions to her life, and it can be said that the offices corresponding to them were those of priest, prophet and king, and they predominated variously at different stages of Israel's history. All of them, however, are equally oriented at once to Israel's relation to God and to the social order consequent upon that. They were called in order to maintain Israel's faithfulness to the covenant. In a monarchy, which Israel became, the function of a king is to dispense justice internally and defend the realm against external threats. And that is what Israel's kings did, or were supposed to do, for the period when she could claim to be an independent state. Those were good kings who focused and expressed Israel's obedience to God and her distinct calling among the nations; and bad kings who followed pagan peoples into religious apostasy and social injustice, which were for the prophets two aspects of the same sin. And so we come to the second institution by which Israel's loyalty was maintained. Prophets indeed predicted disaster, and sometimes salvation as the other side of disaster, but did so in order to recall Israel to her covenant responsibilities. They did not only speak, but acted, combining, as Jesus was later to do, their teaching with politically charged symbolic acts and miraculous healings. They were prophets because they were called by God to both speak and enact his truth in a society where it had been abandoned.

In our world, we are moderately comfortable with our equivalents for kings and prophets, but less so with the third great institution, the priest-hood and the cult which was its responsibility. And yet it could be said that the priests and their sacrifices take us to the heart not only of Israel's relation to God, but of ours also. Sacrifice has and had myriad functions and mean-ings, and that is testimony to its all-embracing character, enfolding within its conceptual variety many aspects of our relation to God and the world. Its heart is in something like this: that those who bring an animal to the altar or place a coin in a collecting box give something of themselves, of their substance, as we say, and in that way alter, be it ever so slightly, the shape of our world. In specifically religious context, a sacrifice reorders the relation between God and his people. Israel's sacrifices were given by God, ordained by him as part of his relation to his chosen people, and were consequently the means by which their life was ordered and reordered in relation both to him and to one another. Closely linked with the notion of sacrifice is that of exchange, which we shall encounter later. Something is exchanged for something else, a coin for a pound of apples, a death for a life. And it is with life above all that sacrifice is concerned, for Israel's God was the God of life. All life was his, and the cult was directed to the living relation of God and the creatures, human and non-human alike, which were his special preserve. Where sin means the rule of death, God's action is designed to restore life.

The value of the concept of sacrifice is that, in contrast with other images used of God's providentially gifted institutions and saving acts, it cannot be restricted to the merely social and human sphere. That is important enough, as we have seen, for the human being is at the heart both of God's purposes and their attempted subversion. Yet, as we have also seen, to be human is to be embodied, to be continuous with the beasts and indeed to be constructed from the dust of the earth. Sacrifice reminds us of, indeed establishes us in, our continuity and involvement with the wider world in which our life is lived out. It reminds us of our ecological entrenchment, the fact that what we do affects both one another and the world of which we are a part. Moreover, it focuses both our calling to offer the creation back to God in thanksgiving and our inability, as we and the world are at present, apart from God's redemptive act, to offer ourselves as a living sacrifice, holy and acceptable to God (Rom. 12.1).

If, as we have seen, sin is that which ruptures the human relation to God and brings personal, social and ecological disorder in its train, all of the institutions we have so briefly surveyed are in part devoted to mitigating the effects of sin, to constraining evil or channelling its effects away where they can do less harm. They help us to understand what can be called the secondary qualities of sin, the symptoms to which the underlying disease gives rise. Kings and prophets remind us that sin takes the form of lawlessness and injustice, the oppression of the weak and the theft of our neighbour's property. (Calvin rightly comments that failure to help our neighbour in need is as much an offence against this law as is positive theft.)[13] We need governments and prophets because we fail to live in love and fellowship with our neighbour. Priests and their sacrifices, however, remind us – whatever we are to make of the form that their offerings traditionally take – that our failure goes deeper, and that the malaise consists not merely in social disorder, but in our sharing in the corruption that threatens all life, that prevents people from being holy, culture from being truly the praise of God and things from being whole-some and good.

§16.   The Achievement of Salvation

How is this human failure and earthly corruption to be righted, the move-ment of creation to dissolution to be reversed? The gospel teaches that,

[13] Calvin, *Institutes*, II. 8. 45.

good though law and sacrifice and prophecy may be, the accumulated misery of the human condition requires, if it is to be healed, nothing less than the personal and saving presence of the eternal Son of God. Reconciliation with God, that is to say, is the necessary condition for reconciliation between people and peace with the environment. Without putting that right, the rest will not happen either. The same point can be put positively. In his person, and through the various acts and phases of his historic career, Jesus fills the offices and institutions of Israel with distinctive and definitive meaning, in such a way as to open up a new and definitive way for lost men and women to make their peace with, and their way back to, their God and creator. Israel's offices are so concentrated in him that the old wineskins are burst open by the new and heady brew: in his person he *is* prophet, priest and king. That is why John Newton's celebrating of Jesus in his well-known hymn as 'My prophet, priest and king' is so evocative; in him are focused all of our relations with our creator.[14]

The New Testament uses a range of ways, from the pictorial to the more conceptual,[15] on which theology has drawn to build up a broad range of articulations of the way by which a human being called Jesus both embodied and achieved what is called salvation. We begin with one that illustrates both the Old Testament roots of our topic and its metaphorical richness. Redemption is a monetary image, illustrated by its use today in commerce. For the Old Testament, the redeemer is one's next of kin whose responsibility it is to buy back from slavery those who have been captured in war. The prophet known as the Second Isaiah transfers the language to God, who, as Israel's 'next of kin' or redeemer, will release them from the slavery of their exile in Babylon. When we come to the New Testament, it is important to bear in mind that it is God who is the redeemer, who pays the price for human sin. But he does it through the life, and particularly the death, of Jesus, who is the 'ransom' he pays. One of the two explicit uses of the notion appears in the dénouement of Mark's account of the dispute among Jesus' disciples about which of them will dominate when he comes in his glory: 'For even the Son of Man did not come to be served, but to

---

[14] John Newton, 'How Sweet the Name of Jesus Sounds'.

[15] All are in different ways both. There are no pure concepts, free of pictorial or metaphorical content; think, for example, even of one apparently so, 'substance'; but nor are the images merely 'pictures', because they are ways of understanding the human condition in all its complexity.

serve and to give his life as a ransom for many.'[16] The facts that in Isaiah it is God who pays the ransom and that this is a metaphorical description of that payment remind us that there are limits to what we can make of it. We must neither play God off against Jesus nor ask to whom the price was paid, whether, as has sometimes been asked, to God or to the devil – and, worse, sometimes answered. Jesus' gift of his life is at the same time God's ransoming of his enslaved people.

The two sides of this one action are also important for our second way of speaking, which is quite closely related. In speaking of the human condition, we often use military imagery, in speaking, for example, of winning a moral victory or in saying of a book – Tolkien's *Lord of the Rings*, for example – that it is a literary depiction of the eternal battle of good against evil. In the Old Testament, Israel's liberation from Egypt at the Exodus is often depicted as God's victory not simply over the Pharaoh, but over forces of nature also. God's right arm, as the psalmist puts it, has won him the victory by taking Israel through the Red Sea. In the New Testament, Jesus, in the power of the Spirit, becomes God's right arm in person. The epistles often portray the cross as a titanic struggle and victory over the forces that hold human life in bondage – what Paul sometimes calls the 'principalities and powers', whose character we must consider when we come to the chapter on eschatology. It is evident that they are not defeated in the sense of being abolished, for this is a victory in the light of which human struggle against evil continues, and indeed has to be intensified: 'Our struggle is not against flesh and blood, but against the rulers, against the principalities, against the powers of this dark world...' (Eph. 6.12). But it is a victory none the less. In what sense?

The answer is to be found in the manner of Jesus' life and of his achievement. His ministry begins with a struggle against temptation, his victory in which is the source of the authority and power which enables him to live the kind of life that he does. Luke's story in chapter 4 of the outcome of Jesus' resistance to temptation indicates that by his victory – the quintessential 'moral victory' – he wins the authority of true speech and effective action. Indeed, it is often the case, as with the prophets, of effective action by means of speech. Through his obedience to God the poor and excluded are offered a place in the kingdom, the sick are healed and the sin which stunts human

---

[16] Mk. 10.45; compare 1 Tim. 2.6 and Rom. 3.24, where slightly different Greek words are used.

development is forgiven. We may in our culture have difficulties with the idea of demons – though we meet the demonic often enough in twentieth century history – but we can see in one encounter between Jesus and his opponents the very heart of the matter. He is accused of casting out the demons in the power of the prince of demons. He replies, commonsensically, that if that is the case, the kingdom of the demonic is divided against itself, with the foreman destroying his workmen. The moral is that Jesus is not the prince of darkness, but one stronger than he, and his healings are the evidence (Mk. 3.22–30). In sum: the eschatological victory of God is begun in Jesus' ministry. By this human victory over evil, in a war waged only by the power deriving from obedience to God, the rule of God over an enslaved world is reinaugurated. The struggle climaxes with the cross, because there the accumulated power of evil and Jesus' final temptation to run away from the battle field are overcome in his refusal to do anything but the will of his Father. His 'moral' victory is the way by which God effectively overcomes the enemy by refusing to use its weapons, as when in Tolkien's modern myth Frodo Baggins is able to overcome the power of Sauron only by refusing to use the ring of power. Jesus' is a divine victory won through the human faithfulness and sheer intransigence that only the empowering Spirit can effect. It begins in his life and climaxes in his death.

But the story has other dimensions as well, dimensions indeed which take us ever deeper into the mystery of the topic of how evil is overcome by a human act that is also God's. Many of the symptoms of sin derive from a failure to obey the law, a failure to love only God unconditionally and so to be able to love our neighbours as ourselves. Here we are in the realm of justice, of divine and human justice, and of the question of how they are realized and related. We have seen already that Torah means more than we tend to mean by law. Similarly, justice has for scripture a far wider embrace than fairness and the proper punishment of offence. Comprehensively, divine justice refers to the realization of God's rule over the creation, and that means the fulfilment of his project that all creation should be perfected and therefore praise him. Human injustice is in that light that which retards the movement to perfection of the world and its constituent people and things. If, then, Jesus is to embody and realize God's purpose, his action must in some way achieve a reordering, a re-establishing of God's just and merciful rule over his world.

So far as human justice is concerned, Jesus is, in Paul's words, 'born under the law', subject to its constraints, and, in a fallen world, its injustices. He is brought up as a son of the law, keeps it, teaches it, at times authoritatively reinterpreting it, and finally accepts its flawed, if apparently justified, sentence. He goes to the cross as a criminal convicted under the law of God. As part of this calling 'to fulfil all righteousness' the New Testament sees Jesus as accepting the law's punitive outcome, because by accepting the death that he does he accepts also, on behalf and in place of others, the consequences of human failure to live by the law. It does not follow that God is punishing Jesus instead of the sinner, but that God in Christ achieves an exchange: that the one who 'knew no sin' – and we must examine the meaning of this in a later chapter – is 'made to be sin' for us (2 Cor. 5.21). For the passion narratives in the Gospels it is patent that Jesus' reluctance before death was more than a natural cringing before the end of life. It was the horror of one going to the death that is the fruit of the human breach with the creator. Jesus dies in the space from which God has taken away his loving presence, to the effect that he bore the just judgement of God upon sin in order that others might be freed not from all judgement, but from the judgement that brings death.

The universal message of the evangelists and apostles is that the death of Jesus is rooted in God's love for the creature – his mercy – and not in his punitive justice. We shall have to say something in another chapter about the place, if any, of punishment in divine and human order; what must be said here is that in some way or other the importance of upholding a just order of things must be maintained. If breaches of the law are in no way righted – if the victims of murder, rape and slander are in no way vindicated – then it is finally an unjust universe. At this place, we must therefore engage briefly with another of the divine attributes which together build up a picture of the kind of God with whom scripture presents us. We have seen that from the outset of the sorry story of human obliquity God's actions have been characterized by a merciful refusal to allow evil to take its full course. We have seen, also, that God's justice is not primarily his punitive act but his purpose to see that right prevail. But if we are to be true to the overall message of scripture, we must also allow that the wrath of God is integral also to his relations with the world.[17] Wrath is the form that holy love takes when it is rejected, and it involves the rejection of the actions of those who put themselves outside the love of God. It is a function of God's

---

[17] I am grateful to Andrew Mackintosh for indicating the absence of any direct reference to this in an earlier draft of this chapter.

love, and so is punitive only in the respect that it accepts that breaches of the law must entail certain consequences, however much these are mitigated in their outcome. (The function of punishment in a loving family offers a proper if limited analogy.) It is, however, not punitive in making punishment an end in itself rather than a means to the greater end of the redemption of the sinner. To obtain some conception of what it involves, we again refer to Jesus' horror before his execution, which is the horror of one encountering God's rejection of all that is unfit to come into his presence. He endures it, however, so that we should not have to suffer the deadly judgement that is the logical outcome of our ways.

For the logic of punishment is precisely what is transformed in Jesus' endurance of divine wrath. The outcome is that God creates a way of righting wrong not by vengeance, but by bearing the consequences of evil himself, by the act of his own right arm. We sometimes say that we 'would give our right arm' for something we really want. God in Christ gives his for us. Another way of explaining the position is that underlying this theology is the conviction that evil can be overcome only by good, for attempting to overcome it by a further evil simply reduplicates the ill. This is a way of characterizing both the divine action and the ethic that is consequent upon it, however lamentably its exponents have often failed to live up to it. Because God in Jesus overcomes evil by good, so should those who follow him (see especially Rom. 12.21). A real change in the situation can come about only if the evil is *overcome*; that is to say, taken seriously in such a way that its reality is displaced by something stronger. To say that God could simply forgive, as is sometimes put in objection, may be true abstractly, but it would trivialize that which causes the problem in the first place. Forgiveness can be made effective only by an alteration of the conditions that created the offence.

If we are to understand aright the notion that Jesus bore the – legal – judgement of God in place of the human sinner, it must never be understood in abstraction from the implications of our fourth image and concept. Just as the life and death of Jesus is God's redeeming and liberating act as (1) at once a divine and a human victory over evil and (2) at once a just act of God and the just action of a man, so (3) it is at once a divine and human sacrifice. The two sides of this matter are brought out, first, by John's well-known statement that 'Greater love has no one than this, that someone lay down his life for his friends' (Jn. 15.13; see also the numerous equivalents in Paul and the other apostles); and second by Paul's equally sacrificial expression that 'He who did not spare his own Son, but gave him up for us all – how will he not also, along with him, give us all things?' (Rom. 8.32). Jesus' self-giving is at the same time God's giving, a giving that expresses, realizes in time, the order of giving and receiving that God is eternally.

In the Old Testament the priest is one who makes sacrifices to God on behalf of the people by bringing the gifts of the people to God. In this new order of things, the priest *is* the sacrifice and his gift to God the Father is that of himself, of his *life*. The lineaments of this are wonderfully expressed by the author to the Hebrews. His Jesus is the eternal Son, mediator of creation, who as man offers not the sacrifice of animals, which cannot 'cleanse the conscience from dead works' (Heb. 9.14), but a life of perfect obedience to the Father. The mystery of salvation is that those who have by their unholy living put themselves outside the way to life may through their relation to this man come before God as his holy people. The outcome, which we shall treat in more detail later, is a new understanding of the meaning of sacrifice: not a dead animal, but to repeat Irenaeus' words, a human being truly alive. Paul draws the conclusion in the text we have already met: a human life in response is 'a *living* sacrifice, holy and pleasing to God...'. Once again, we reach a recurring theme: that the point of our creation is the perfection of our whole persons, body and spirit, in praise to God. The heart of the Christian theology of salvation is that because the Son of God has been through it before and on behalf of and in certain respects instead of us, he is the 'pioneer and perfecter' of our faith, on whom we can rely for everything. The early Christian writing known as *The Letter to Diognetus* sums up the saving mystery of the life and cross of Jesus in words that cannot be bettered. 'O sweetest exchange... The sinfulness of many is hidden in the righteous one, while the righteousness of the One justifies the many that are sinners.'[18] But who is this apparently hybrid being, both eternal Son of God and human way to God? Who he is and what he did and does will be the topic of our next two chapters.

[18] *Letter to Diognetus*, 9. 5.

Chapter 5

The Identity of Jesus Christ

§17. To Set the Scene

Recent theology is virtually unanimous about the importance of stressing the humanity of Jesus, even though it is by no means agreed about the best way of going about it. The complaint is frequently on the lips especially of those who wish to stress the gulf between ancient and modern conditions that ancient theology was 'docetic', that is, presented a Christ who only appeared to be human. That this was by no means always the case in premodern times is evident to anyone who has seen one of the mediaeval mystery plays or the pictures in art galleries. Yet it is true that the tradition has for the most part been able to present the divine Christ, awesome judge of the living and the dead, more vividly and effectively than the human, as some early Christian art and later musical expressions of the *Dies Irae* in the Requiem Mass also vividly witness. That is something we shall have to bear in mind as we consider the matter of the person of Christ – the question of his identity – if only because the way it has been depicted contains the reasons for the offence that is sometimes taken at the claims of the gospel. (To be sure, there is a necessary offence, both moral and intellectual, involved in the gospel. It offends against many of our deepest intuitions that the key to the meaning of our life and death should be the death of a man on a cross. But it is important that the offence be the real one, and not something misleading or irrelevant.)

Another cause for offence in the modern world is the doctrine of 'two natures': that Christ was, according to the language of the tradition 'one person in two natures'. This has sometimes led to the appearance of a kind of hybrid being, two contrary realities stitched together, like a centaur, suggesting two persons rather than one person in two natures. That this teaching has since early times been labelled 'Nestorianism' and officially rejected has not prevented some from speaking and writing as if it were true. When, for example, it is suggested that when Jesus was tired and wept he did so as a man, whereas when he performed miracles or forgave sins he acted as God, we may be near to such a transgression. Our principle when speaking of Jesus must be to hold in mind the biblical portrayal of him, for as we read that we undoubtedly meet someone who was by almost any standards unusual, but not unusual in the way that some use of the two-nature language suggests. Here is one who is a unity, so that if he performs divine acts, he does so as one who is truly human, whatever else we may also wish to say – as we do have to say other things also.

Our topic is particularly difficult because the truth of historic Christianity depends upon the confession that Jesus of Nazareth is the eternal Son of God. The chief *historical* basis for this is provided in two facts: that from earliest times he was confessed in terms that identified him with the God whose servant he was, and that his disciples worshipped and were prepared to die for him. Similarly, the chief *theological* basis for those who make the confession thereafter is to be found in what we reviewed in the previous chapter. Christianity is a religion of salvation whose character is inseparable from the teaching that salvation is mediated by what I shall summarize as the career of this one man. By 'career' I mean the whole of what happened to Jesus and what he did, does and will do, from his birth to Mary, through his life of teaching and action, to his death, resurrection and the ascension, with its implied promise that this same human being will return in glory to complete that which began at the creation of the world. It is this career, set out as a narrative as it is, which is the place where God both reverses the accumulated history of sin and evil and re-establishes the creation's movement to its promised perfection. The theological heart of the Christian faith, therefore, is to be found in the affirmation that this historical human being, 'despised and rejected of men', is identical with – the same person as – the eternal Son of God through whom God created the world. His earthly career, accordingly, must be understood as God's personal action in his world to renew and complete the plan of creation once begun but since disrupted. It is the means by which God the Father re-establishes through the perfecting work of his Spirit the *rightness* of the creation. In order to show just how this can be, we shall need to draw on the resources with which the Christian tradition, itself drawing on scripture, has so generously endowed us. I therefore begin a discussion with some summary points from scripture.

There is far more to scripture than narrative, because, as we have seen, it presents a stable and established creation as well as a history of providence and salvation taking place upon its stage. Yet because we are here occupied with God's perfecting of the world through time and in space, it remains the case that it is the narrative with which we are chiefly concerned. In the books of the Old and New Testaments the course of what is technically called the *economy* of God's action in the world is laid out.[1] There, what can be called God's story and that of the world are told not in parallel but in an interweaving of such a kind that it is often difficult to disentangle the threads. Distinct threads there are because, as we have also seen, the created order has its own distinct reality, and it is other than God's. But they are also interwoven, because that distinct reality comes only from God's providential action towards and in the world. And, for our purposes in this chapter, they begin their interweaving in the story of God's call of, and involvement in, the people of Israel. Israel, we might say, provides the logic of christology, so that the Old Testament lays down the framework within which both Jesus himself, so it would appear, and his first interpreters understood his significance.

Much effort has been expended in recent centuries to reconstruct the story of Jesus, particularly by historical investigation of the Gospel stories and their background. By this method, however, the man remains elusive, and the Roman Catholic theologian George Tyrrell, no advocate of a rigid traditionalism himself, famously jibed that the Jesus that had been constructed in the nineteenth century was 'only the reflection of a Liberal Protestant face, seen at the bottom of a deep well'.[2] Equivalent points could be made about recent attempts to do the same, so that Marxists find a revolutionary Jesus, feminists a feminist Jesus and some modern western thinkers a politically correct Jesus in their own image. There are, to be sure, more careful and theologically informed attempts, but if they are to be more than narcissistic reflections in a mirror they must hold on to the fact that the

---

[1] 'Economy': literally, the way by which God organizes his household.

[2] Cited by D. M. Baillie, *God Was in Christ. An Essay on Incarnation and Atonement* (London: Faber, 1956), p. 40.

real Jesus (1) was formed by Israel's scriptures, (2) was interpreted by his first followers in their light, and (3) in turn became for his followers the key to those scriptures. The identity of one book that is heavily determinative can be ventured, and it is the collection of narratives and prophecies collected as the book of Isaiah. New Testament scripture is so replete with allusions to and citations of this book that it clearly was, and remains, a key to Jesus, whose contours become clearer when we view him in its light, not more obscure and disputed as is the case with most modern historical reconstructions. More: those reconstructions, which rightly sought to find a more detailed picture than was provided by the summary form of the traditional dogmas, might have been unnecessary had the tradition been more careful of Jesus' Jewishness and less anxious to cut him off from his historical context and formation. We shall return to this problem in the next chapter.

The earliest biblical evocations of Jesus' significance, developed in a time when eye-witnesses were still alive, take two overlapping but distinct forms. First, are brief historical summaries of the story and its meaning. If, as cannot be finally established but remains likely, the speeches in the Acts of the Apostles truly reflect the early Christian preaching they purport to record, we have an indication of an early response to the resurrection.[3] Acts 2.22–4, tells a story that is both Jesus' and God's. The wicked human act of murdering Jesus both took place according to God's purpose and was reversed by God's raising him from the dead. The same chapter later interprets this in trinitarian terms: 'Exalted to the right hand of God, he has received from the Father the promised Holy Spirit and has poured out what you now see and hear' (Ac. 2.33). Galatians 4.4 and 1 Corinthians 15.3–5 indicate different aspects of the one narrative. 'When the time had fully come, God sent forth his Son . . .'; ' . . . Christ died for our sins according to the scriptures, . . . he was buried, . . . he was raised on the third day according to the scriptures, and . . . he appeared to Peter and then to the Twelve.' At greater length is Philippians 2.5–11, which interweaves so tightly the story of divine act and human career that the two are both inextricable and endlessly the source of both profound insight and scholarly dispute:

Christ Jesus, who, though he was in the form of God, did not count equality with God a thing to be grasped, but emptied himself, taking the form of a

[3] G. N. Stanton, *Jesus of Nazareth in New Testament Preaching* (Cambridge, UK: Cambridge University Press, 1974), chapter 1.

servant, being born in the likeness of men. And being found in human form he humbled himself, and became obedient unto death... (vv. 5–8)

Jesus Christ, who was truly God, first took the form of a servant and then behaved, by going to the cross, in ways expressive of that servanthood.

The Gospels, particularly the first three of them, fill in the narrative details underlying these confessions. Each has its own theological perspective and stress, but all depict the human life of Jesus as divine action for the salvation of the world. It has been opined that they are in large measure stories of the passion with prefaces and conclusions, and that is particularly illuminating for Mark, where from the beginning Jesus is destined for death, with conflict being aroused by his very first words and actions. Offence is taken especially at his claim to forgive sins, an arrogation of divine privilege, and later by his violent cleansing of the temple. The Gospel begins with affirmation of his significance as the Son of God, and moves to that very confession on the lips of a Gentile (15.39). Matthew and Luke trace the beginnings of Jesus' story back to his birth, with divine sonship important for them also. The articulation of Jesus' unique significance is central for them all. Luke's penultimate verse reports that the disciples worshipped the ascended Jesus, while Matthew ends with the risen Jesus' claim to have been given 'all authority' by God. Matthew 11.27 is of major significance in producing a trinitarian shape similar to that we have met in Acts, that 'All things have been committed to me by my Father. No one knows the Son except the Father, and no one knows the Father except the Son, and those to whom the Son chooses to reveal him.' Whether or not such words were actually on the lips of Jesus – and who knows? – they are there to indicate Matthew's estimation of his significance.

It has often been noted that this – the 'Johannine thunderbolt from the Matthean sky' – appears to echo some of the things said in John's Gospel, a large part of whose message the verse so precisely summarizes. The case being argued here does not depend on a claim that Jesus said precisely the things placed on his lips in that Gospel, although there is no good reason to doubt the authenticity of the historical tradition with which John works. The heart of this Gospel's theology rather derives from its distinctive perspective, which is of Jesus viewed from the standpoint of those who have for some time lived in the light of the gospel he embodies, and especially of the Spirit's teaching about him. The Jesus who weeps at the death of a friend is also the one who says, 'Before Abraham was, I am' (Jn.

8.58), and who is confessed as 'the holy one of God' (Jn. 6. 69); and, after his resurrection, by Thomas as 'My Lord and my God' (Jn. 20.28). This is precisely parallel to the theology of the Letter to the Hebrews, which, like John's Gospel, prefaces an account of the human action and passion with an identification of it as the career of the one through whom the world was made and is upheld.

So much, then, for our first group of New Testament evocations of Jesus' significance, the summaries of his story. The second form taken by the early witnesses is of often fragmentary credal confessions which outline not so much the story as its significance, and especially the significance of its chief human actor. Romans 1.3–4 places in parallel Jesus' human descent from David and his divine significance as the Son of God. Of similar significance is 1 Corinthians 8.4–6, a confession which glosses and so reinterprets in the light of Jesus an Old Testament confession – perhaps we should say the classical confession – of the oneness of God. Deuteronomy 6.4 says, in its statement of the law: 'Hear O Israel: the Lord our God, the Lord is one', and this is cited in v. 4 of the Corinthians passage. Two verses later comes its glossing by Paul: 'For us, there is but one God, the Father, *from* whom all things came, and *for* whom we live; and there is but one Lord, Jesus Christ, *through* whom all things came, and *through* whom we live.' The significance of this can scarcely be exaggerated. Not many years after the death of Jesus he is being placed alongside God the Father, subtly differentiated in the form of his relation to the world but clearly also – despite what some commentators have claimed – given equality of divine being and status. Later New Testament confessions, which we cannot examine in detail, reinforce and expand that status, but never in such a way as to deny that it is the human Jesus of whom they are speaking. He it is who is the mediator of God the Father's creating work, become flesh for the salvation of the world.

> In the beginning was the Word... Through him all things were made; without him nothing was made that has been made. ...And the Word became flesh, and lived among us, full of grace and truth.[4]

As the critics will remind us, however, there is no uniformity in the expressions, and one cannot say that there is a single New Testament

---

[4] Jn 1.1,3,14. Compare 1 Cor. 8.6, Eph. 1.3–10, Col. 1.15–20, Heb. 1.1, 13.8, Rev. 1.7, 21.6.

christology. But neither does it follow that there is such a diversity that no general theological conclusions can be drawn. Much depends upon the kind of unity which is being sought, and that in turn depends upon the type of theology underpinning the search. Neither in the gospels nor in our understanding of God is the unity that we are seeking a bare mathematical one. That is because, as we have seen, the relation of God to the world, though that of one God, is realized in a rich variety of acts and forms. In that light, we shall not expect all the confessions to describe Jesus and his significance in precisely the same way. Yet the texts whose message is being so briefly summarized do have common features. The first is that none of the things said of Jesus, even the most exalted, is considered by the writers to compromise in any way the monotheistic faith of Israel. The oneness of God to which Deuteronomy bore such categorical witness is a oneness that brooks no rivals, not one of bare mathematics. The God who according to Old Testament teaching relates to the world in many and various ways is the one now identified as a result of and through what happened with Jesus. It is Jesus who, through the Spirit, now personally mediates the divine action which the Old Testament refers to with the help of various terms, in its speaking of God's word, law, wisdom, glory and name.

A second feature common to all the New Testament witness to Jesus is a conviction that it is the whole story, not any single part of it, by which the Father's saving action is effected, and it embraces birth, ministry, passion, resurrection, ascension and return in glory. Common to all the theologies and stories, in their variety, even with their tensions and contradictions of detail, is that they mysteriously converge in this unique episode in human history which they hold to be definitive for the destiny and meaning of the whole of creation. Despite this, none of the unique significance that is attributed to Jesus in the Epistles and Gospels detracts from the humanity of the agent who mediates the saving action. The one who teaches, proclaims the nearness of the kingdom and performs healings and miracles in the power of the Spirit, is authentically and recognizably a human being, doing nothing without parallel in the records of the great figures of the Old Testament. There is in that respect a precise parallel between what one scholar[5] has called the *Christusbild*, which refers to the historic shape of Jesus'

---

[5] Werner Elert, *Der Ausgang der altkirchlichen Christologie* (Berlin: Lutherisches Verlagshaus, 1957), pp. 15–19.

life, and the *Christusdogma*, that is, the theology of the church that seeks to summarize it. Like the two sides of the confession of Philippians 2, they are two sides of the one historic nexus of events. The human career is as such the saving action of God. The third feature that the texts all have in common, therefore, is that they all base their assessment of Jesus' significance in the twofold narrative, according to which Jesus' story is also the story of God present to the world to heal and save. It is this that the first theologians sought to summarize and defend in the rather different world in which they did their praying, living and thinking.

§18. The Framework of Christology

As we have seen, there are two overlapping forms of New Testament descriptions of Jesus, credal confessions, often fragmentary, and narratives. We shall explore in this section the implications of the summary credal confessions found in scripture as they gave rise to the fuller and more systematic development of the creeds in the first centuries of the church's life, before in the next section looking at some modern use that has been made of the christological narratives. This may appear to be a backwards way of going about the task, especially in view of the greater attention given in scripture to narrative and the modern concern to do justice to the human Jesus. Yet there is a reason. Scripture is never approached without some presuppositions or expectations, even though they may be undermined or revised when the text is studied. Modern readers tend to approach the Bible with, so to speak, spectacles shaped either by modern criticism of the creeds or by a more or less confident expectation that the ancient summaries are indispensable to our understanding. I take the latter approach, because I believe that in their struggles to articulate the implications of the faith in a hostile and often uncomprehending environment – just like today's, we may say – the Fathers of the church laid down guidelines for the interpretation of scripture which we neglect at our peril. Another advantage is that, far from involving an uncritical reading of the tradition, the approach enables us, with the benefit of a wide view of the scene, to discern where the tradition was weak and where a modern christology must seek to revise or supplement some of the things there said. To review the way that some of the developments took place, therefore, is essential for an understanding of this difficult and complicated topic.

Two preliminary remarks need to be made. The first concerns the concept of heresy. This is not a fashionable concept; indeed, it smacks of the irredeemably politically incorrect, and for good reasons. It became during a large part of Christian history a political as much as a theological concept, and was improperly used to persecute, far too often to burn at the stake, those supposedly guilty of it. About heresy it must be said, first, that as a theological concept it refers to those teachings, internal to Christianity, which are judged so to distort the faith from within that it ceases to be authentically Christian. It is therefore indispensable in theological discussion because the gospel claims to be true and its truth therefore requires defence against teaching judged to be false.[6] The disputes between rival versions of – say – Darwinian or Marxist theory are in that respect precisely the same, even to the extent of constituting, with some of the more ideological of their exponents, differences about the character of saving dogma. But, second, the chief reason for including a reference to heresy here is its positive function in evincing hard thought, compelling theology, as it does, to think through the implications of the faith for its understanding of God, the world and human life within it.

The second preliminary remark is that in the disputes of the first five centuries and beyond about the significance of Jesus two principles were at stake, as they still are. They both concern the reality of salvation. The first was that because only God can save, Jesus' reality as God in action must in some way be preserved in whatever was taught about him. Bound up with this were both a confidence that the gospel was the way to full and genuine salvation and a conviction that the seriousness of the human condition required so radical a form of action. That the early Christian Fathers also believed Jesus' divinity to be taught in scripture does not lessen the importance of this principle. It was something which they believed that they had received from scripture and which in turn provided a key to the way in which they read the Bible. That was not a circular process of argument so much as a conversational one in which the two standpoints mutually

---

[6] It is never right to oppose heresy by process of public law or any form of violent coercion. The need and right of any voluntary association, however, to exclude or discipline members judged to place themselves outside the community is quite another matter. The great theologians refuted heresy by argument, though, it must be confessed, some also used additional methods which did not conform to Jesus' behaviour in going to the cross rather than calling for legions of angels to resist his oppressors.

enriched one another. Scripture's teaching was clarified in the light of thought about the character of the gospel and the forms of life to which it gives rise. The second principle also contained deep-seated assumptions about the nature of the Bible's God and the way in which he acted. It is that unless Jesus is also fully human salvation is again not guaranteed. This is a repetition at another level of a point which has been made throughout the book so far. God's action is not against the world, not coercive of it, but concerned to establish it as genuinely itself. The point in christology is that if human being is to be restored to its right condition, the change must happen from within, taking account of human freedom rather than forcing people into an alien pattern. These two principles were preserved by insisting on what we have seen the New Testament to teach, that Jesus is the eternal Word of God in person, yet without being in any way less human than we are; in fact, being more truly human.

In the ancient world, as in ours, the two principles ran up against deep-seated assumptions which appeared to make it necessary either to choose between something's being human or divine or to place it somewhere midway between the divine and the human. I shall call this dualism, and mean by it an assumption that the divine and the human are *opposing* realms, related to one another only in terms of logical contradiction, such that to say that Jesus is both human and divine offends not simply against what we feel to be likely, but against logic. This book began with an outline of the doctrine of creation in part to show that dualism of this kind is unnecessary and wrong. God's creating action, as expressed in the spacious movement of Genesis' six days, is that of a God who is not negatively related to the created world but rather gives it its distinctive shape by involving himself in it personally and – we might say – at length. Further: because he creates it by the mediation of his two hands, both of whom demonstrate his personal involvement in and over against the material world, the ground is laid for our understanding, or at least not rejection out of hand, of the teaching that one of those hands becomes present in person in and to the world through the action of the other.

Among the early heresies were two which offended, respectively, against the two principles. The first was Ebionism, or the similar and more sophisticated Adoptionism, which taught that Jesus was not God in person but either the greatest of the prophets or simply a man adopted as God's Son. The second was docetism – 'seeming-ism' – which held that Jesus only seemed to be human, but was in reality a divine being only pretending to be such. In the early credal statements, known as the 'rule of faith' or 'rule of truth', these were ruled out by two devices: affirming that Jesus Christ was eternally the Son of the Father who was made man, and that he took to himself a genuinely human body. Already by the time of Origen the suffering of Jesus was becoming the crux of the problem. Greek philosophy and Christian theology alike taught that God was 'impassible', in no way subject to the passions which so buffet our human bodies. Plato had taught that the Greek poems showing the gods as subject to the passions of jealousy, anger and sex were inappropriate tools for the education of the young and must be replaced by a more elevated and philosophically conceived deity. However, turn this into an abstract principle and you invent a deity who cannot even allow himself to be touched by those movements of mercy and love which we have seen to be characteristic of the Bible's God. In particular it becomes difficult to do justice to the fact that on the cross the Son of God did suffer, and suffer in a way that was essential to the gospel's understanding of salvation. Docetism appeared to solve the problem by arguing that the inner deity did not suffer, only an unreal outer shell. But it is a solution that is no solution.

Two theological principles must be maintained here if we are to maintain the twin principles which guarantee that this is truly salvation. The first is that unless God is impassible in one sense, his very being is at risk on the cross, so that the cross rather than being his saving *action* becomes something that happens to him, beyond his power. History then controls God, not God history. In that respect, theology needs the doctrine of impassibility to ensure the maintenance of the principle that the Bible's God cannot be pushed around; his fundamental being is secure. But, second, the doctrine cannot be extended so far as to produce a dualism which excludes God from interaction with the world. In so far as a rigid doctrine of impassibility controlled christology, forms of teaching emerged which distorted the biblical teaching that in Jesus Christ, even when he suffers on the cross, we encounter the eternal Son of God who is also, without threat to his divinity, fully and genuinely human. In sum, in the heresies we shall meet theology came to be controlled by an abstract philosophy that prejudged the issue of what was happening on the cross. In face of such threats, there were three main tendencies which the church after much debate, and some undoubtedly disgraceful political behaviour also, decided must be rejected if the heart of the gospel was to be maintained. All of them in some way derived from dualism, the refusal to accept that the Son of God was able, because he was the right hand of the creator of heaven and earth, to involve himself personally in the creation without loss of or threat to his eternal divinity.

The first tendency attempted to evade the scandal by placing the Son of God midway between creator and creation. Because, it was held, the eternal God was immune to interaction with the world, that interaction must take place through one who was nearly God, but not quite. Known as Arianism, it found in Athanasius of Alexandria its intellectual nemesis. His great contribution is to the doctrine of God, for he realized that if the gospel is true, then God cannot be as the Greeks said he was, an absolutely transcendent and unitary being, closed off from relations with the creation. One of his arguments is anti-dualistic, to the effect that both of his main opponents on what might be called the right and the left shared the same assumption: that the saviour's human attributes rule out his being divine.[7] But it is precisely that assumption which has to be rejected in the interest of a theology in which God is not a blank unity, but has it within his power to enter his world savingly, not at the expense of but in expression of his divinity. Divine being can be shared being. Athanasius argues from the state of things as he sees them in Bible and church in order to reject beliefs about God which had been adopted by his opponents before the person of Christ had even been taken into consideration. His positive arguments were to the effect that scripture shows us that Christ performs the divine actions of creation and salvation. Only God can create and save, and it must therefore follow that God the Son is as truly divine as God the Father.

Athanasius' theology was confirmed at the Council of Nicaea in AD 325, with its teaching that God the Son is 'one in being' with God the Father, although it took some time before that was everywhere accepted, or, indeed, its implications understood. But a reaction often takes the form of an overreaction, and that was the case here. The Athanasian theology of Christ's divinity helped to generate the second of the two evasions of the scandalous teaching that Jesus is both God and man. In this, the divinity of the saviour was stressed so strongly that his humanity was in danger of being swallowed up by it. That takes us to our second typical heresy, that of Apollinaris, who taught a doctrine of what one commentator has called

---

[7] 'For the Jews say, "how, being a man, can he be God?" And the Arians, "If he were very God from very God, how could be become Man?" ... Thus both parties deny the eternity and Godhead of the Word in consequence of those human attributes which the Saviour took on him ...' Athanasius, *Against the Arians*, 3. 27.

'divine irruption'. Jesus is God's irruption into the world to save, but he irrupts so vigorously that he deprives Jesus of a human mind or soul.[8] Apollinarianism was in its turn rejected, for it was again, rightly, argued that unless the whole of our humanity is taken to himself by the Son of God, then the whole of our humanity is not healed. In later centuries, indeed even until now, Apollinaris had some successors in the tendency to over-stress the divine in Christ. This is the teaching, often dubbed 'monophysite', sometimes, misleadingly, 'docetic', which — speaking very generally — is a recurring tendency to stress the divine Christ so one-sidedly that the humanity becomes little more than a cipher. Once again, a choice appears to be demanded between the divine and the human, and this time it is the human which gives way.

So far, it might be thought, so good. But a third problem remained in a more explicit dualism. One can affirm both against Arius that Jesus is fully divine and against Apollinaris that he is fully human, and yet continue to find difficulties. The chief one centres on the unity of Jesus' person and emerges when one asks what happens on the cross, with its apparent threat to God's impassibility. If Jesus is the eternal Son of God, must we not say that when he suffers, God suffers? One answer, which came to be called Nestorianism, tended to say that the human Jesus suffers on the cross but that God the Son or Word remains, in one expression, 'cautiously remote'. Our third heresy, then, is to suppose or imply two persons, almost side by side, with the Son or Word of God *lodged* or ensconced in a human body rather than truly having *become* human. This tendency, accordingly, is a threat to the integrity of the person of Christ, who must not be conceived as a hybrid, but as the unified person by whom we are met in scripture as Jesus Christ.[9] And so we must say something about the language of 'person' and 'nature' that was so important in these early debates.

All christologies, whether ancient or modern, tend in one of the three directions we have identified, to endanger or impugn the integrity of the deity, of the humanity or of the person. At the Council of Chalcedon in 451 an attempt was made to lay down principles which excluded all three: the one Christ is (1) one in being with God the Father; (2) one in being with us, sin apart; and (3) 'concurring into one person' in the integrity of both divine

---

[8] G. L. Prestige, *Fathers and Heretics* (London: SPCK, 1940), Lecture 5.

[9] This form of dualism is at least near the surface when it is said that 'the divine nature' did one thing, the 'human nature' something else, as happens far too often.

and human 'natures'.[10] The one term, 'person', thus denotes the unity of Jesus Christ, the other, 'nature', the fact that here we meet one who is genuinely and properly both divine and human. Yet, as we have seen, the language of 'nature' can be dangerously misleading. The word is best understood to work in this context more as a verbal adjective than a noun. Natures are not separate entities, but ways in which Jesus of Nazareth is fully divine and fully human, in a relationship we shall have to explore. Chalcedon's Definition has never been accepted by quite every branch of the church, but serves as a useful measuring rod, for, as we have seen, we need all three of its central doctrines if we are to be true at once to scripture and to the claims made in it for Jesus. Yet it has also led to endless debate, and often appeared to be merely abstract, even to some who wish to remain basically loyal to it. What are the problems? They can be examined by looking at some of the debates which have arisen since the Reformation and the Enlightenment, movements which in very different ways threw into question what had for centuries been accepted by most western Christians as unquestioned bases for belief.

§19. The Problem of Dogma

The problem for the modern world lies in the very concept and nature of dogma. For the Reformation the suspicion of dogma is not radical and in its main streams this movement did not question any of the articles of the creed. It was the teaching and defence of mere dogma, of which they tended to suspect their mediaeval predecessors, which the Reformers rejected. Their wish was to return to a more directly biblical teaching, supported by and supportive of the church's teaching, and directed less to intellectual complexity and more to the heart. There was little christological controversy in the Reformation, except in one respect, that concerning the presence of Christ in the Lord's Supper. Luther and the Lutherans tended in a more monophysite direction, with Luther holding, for example, that Christ was present in the body and blood by virtue of his capacity to be anywhere and everywhere – his 'ubiquity'. This depended on a strong stress

---

[10] '. . . not as if Christ were parted and divided into two persons, but one and the same Son and only-begotten God, Word, Lord, Jesus Christ; even as the prophets spoke concerning him . . .'. *Definition of Chalcedon.*

on Christ's divinity. Because God can be everywhere, and because Christ is God, then it must, they held, follow that Christ can be everywhere. Against this, Calvin held that because Christ was human, and continued to have a human body, this must, like all bodies, be located somewhere, and so could not be everywhere. We cannot here explore all the ramifications of this dispute, but must mention it because it had immense historical influence, as we shall see. Before coming to that, however, we must look at another, this time more destructive, influence on modern christology.

The Enlightenment was deeply suspicious of dogma as a whole. Confident in human reason's capacity to discover the truth for itself, it was in principle suspicious of anything taught by authority in the name of tradition.[11] It was the christological and trinitarian dogmas which it subjected to the most savage rational critiques, and in doing so returned to the very dualism which had been at the root of the heresies we have reviewed. Because 'God' and 'man' were, as the enlightened claimed, incompatible predicates, the orthodox teaching was rejected on the grounds that it is self-contradictory, as it still is rejected, sometimes also from within Christian theology itself. The divine Christ therefore tended to be replaced by a human figure, a teacher or example, but not one who saved. It was not, however, all loss, because once again the denial of the credal teaching served a useful purpose. By exposing the weaknesses in the tradition, the critics called attention to things that had been neglected, and needed to be thought through. One of them was the humanity of the saviour, endangered as it undoubtedly was by some of the dogmatic developments. No doubt Chalcedon had taught that the saviour is one in being with us, fully human, sin apart. No doubt Chalcedon's successors had struggled long and hard, in rigorous intellectual developments which we do not have time to follow, to preserve the teaching. Yet the historic failure to give full weight to the human figure depicted in the Gospels, increasingly coming to light as the new critical studies of scripture developed, was coming home to roost.

The weakness had been exacerbated by the Lutheran christology which we have met, because it was the tradition in terms of which modern debate, mostly centred on Germany, was often conducted. Suppose that we attempt to hold in tension two approaches, a very strong assertion of Jesus' divinity

---

[11] The supreme irony of this is that it has become an authority and a tradition in its own right, generating in reaction the even more anti-traditional range of dogmas loosely grouped as postmodernism.

and a modern counterassertion, rooted in a new approach to scripture, of his humanity. Either something tends to give, or a device is sought to reconcile the two. A favourite device, and one which aids our understanding of the matter at issue, is that of *kenosis* or emptying, deriving from the affirmation in Philippians 2.7 that Jesus 'emptied himself'. There, as we have seen, it refers more or less simultaneously to two things, Jesus Christ's becoming human and his movement to the cross. In early modern theology, however, it was used as a device to account for the apparent change involved in an eternal person becoming man. We shall explore something of the becoming in the next chapter; here we are restricting ourselves to consideration of the relation of divine and human in Christ – in traditional parlance to the relation of his divine and human natures. Our consideration involves examination of another traditional divine attribute, God's immutability or changelessness. Like impassibility, this is an essential theological concept. The Bible's God is reliable, trustworthy, true to his promises, in James' expression, 'without shadow of turning' (Jas. 1.17). If we are to rely on him it cannot be the case that his being or purpose is threatened from without. If, for example, the eternal triune being of God were alterable, how could we rely on his promises concerning the stability of the earth or the future reconciliation of all things? In terms of the doctrine we are discussing, we must therefore say that such changes as this unique historic act inevitably imply for God can represent only the outworking or expression and not the overturning of God's immutability. It follows that if what happens in Jesus is genuinely God's doing, it is an event in which God is true to his deepest reality, consistently the one who creates and provides.

And yet if the concept of immutability is used rigidly, it rules out attributing any decisive significance for our understanding of God – and especially of God the Son – of the series of events which I have called the career of Jesus. If we were to construe it in an absolute sense, it might suggest the kind of divine rigidity that would make it impossible for God the Son to become man without contradicting his divinity. If, moreover, we are to be true to scripture's presentation of God we must make allowance for what can exaggeratedly be called God's flexibility in relation to his creation. Once there are creatures who can talk back, and are indeed encouraged to do so, a rigid immutability is ruled out.[12] Of all the early fathers, Cyril of

---

[12] In promising to answer prayer, for example, God shows that in some way or other men and women are incorporated into his gracious government of his universe.

Alexandria (c. AD 375–444) came the nearest to a solution of the problems we have met. Not only did he say that on the cross Christ 'suffered impassibly'[13] – the paradox enabling him to say that the suffering was real but does not compromise God the Son's integrity as a person; he also offered a solution to the puzzle of unchangeableness. There is an emptying by God, a movement into the lowliness of human being; but this *kenosis* rather than *depriving* the Son of his divine being 'adds' something to it, enriches it, we might say, by taking historic form.[14] From another perspective, we can say that the Son's human career represents the concentration of something that is there all the time: 'The Word of God came to our realm; not that he was far from it before.'[15] This is the creating Word 'who is always present with the human race', now present in person as Jesus of Nazareth.[16]

The modern kenotic theory was an entirely different kettle of fish, being designed rather to evade the challenge of the divine and human united in one person. There were various forms of the theory, but they held in general that in order to become man the saviour divested himself of some or all of his divine attributes. Where they failed was in rendering Jesus a depotentiated deity rather than the Son of God in action. The eternal Son became in most versions a temporary and mythical visitor, not truly himself for a while, only returning to his full deity when, so to speak, he is safely back in heaven. If Christian faith is true, however, this historic divine-human person must be understood to be the *concentration* of God's reality, the Son of God in his essential unchangeable power and love, present in person to his world, and, moreover, the humanity must be a permanent, not temporary, 'addition'.

The outcome of this brief discussion of the divine and human in Christ can be illustrated by two examples which will together serve to bring out its point. The first comes from P. T. Forsyth (1848–1921), perhaps the theologian nearest to making a reasonable fist of the kenotic theory, largely because his conception of God freely self-reduced to the human condition was able to conceive the incarnation as the expression of the fullness of God's love, not the reduction of some abstractly conceived deity. His way of putting it is worth citing:

---

[13] A play on words in the Greek: *apathôs epathen*.
[14] Prestige, *Fathers and Heretics*, Lecture 7.
[15] Athanasius, *On the Incarnation*, 8.
[16] Irenaeus, *Against the Heresies*, 3. 16.

What we have in Christ, therefore, is more than the co-existence of two natures, or even their interpenetration. We have within this single increate person the mutual involution of the two personal acts or movements...[17]

To see Jesus as the coming together of two acts or movements assists greatly, though it is better, I believe, to say that we have a single personal action – that of Jesus Christ, the Son of God in the flesh – which is at once God's action and that of one who is fully human. This consideration takes us to our second example, which indicates a way out of the problem first raised by the Lutherans. It centres upon another concept which any serious treatment of our topic must at least mention, the so-called communication of attributes.[18] The Lutheran argument, which has deep roots in the tradition, went to the effect that if God and man are truly united in the person of Christ, there must be a sharing of the divine and human characteristics of such a kind that everything we attribute to one 'nature' must also be attributable to the other. For example, if the human Jesus dies there must be a respect in which God can be said to die; if God is omniscient, there must be a sense in which Jesus is so also. This is in large measure the answer to a foolish question, but did have the merit of evoking from the opponents of the Lutherans a suggestion which shows why. We are in this discussion not engaged in an enquiry about the relations between two separately conceived natures, because natures – to reiterate a point already made several times – are not things but refer to ways in which Jesus is and acts. The suggestion, then, is that we have in this case not a communication of 'attributes', but of actions. The idea has already been implicitly drawn upon in this chapter: that Jesus' acts as scripture presents them are at once God's actions and those of a human being. How does this solve the problem of the question of Christ's integrity? It takes us back to the concept of the person.[19]

---

[17] P. T. Forsyth, *The Person and Place of Jesus Christ* (London: Independent Press, 1909), pp. 343–4. Forsyth continues:

> ...the one distinctive of man, the other distinctive of God; the one actively productive from the side of Eternal God, the other actively receptive from the side of growing man; the one being the pointing, in a corporeal person, of God's long action in entering history, the other the pointing of man's moral growth in the growing appropriation by Jesus of his divine content as he becomes a fuller organ for God's full action on man.

[18] In the original Latin, *communicatio idiomatum*

In Jesus Christ, we meet a single person whose acts are at once human and divine, not a cobbling together of two externally related quantities. This was Cyril's approach: '. . . [W]e do not distribute the Words of our Saviour in the Gospels to two several substances or persons. . . To one person. . . must be attributed all the expressions used in the Gospels, the one incarnate Person of the Word, for the Lord Jesus Christ is one according to the Scriptures.'[20]

And so we close this stage of the discussion with a reference to what is perhaps the most important of the patristic conceptions. Jesus is one person, because he is the hypostatic or personal union of God the Son with the man Jesus of Nazareth. Like everything we have so far explored, this is rooted in God's love for his creation, on this occasion his love for the creation in its lost and endangered condition. The depth of the need demonstrates that the adoption of a good man, independently thrown up by evolution or history, was not enough; we are not saved by the cosmos or by history, but by their sovereign lord and disposer, God in person. And so the eternal Son of God empties himself by adding humanity to his being, in obedience to the Father and by the enabling of his Spirit, to bear his own human body, to *become* human as the God-man who is the agent of our salvation. He is thus one person who is at once the Son of God and, in the Fathers' adaptation of the biblical expression, the Son of Man. But how can this thing be? How can it be that the flesh borne by a divine person is truly human? That is the burden of the next chapter.

---

[19] Bruce McCormack, *For Us and Our Salvation. Incarnation and Atonement in the Reformed Tradition* (Princeton, NJ: Princeton Theological Seminary, 1993), pp. 7–8. I am grateful for this piece, which took me back to the solution which was, I believe, already to be found in Cyril of Alexandria.

[20] Cyril of Alexandria, 'Third Letter to Nestorius', J. Stevenson, (ed.), *Creeds, Councils and Controversies. Documents Illustrative of the History of the Church 337–461* (London: SPCK, 1972), p. 284.

Chapter 6

'And Was Made Man':
The Incarnation and Humanity
of Christ

§20. The 'Becoming' of God the Son

The doctrine of the incarnation is succinctly stated already in scripture: 'The Word became flesh, and lived among us . . .' (Jn. 1.14). We have explored in the previous chapter something of who this Word is. He is, first, the eternal Word of God, who is with the Father eternally. And second, he is Jesus of Nazareth, of whom the Gospels speak in rather varied ways, some of which we shall now seek to bring together into something like a coherent pattern. The creed describes the event in which this took place with the words, 'He was made man', a form of expression we should not alter to 'he became human' or 'he became a human being'. The reasons for this apparently offensive attachment to the past will enable us to see something of what is involved. The first is that the word 'man' encompasses both the particular and the universal. This is a particular human being who also in his own way embraces the universal, man and woman alike. The moral and social implications of the universality were drawn by Paul and other Christian thinkers, inaugurating an era of movement towards the equality of men and women in the church which was, unfortunately, short-lived by virtue of the contamination of early Christian theology with ideas drawn from Greek suspicion of the body and Aristotelian teaching that women were inherently inferior to men.[1]

The second reason for the inadequacy of 'he became human' or '... a human being' is that they both suggest precisely what the early theology so carefully sought to avoid, that when the Word became flesh it meant a change in the nature of the Word, that in some way or other there is transmogrification of the Word into something else. That would make the doctrine of the incarnation like the myths of the religions, according to which one of the gods dons a temporary dress of some kind in order to mate with a human, or whatever. The subtlety of the expression 'he became man' is that it is possible to construe it so that mythological transformations are avoided, and that the human Jesus becomes not something foreign to the Word, but the Word of God in person. The incarnation of the Word in Jesus of Nazareth is the realization of a relationship that is eternal in being, rooted in God's continuing relation with the world. Christ, as we have seen, is the mediator of creation, the one in whom God the Father holds together all created reality. There is already and always a relationship between the Son of God and the world and it now, uniquely, takes the form of a personal presence.[2]

For whatever reasons, and there is a range of them, theology has found it difficult to do full justice to the humanity of Christ. The quest of the historical Jesus is witness to a genuine anxiety to do justice to Jesus' human reality in a way that goes beyond the mere dogmatic summary of the Chalcedonian creed. But the failure of the quest, already referred to in the previous chapter, is ironically that it often presents Jesus as a divinized

---

[1] Not only does the Acts of the Apostles show that women moved naturally into positions of leadership in the Christian community, but Paul, when arguing with himself about the role of women in leading worship – which he clearly presupposed in the passage under review – came to the conclusion that 'In the Lord ... woman is not independent of man, nor is man independent of woman' (1 Cor. 11.11). The modern proposal to remove sexist language from theology is a proper attempt to re-establish the logic of early christology; it just happens not to be a satisfactory way to achieve it.

[2] He did not become other than Himself on taking the flesh, but, being the same as before, He was robed in it; and the expressions, 'He became' and 'He was made', must not be understood as if the Word, considered as the Word, were made, but that the Word, being Framer of all, afterwards was made High Priest, by putting on a body which was originate and made ... (Athanasius, *Against the Arians*, 2. 8).

man or as some kind of ideal figure rather than the flesh and blood human being of the Gospels. How then shall we understand the incarnation? On the one hand, we must accept from the outset that we shall never understand it in the sense of fathoming it without remainder, of making final sense, as of some mechanism. It is doubtful whether we shall ever be able to achieve that with the atom and the cell, let alone this most mysterious of events. We must always bear in mind Kierkegaard's warning, that when the eternal and the temporal come together, something inevitably happens which defies all merely human logic. If this is God, then it is necessarily God incognito, and all attempts to penetrate that incognito will fail. But, on the other hand, that is not to say that it defies all logic. One of the implications of Athanasius' doctrine of God as we met it in an earlier chapter, is that God submits himself to the logic of our human condition, to save, indeed, but also to reveal, in such a way that we may both encounter and know him. In Jesus of Nazareth, as he had done with Israel, God lays out his own logic within the frame of ours, and by his Spirit enables us to understand it, according to his and our limits. The reference to the Spirit is crucial, for everything happens only by the Spirit's action and is made understandable in its own way only by his gift. If we are to understand what is going on first with Jesus and then with the human response to him, the central place of the Spirit cannot be ignored.

'He was incarnate by the Holy Spirit of the Virgin Mary.' Like so many doctrines of the faith, this too has suffered from the less than tender mercies of its exponents. It has two possible functions, which are incompatible. The first is to treat it primarily as a means to isolate Jesus' humanity from ours. At this place I must make clear my difference from Roman Catholic theology, in order to indicate both what are the issues which still divide the churches and what is theologically at stake. To teach that Mary was immaculately conceived, that in some sense her being contained an immunity from sin so that the saviour should likewise be immune, prevents the doctrine of the humanity of Jesus from performing its saving function. It is no surprise that Mary has tended to replace Jesus as a focus for human devotion, to the effect that her Son was displaced to be the fearsome judge, to be pleaded with by his mother, in explicit contradiction of scripture's claim that he is the one who represents us before the Father. Rather, we must concentrate on the second function of the doctrine, which is to show that Jesus' humanity is continuous with ours in a more radical way than is often allowed. The point can be approached by way of a rejection of another distortion, this time found in Protestant theology of recent centuries, in which the doctrine of the virgin birth of Jesus has been deployed as a miraculous proof of his divinity. For it must be insisted that the teaching is at least as much, if not more, concerned with the humanity of Jesus as with his divinity.

To show how this can be so, let us begin an exposition of what is called the doctrine of the incarnation. We have met the lapidary claim that the Word became flesh, and we can begin to expand its meaning with the help of Paul's parallel assertion that 'when the fullness of time had come, God sent his Son, born of a woman, born under the law...' (Gal. 4. 4). We must here emphasize the fact highlighted in the text that it is in and through time that God works out his purposes. Two comments can be made. The first is that although Paul does not refer to anything miraculous beyond this mysterious sending by God, neither does he – along with the other New Testament writers – ascribe the birth to begetting by a human father. We cannot read too much into this, but if the birth was indeed from a virgin, it simply reinforces the point made by 'when the time had fully come'. The renewal of the creation can begin only by a new and miraculous act of God, the making new of our humanity, which had become soiled and tired. It would be satisfying if Barth's comment about this were also true, that it shows that in this event God does not need the male, the one who tends to think that all depends upon his initiating action.[3] In the conception and birth of Jesus, God initiates what only he can do, especially given the condition of things.

The second comment arises from Paul's 'born under the law', and this must surely include a reference at least to the full conditions of life in the body and in society. This child is born into Israel, the people which carries the promise and the burden of fallen human life. Personal life in society requires a body, and that too is implied, so that 'born of a woman' means precisely what it says, that the matter of which Jesus' flesh consists is a sample of that from which all life is built, the dust of the earth. It is therefore, like every human life, particular, and this means that a particular genetic – in this case *Jewish* genetic – inheritance is involved. This is not ready-made, perfect flesh sent down from heaven, avoiding the messiness of involvement in sin and evil. He comes 'from heaven' indeed, but only by means of a full embodiment in the matter of the fallen world he came to save. Only so

---

[3] Karl Barth, *Church Dogmatics*, translation edited by G. W. Bromiley and T. F. Torrance (Edinburgh: T. & T. Clark, 1957–75), vol. 1/2, pp. 192–4.

are we enabled to engage with the chief question arising here: if Jesus' body is indeed constructed not from immaculate but from definitely maculate material, the same material as ours, what does it entail for his sharing of the human condition? Is he, like us, liable to sin?

A pair of texts will enable us to sketch an answer. In Romans 8.3 Paul says that God sent his Son 'in the likeness of sinful flesh'; and in 2 Corinthians 5.21 that 'God made him to be sin who knew no sin.' Both of these expressions of Jesus' involvement in the conditions of human fallenness appear to entail, when taken in their contexts, a reference to Jesus' birth, to his life, and to the death which was its outcome. The 'likeness' of sinful flesh may well make a similar point to the later credal expression, 'like us in all things, sin apart', but in any case, full involvement in the human condition is manifestly affirmed. He is not only fully human, but in some way also shares our fallen condition. It is similarly the case that the Gospels depict someone whose life was bound up with that of a corrupt social order, whose conditions his actions exacerbated as much as healed.

From the beginning of this book it has been argued that a theology of trinitarian mediation is indispensable for a grasp of the shape of God's manifold action in the world. Of the first 'hand of God' – often referred to as the second person of the Trinity – we must reiterate that he is the focus of God's involvement *within* the world's structures. That involvement, as we have seen, comes to a climax in the begetting and birth of Jesus: 'when the time had fully come' (Gal. 4.4). But without the equal and simultaneous activity of the other hand of God in the single act of the one God, we can understand neither God's action in the world in general nor this instance of God's involvement in the world in Jesus in particular. We must now pause briefly to sketch something that will be further elaborated in the final chapter devoted to the doctrine of God. Because the Son and the Spirit are God the Father in action, it has been argued almost from the beginning of Christian theology that they are intrinsic also to God's eternal being. What God is in his relations with the world, he is also in his eternal being, because there is no breach, as there is with fallen creatures, between what God is and what he does. Because the Father's action is mediated by the Son and the Spirit, the Son and the Spirit are correspondingly intrinsic to God's eternal being. It would follow that the relation of the Son to the Father in God's inner being is in some way mediated by the Spirit. The Son is – we might say – enabled to be the Son by virtue of the way the Spirit realizes and perfects the love between him and the Father. Only so are the three truly one God.

If we apply that to our particular case, we shall see that the Spirit does here in time what he does eternally in the being of God. In the stories of Jesus' birth in Matthew and especially Luke the agency of the Spirit is made explicit. It is by the power of his Spirit that God the Father shapes a body for his Son in the womb of Mary, enabling *this* sample of human flesh to be that which it was created to be, in distinction from all other created persons and things. Two features have here to be held in tension. The first is, to repeat, that the material for Jesus' body comes from the common stock from which ours and that of other living creatures is constructed. The Word becomes *flesh*. It is in this regard that, to his cost, Edward Irving, using language too subject to misunderstanding, spoke of Christ's 'sinful' or 'fallen' flesh.[4] Because it is people, not flesh, who sin and are fallen perhaps it would make the point more adequately if we were to say that the matter from which the Spirit builds a body for the Son is that same corrupt matter as that which constitutes the persons of other human beings. In an earlier chapter, we noted that the Hebrew word for flesh refers to 'weak and needy man' and it is that flesh which the saviour assumes. 'The Word became flesh', says John, and he is perhaps taking up that very point. Jesus, a man in need of divine support and guidance like all human beings, shares in human flesh in all its weakness and need. The second point, however, is that the Spirit's action is a renewing action, and therefore makes perfect that which enters the process marked by the accumulated corruption of the ages. The recreation of the world is begun, but first only as the renewal of a representative sample of that which is fallen. The Spirit is the one who makes Jesus of Nazareth to be the particular human being that he is. And so we come to Jesus' life after his birth.

§21.   Death and the Kingdom

When we come to speak of the life that arises out of this beginning, we must at all costs avoid speaking of a life that is somehow effortless, somehow immune from the struggle that marks all human life. Rather, we must realize that the whole of Jesus' life was the bearing of a cross. Once again, two points have to be made. The first is in answer to the question of how this

---

[4] See Colin E. Gunton, *Theology Through the Theologians* (Edinburgh: T. & T. Clark, 1996), chapter 9.

human being remains what Luther called the 'proper man': fully human, and yet true to the destiny that is God's intention for all men and women. And it is: by being maintained by the Spirit in right relation with the Father who sent him. We should beware of suggestions that Jesus was in some way pushed around by the Word, by his 'divine nature'. He *was* the Word, but the Word become truly and fully human, God the Son self-emptied into the condition of the flesh, the while remaining fully himself. We therefore conclude that it is by the power of the Spirit that the incarnate Word is maintained in faithfulness to the Father while being truly 'weak and needy man'.

The second point is similarly an answer to a question: what does Jesus in that case share with the others with whom he is one? And the answer is that he also works out his human calling through time and by means of the Spirit's leading. The Letter to the Hebrews is a leading exponent of the mystery of this twofold relation. Jesus was, says this author, like us in all things sin apart (Heb. 2.17, 4.15); yet 'although he was a son, he learned obedience by what he suffered, and, being made perfect, became to all those who obey him the source of eternal salvation' (5.8–9. Note the parallel he draws between Jesus' obedience and that of the disciple). This may appear to narrow things to the strange claim that Jesus was made perfect in his passion and cross, but attention to the wider meaning of the Greek word translated 'suffering' suggests a broader perspective. If by 'suffered' we translate 'what happened to him' – the cross that he bore throughout his ministry – then we shall understand that it is by the whole course of his life that Jesus' humanity is perfected as the Spirit maintains him in obedience to God the Father. A satisfactory account of Jesus' humanity therefore requires attention to the beginning, continuing and ending of his particular human career.

We begin with one of the fragments that Luke thinks it worth our hearing about his childhood. According to this evangelist, even the one who had come from impressing the learned doctors with his insights was afterwards 'obedient to [his parents] . . . and grew in wisdom and stature, and in favour with God and man' (Lk. 2.51–2). This is part of the broad presentation in the Gospel accounts of one who lives in a special relation to both God and his own people. Throughout the narratives, we are shown a man who is led by the Spirit, and we learn much about the shape of that leading in the episode, contained in all the Gospels, of Jesus' baptism by John the Baptist. John was pronouncing judgement on disobedient Israel, and it is when Jesus accepts for himself that judgement that we read of the Spirit's descent upon him (Mt. 3.13–17). That is to say, Jesus' acceptance of solidarity with his people under judgement is the occasion for the Spirit, by whom the Father formed his body in the womb, to become personally present in full measure.

The outcome of this baptism, calling and gift can be understood only if we pause to sketch the two focuses, both in their different ways eschatological, through which this unusual life must thereafter be viewed. The first is death. It has already been noted that the passion narratives play a prominent place in the Gospels' presentation of Jesus. From the very beginning, as is shown even by the birth narratives, Jesus moves toward death by political machination but also by divine will and permission. In a fallen world, death is the place where man meets God's judgement. It is not that, or not only that, after death there is divine judgement on human wickedness; it is rather that death itself is a form of destroying judgement, which is why for Paul it is the last enemy which must be destroyed (1 Cor. 15.26). Death is that which frustrates God's purposes for the creation, and so is the ultimate enemy to be overcome, and Jesus goes to it with eyes wide open.

The second focus is precisely coincident with the first. As has been much stressed in recent centuries, the proclamation of the kingdom of God is central to Jesus' word and act. At least since the nineteenth century, the eschatological character of the kingdom has been much debated, for it is clear that in some sense or other it is taught in the Gospels that in Jesus the kingdom has – in different measure according to varying interpretations – drawn near, been anticipated, inaugurated or realized. It seems, to me at least, that, first, the reference is to the inbreaking of God's rule over the creation, and, second, that the centrality of the concept of the kingdom in Jesus' teaching and activity entails two important features of that inbreaking. First is that in what he says and does Jesus re-establishes the sovereignty of God over his creation in face of the fact that it has been, and continues to be, disputed by the creation. Second is the eschatological note that he sounds. That which is here being reasserted will, in God's due time and by his due process, be completed. The project of creation is being taken up again by its original mediator, become man. It is with this double focus that we shall outline the shape of the narratives.

The outcome of Jesus' baptism can be understood through the twin focus of death and the kingdom. Because he lives in the world of death, his is not an automatic saintliness; instead, he is tempted, in one of the episodes without which we cannot begin to understand him, to be other than he is called to be. The words of God, taken from Isaiah, with which the evangelists interpret the baptism – 'You are my beloved Son, in whom I am well pleased' (Mk. 1.11, cf. Is. 42.1) – declare the divine sonship of the one voluntarily subjecting himself to John's prophetic and eschatological judgement. When Jesus has heard this, the Spirit *drove* him – on one account (Mk. 1.12), possibly containing undertones of compulsion – out into the desert, the place of Israel's historic testing, to be tempted. This temptation of Jesus, so important for the author to the Hebrews, is clearly central to his learning of obedience, because it concerns, at two of its many levels, both what it means to be a true Israelite and what it means to obey God rather than the devil. Overall, the temptation and its outcome indicates the meaning of the sonship to which Jesus is called: he is a son by obedience, not by Adamic self-assertion. As Adam fell, so Jesus stands and walks with God. It also brings to the fore the question of the sinlessness of Jesus, of which the tradition again has two opposed interpretations. The first is summarized in the Latin sentence, *non potuit peccare*: 'he was *unable* to sin'. This suggests that because he was the Son of God he was, so to speak, constitutionally unable to accept the temptations of the devil to court success, popularity and power.

The weakness of this position is that it can undermine Jesus' full humanity. Is there not near to the surface at least a hint that the human nature was in some way so driven by the divine that he was automatically immune from doing wrong? Yet if the temptations were real, and if the temptation to run away on the night before his death was also real – and Luke links the two – must we not avoid such a suggestion? As we have seen, there are not in Jesus two natures in the sense of rival principles. His action is God's action *only* as the action of one who was fully human, and nothing must be said which might undermine that humanity. The second option offered by the tradition, however, is equally problematic. If we say, *potuit non peccare* – 'he *was able* not to sin' – we have equal difficulties. Can a human being, even this one, do the will of God in his own strength, without divine grace? It is certainly not the case generally with human beings after the fall, whatever we might make of their hypothetical capacities before it. Our situation being what it is, we therefore need, if this man is truly to be the author and pioneer of our faith, a stronger sense of the fact that the incarnate Word is like us in requiring divine enabling if he is to remain faithfully human. Must we not say rather, in a third formulation, that 'He *was enabled* not to sin', enabled, that is, by the Spirit, the mediator of all God's perfecting action?[5]

If we take that course, we shall be able to understand the ministry of Jesus as that of the true Israelite who did the will of his Father because the Spirit maintained him, *as Son*, true to the Father from whom he came and to whom he was to return. There are therefore two levels at which his action must be understood. The first is that of one mediating the actions – the merciful, providential, redemptive, forgiving, renewing, healing actions – of God the Father himself. This Jesus is an eschatological prophet, with loaded actions to match, endowed with the power and authority to perform acts – like the cleansing of the temple – consequent on his status. In that regard, everything that he does is the work of God, because he is the eternal Son of God made man. But that is not the main focus of this chapter, which is to address the question of the respects in which all this is also, at its second level, authentically human achievement.

In what he does and teaches, this Spirit-inspired prophet concentrates in himself the work of the lawgivers, prophets, kings, priests and indeed wisdom teachers of Israel. Their work comes to a head in him. His continuity with the first three is evident from a reading of the Gospels, where Jesus mediates the law, God's covenant relation with Israel and his rule over her and the world. The fourth – priesthood – we shall consider in the next section. A reference to the fifth, wisdom, however, enables us to say something of the character of Jesus' human ministry. The unique character of the parables, for example, adapted to church use as some of them clearly are by the time they come to be recorded, shows that he was a wisdom teacher in the tradition of the Old Testament. More than that, he was steeped in that book's theology of creation. As Francis Watson has shown, the Gospel writers drew on or alluded to all seven days of the story of creation in their accounts of Jesus' life, ministry and teaching.[6] This point enables us to understand something of the comprehensive nature of Jesus' teaching and actions, re-establishing in all that he does the rule of God over his world. If we are to be true to the theology of creation which forms the foundation for everything else, we must hold to the insight that as the minister of God's kingdom this man re-establishes God's writ over the

---

[5] I owe this way of putting it to Tom Smail.

[6] Francis Watson, *Text and Truth. Redefining Biblical Theology* (Edinburgh: T. & T. Clark, 1997), pp. 237–9.

whole of the fallen creation, not merely the religious or spiritual. His actions in healing the sick in body and mind indicate that God's providing is for the whole person in the world, prominent in some accounts being Jesus' sheer anger at the disfiguring effect of evil on human life and compassion for its victims. (Someone once described the Jesus of Mark's gospel as being rather like a bad-tempered faith-healer; the wrath of God in action, we might say.) In that respect, the miracles are not those that Jesus was tempted by the devil to perform, but rather acts which break the entrenched dominion of the enemy over man and nature, anticipating their eschatological redemption.

The account in Luke 4 suggests that the result of Jesus' victory over temptation was that he was able both to speak the truth and to heal the sick. Because he obeyed, he was endowed with authority. The healings, along with the so-called nature miracles, bespeak Jesus' authority over the created world in all its variety. Here is creation's lord returning to his realm to reclaim his own, to redeem a lost world from bondage to dissolution. The healing of those possessed by demonic powers witnesses to a broader bondage than the merely psychological; notice the parallel, that modern medicine seeks variously to heal the mentally sick by both chemical and psychological means. Similarly, on a holistic understanding of the person, we do not need to choose between diagnosing the social and psychological causation of, say, depression, and the imbalance of chemicals in the brain. Both may be symptoms of the broader breach from the creator which can be understood in its fullness only theologically. The stilling of the storm, in which Jesus uses an expression suggestive of exorcism, is another way of showing that human life and its world are so intricately interwoven that their fallenness and its healing can be understood only as both are called back into the hegemony of their creator (Mt. 8.26–7). It would be a mistake, however, to move from there into a politically or ecologically led conception of the ministry of the incarnate Son of God. He is not primarily a political reformer or ecological visionary, but one who proclaims and realizes God's reconciling action. A right political and ecological ethic can only be the consequence of this gospel, not its justification or criterion, because the relation of the world to God must control our understanding of relations within that world. Because Jesus is who he is, and because he is obedient by the Spirit to the One to whom he refers all his actions – and notice Jesus' orientation to prayer, especially at the crises of his ministry – the primary purpose of his ministry is to call the fallen creature back to God.

Reconciliation with God is the condition for the reconstruction of order and freedom within the world.

In what sense, then, is this the work of one who is sinless? Did Jesus have 'sinful impulses', as is often asked? That depends upon what is meant. If entertaining the suggestion that he might worship the devil – seeking to attain power and influence by using the weapons of the fallen world – is a sinful impulse, then he did. What is at stake is not what was entertained, but whether what is entertained involves already the broken relation to God in which sin consists. The point of the confession 'like us in all things sin apart' is that the one who brings redemption is not himself in need of redemption, but lives victoriously in the realm of death as its conqueror.

We end this part of our account of the humanity of Jesus with a brief reference to two incidents through which the writers of the first three Gospels in particular punctuate and so interpret the story. The hinge on which the accounts turn is the story of Jesus' enquiry to the disciples about who they think he is, and Peter's subsequent confession that he is the messiah of Israel (Mk. 8.27–33, and parallels). It is the hinge, because it makes explicit Jesus' movement to the cross which had been implicit from the beginning. Jesus' insistence that his messiahship involves suffering and death brings to fulfilment the message of the baptism and temptation, which already point to it. Peter's attempt to dissuade Jesus from his movement to death in Jerusalem represents a reiteration of the devil's suggestion that he should be a son of God different from the one directed by the Spirit of the Father, because to accept it would be a failure of Jesus to be obedient to his particular calling and vision. The strange episode of the transfiguration which follows accordingly represents God's validating of both the baptism, to which it alludes, and the outcome of the second rejection of temptation which the rebuke to Peter's urging represented. Yet Peter's sin does not invalidate the truth of his confession. He is among the disciples who are granted an advance vision, given in the presence of the two Old Testament figures, Moses and Elijah, of the saviour's eschatological glory, later to be confirmed by his resurrection from the dead: 'This is my Son, whom I love. Listen to him' (Mk. 9.7). The transfiguration is not a religious experience – as it is often made – but a revelatory event in which Jesus' ride to death is shown to be, despite all appearances, the path of a king to glory. The Father's pronouncement to Jesus at his baptism – 'You are my beloved Son, in whom I am well pleased' – is now confirmed and filled out. The one who goes to his death is the eternal and beloved Son of God, the king moving to take his throne, and his word must be heard.

§22. Priesthood Realized

The Spirit-led man is elevated not to glory, but on a cross; or rather, to use the beautifully nuanced account in the Gospel of John, he is elevated to glory on and through the cross and its outcome. This is the particular place of his saving work, because it concentrates all that has gone before. Obedience to the will of the Father leads, if not always and universally, yet certainly in this case, to death. As we have seen, that death is presented by the New Testament as the heart of that movement of the Son of God into time and history in which God reinaugurates the creation's movement to its final redemption. Historically, it results from Jesus' blasphemous and politically subversive behaviour. By the words and actions which both implied a divine authority and threatened the order of things, he was himself the catalyst of the reaction which took him to the cross. That this was the providential action of God does not, as we have seen, make it in any way cease to be voluntary human wickedness. For us, however, it does raise the question of what is taking place theologically when Jesus goes to his death.

One of the much contended questions in the centuries after Chalcedon was that of the relation of the divine and human will in Jesus' actions. If Chalcedon was right in saying that Jesus Christ is one in being with both God the Father and with us, are we not bound to say that he has also both a divine and a human will? The church decided that he does, and for a good reason. He must have a divine will, because it is God's will that is being done. But if he does not also have a human will, he is not acting freely, and therefore not truly human. There are, to be sure, dangers in speaking of two wills in Jesus, just as there are in speaking of two natures. To us, it seems, to use a rather tired metaphor, schizophrenic. But we shall be able to recognize the elements of truth in the ancient decision if we refer it to the text which was at the centre of the historic debate. In the Garden of Gethsemane, Jesus prays to be released from his coming death, but, 'not my will but yours be done' (Mk. 14.36). The outcome of his prayer is that he freely, *willingly*, accepts what he believes to be his Father's will. Clearly, there are two wills involved, and one accepts the decision of the other. But there are not two wills *within* Jesus, only two at work in his career, his will and the will of his Father. The incarnate Lord, through the Spirit and assisted by the ministering angels, accepts the will of his Father and goes to the cross. The Father's will is fulfilled by the free human willing of his incarnate Son in the power of the Spirit. Forsyth, once again, comes near to expressing the dynamic with which we are concerned, speaking of the 'reconquest', by moral conflict under the conditions of human rebellion, of a province, even within himself, that 'was always his by right'.[7]

We need a theology of the Spirit to make such sense as we can also of the succeeding events. The cross follows the logic of God's providence, of Israel's and Rome's politics and of Jesus' own actions. It is the confluence of divine action and Jesus' human determination to persevere in face of fallen political and religious forces. As a fulfilment of Jesus' baptism, it represents his full identification with Israel and ultimately with all men and women in their self-inflicted sundering from their creator. That is the realm of death as judgement. The Father abandons Jesus to the cross so that he may share our condition in its uttermost depths. When Jesus dies, he 'gives up his spirit', or, possibly, 'the Spirit.' (The Gospels present it variously, but leave either interpretation open.) The two amount to the same thing, for to lose one's spirit is to enter the realm where God is not, where death and hell hold their hegemony, and where God's Spirit has been taken away. We should here beware of expressions which imply that God is passive in the event of the cross, as in some of the sloppy recent talk of the suffering of God. There is indeed a kind of suffering on the part of God the Father, for he gives up, 'sacrifices' his Son. But if we go so far as to conceive this as involuntary suffering, we offend against the truth of the doctrine of impassibility, and risk subjecting God to the vagaries of history. The cross of Jesus is the power and the wisdom of God (1 Cor. 1–2), God's powerful act in which he overcomes evil by entering its realm in the person of his Son. Through the Father's abandoning of Jesus, his saving purpose is achieved.[8]

---

[7] P. T. Forsyth, *The Person and Place of Jesus Christ* (London: Independent Press, 1909), p. 308. I have quoted selectively in order not to suggest an adoption of the form of the concept of kenosis which Forsyth is expounding.

[8] This is not a breach in the being of the triune God, as is implied by some recent talk of the 'bereavement' of the Father, because it remains the concerted act of Father, incarnate Son and divine Spirit. Any suggestion of conflict within the being and act of God undermines everything.

The significance of this description of the cross is that it is an act of power which only appears to be weakness (1 Cor. 1–2), the only power that is competent to meet the enemy except on its own terms. The validity of the claim is demonstrated by the resurrection of Jesus from the dead. This, too, is achieved by the Father through his Spirit. It is an eschatological act, in that it transforms the body of Jesus to the condition to which all will finally be brought at the end of the time of creation. It is thus an anticipation of the life of the age to come: neither a resuscitation, like that of Lazarus, who was raised only to die again (Jn. 11.1–44), nor the departure of an immaterial soul from a material body. It is, in sum, a perfecting through transformation, a completion of the renewal of this piece of the created world begun with the conception of Jesus. The risen Jesus eats and drinks, but is also mysteriously transcendent of the normal limits of time and space. Essential to an understanding of this is the point that Paul makes, that Jesus is not disembodied, but elevated to a new form of embodiment (1 Cor. 15.42–53). As the first-born from the dead, Jesus remains bodily human, albeit mysteriously so, and thus a promise of the resurrection of others.

We shall take up the implications of that promise in a later chapter, but must here lay their basis in an account of the meaning of the resurrection for Jesus himself. I begin by reiterating that God the Spirit is the mediator of God's eschatological action *over against and toward* the order of his creation. A number of passages suggest that God raised Jesus from the dead by the agency of his Spirit, for example Romans 8.11, 'the Spirit of him who raised Jesus Christ from the dead', and 1 Peter 3.18, 'He was put to death in the body and made alive by the Spirit'. The point of these allusions is reinforced by the fact that in the New Testament talk of the power, glory and energy of God are also ways of speaking of the Spirit. And when we read Paul saying that 'the Spirit gives life' (2 Cor. 3.6), we should recall the resurrecting action of the Spirit in Ezekiel's great vision of the bones. One passage, however, will enable us to recapitulate the significance of Jesus' career as we have outlined it so far: 'He was justified – or vindicated – by the Spirit' (1 Tim. 3.16).[9] Those words appear in a summary of Jesus' life from his incarnation to his being taken up in glory. They are an essential part of the story, for they show that the one who accepted baptism, 'in order to fulfil all righteousness' (Mt. 3.15), has done precisely that. What he now

---

[9] I am indebted here to Lyle Dabney, 'Justified in the Spirit. Soteriological Reflections on the Resurrection', forthcoming in the *International Journal of Systematic Theology*.

'suffers' or experiences is God's declaratory confirmation of the meaning of his whole life. Here is the one just and true human being, vindicated as such by the act of the eschatological Spirit.

And there is one more step that we must take before ending this lightning tour of the doctrine of the humanity of Jesus Christ. That the resurrection is a continuation rather than the abolition of Jesus' particular humanity is demonstrated by his ascension. In considering the significance of this event, we must lay on one side worries about the spatial and meteorological imagery in which it is couched in some of the accounts. The symbolism is designed to highlight both the mystery and the promise of the event. The Jesus of John's Gospel explains that his continuing significance depends upon his departure from his historical way of being present. The new dispensation depends upon Jesus' absence, which is to be succeeded eventually by his return in glory. In the meantime his significance is mediated by the Spirit (Jn. 16.1–16). We shall engage with the problems of absence and presence in later chapters. The point of the bodily departure, however, is laid out in the Letter to the Hebrews: that the one who has returned to 'the right hand of the Father' is now permanently and universally the means of human access to God. Jesus' significance is made universal, but still as the particular person that he is.

The point is this. We have seen that the notion of sacrifice is central to an account of the way by which human life in the world is brought into salutary relation to God the creator. For Hebrews, Jesus is the one authentic priest who, as such, has offered not a series of victims but his whole person in obedience to God and love to man. This author's treatise is therefore an extended account of the words 'vindicated by the Spirit'. Jesus' life as a whole is an expression of that priesthood over creation that is the human calling outlined in Genesis 1.26–8 as the calling of those created in God's image. 'As it is', writes our author, 'we do not see all things in subjection to him [man]...But we do see Jesus' (Heb. 2.8–9), whose life and death are the giving of himself, at once *to* God and *for* those made in God's image. His whole life and death are an offering to its creator of a sample of created being, made perfect through the Spirit. In priestly fashion, as God made man, he brings together loving creator and hostile creature. That priesthood is now permanent and eternal, a living way for others to go confidently before their maker. Notice in the following passage how central the Spirit is in what happens:

The blood of goats and bulls and the ashes of a heifer sprinkled on those who are ceremonially unclean sanctify them so that they are outwardly clean. How much more, then, will the blood of Christ, who through the eternal Spirit offered himself unblemished to God, cleanse our consciences from acts that lead to death, so that we may serve the living God! (Heb. 9.13–14)

Jesus' act as at once priest and victim takes place in the interest of the renewing of the human heart, that sometimes desperately wicked organ of our humanity, so that it may be free to make its self-offering to God. The author of Hebrews does not wish in all this to reject the meaning of Israel's heritage, but to concentrate it in this one man. The human service of the living God that is the outcome will exercise us in the next part of the book. However, before that some strands must be brought together in completion of this part, and in order to enrich the doctrine of God that is being constructed as we follow the course of his creating, providential, and redemptive action.

§23. Conclusion to Part 2: God the Son

The career of Jesus is a unique act of God – this is God himself – which is also a truly human life. Equally, we have a truly human life which is as a whole God's action in the world. This is something which both can and cannot be understood. It can, because we can see in it the completion of the logic of God's action in and toward the world which is founded in the doctrine of creation. Indeed, although it is there founded, we can now understand the nature of the foundation only in the light of this personal presence of God the Son in the flesh. It cannot, however, be understood because this is the Son become *fully* human, God incognito, an incognito which cannot be broken through by the human mind, except through the Spirit's gift. This reduces to a point the two sides of the concept of God's unknowability which were sketched in the first chapter. God makes himself present, and therefore knowable, in his Son and through his Spirit. And yet the mystery is such that this knowability, though real, can never be explained or plumbed.

We have seen from the beginning of this book that God the Son or Word is the focus of God's involvement, without loss of or threat to his essential being, within the structures of created reality. Jesus is the eternal Son of God emptied to the conditions of humanity, become poor so that his creatures should become rich. This is the full presence of God the Son in bodily form, and yet not the *abandonment* but the *expression* of the Son's eternal being. We must not, however, construe this in the concepts of Newtonian mechanism, and see space and time as a container into which God, so to speak, dips his hand. The universe is rather to be understood as a system of energies generated and upheld through the trinitarian energy of God. That energy is expressed outwards in the created order by the work of the Son, who is thus able, by the Spirit, so to concentrate his being that he becomes timely while remaining eternal. In this dynamic, the impassible becomes passible, the eternal temporal, while remaining truly himself.

Just as in the equivalent section at the end of Part 1 something was said about God's eternity – his relation to the world of time – so here remarks about his infinity are in order, for our theme is with God's entering of space while remaining infinite. The action we have reviewed entails that God is utterly distinguished from our spatiality, and yet not in such a way that it is foreign to him: 'he comes to his own realm... .' God's capacity to be present to and in particular places, therefore, is grounded in his omnipresence, the dynamic relations to everything which we have seen focused in his providential action. Forsyth puts this well:

> Omnipresence, as absolute independence of space, means that God is not hampered by space, but can enter spatial relations without being tied to them, can exist in limits without being unfree, or ceasing to be God. ... If the Creator could not have become immanent in creation, His infinity would have been curtailed by all the powers and dimensions of space. ... If the infinite God was so constituted that he could not live also as a finite man, then he was not infinite. There was a limitation in his power's infinity.[1]

In this historical figure we encounter the infinity and omnipresence of God in action.

How, then, is God the Son differentiated from God the Father? He is like the Son of a human Father solely in being personally and so 'genetically' related to him. The tradition says that he is begotten, not in time as is a human child, but eternally, for both the Father and the Son are what they are eternally and immutably. There is also a measure of reciprocity in the relation. The Son derives his being from the Father, yet in such a way that the Father is only himself as Father of *this* Son.[2] There is no other God than the one we meet in the self-giving and reconciling figure Jesus of Nazareth. Such a consideration demonstrates the point of such speculative theology, and it serves to reinforce Forsyth's point that what happens in history is

---

[1] P. T. Forsyth, *The Person and Place of Jesus Christ* (London: Independent Press, 1909), pp. 309, 314–15.

[2] In that respect the Son *is* passive; or rather, better, he is passive in order that he may be active, through the Spirit, as the Son of the Father, the one who mediates the Father's creating and redeeming action in the world.

rooted in the eternal and infinite being of God. God the Son is God in action in the world, because he is constitutive of God's being eternally. This has a number of important implications for human life, consequent, for example, upon Barth's contention that all this shows that it is as truly Godlike to be humble as it is to be high.[3] As we have seen, the question of human being is the question of how rightly to be godlike in the world. The self-humiliation of the Son of God shows that the poor and the weak truly are more able than the rich and powerful to do the work of God in the world, among other reasons because they are not liable to confuse their power with the power of God. Especially does the being of the Son shape our understanding of glory. If the glory of God is reflected not in the powerful of this world, but in the face of Jesus Christ, we are returned to our contention that God's glory, eschatologically considered, is that which the creatures indeed serve, but only so become truly themselves. To serve this master is not to be a slave, but free.

[3] Karl Barth, *Church Dogmatics*, translation edited by G. W. Bromiley and T. F. Torrance (Edinburgh: T. & T. Clark, 1957–75), 4/1, pp. 190–1.

Part 3

The Perfecting Cause:
'And in the Holy Spirit'

Chapter 7

Christian Community and Human Society

§24. *Some Lessons of Christian History*

God the Spirit is, as we have seen, the perfecting cause of the creation. God the Father perfects his creation in and through time, through his Son and Spirit enabling particular acts, events and things, from bits of pottery to noble and self-giving actions, to be themselves, and thus to be particular anticipations of the final perfecting of all things. In the New Testament much is also made of the Spirit's work in relation both to the church and to the particular Christian, who are in some way prominent among those created beings who are enabled to share in the perfecting. The reference to the church in connection with the idea of perfection may well induce a hollow laugh in the modern world. Can not the Spirit do better than to centre his work on this odd and, apparently, historically discredited institution? In a work dedicated to as concise as possible an account of the faith of the church, too much space cannot be spent on apologies for things not being as they ought to be. But something must be said about how and why things are as they are, in the West at any rate.

The effect of the resurrection of Jesus was to convince those who had been in Jesus' immediate company that he was of universal significance: that his significance extended from Jerusalem to the ends of the earth. It may or may not be the case that Jesus had intended something like the church to emerge. (Loisy's famous saying that 'Jesus announced the Kingdom, and it is the church that came' can have a cynical ring to it.)[1] Certainly, there is little doubt that Jesus' attention was centred on a call to Israel truly to be the people of God, and it is probable that the symbolic choice of 12 disciples arose from that. But the resurrection put things in a different light, and it was in their new-found confidence in the universality of the gospel that the early Christians set out to conquer the world. A combination of confidence, prayer and holy living, allied with sometimes ruthless organization and outstanding intellectual power, achieved something of that. That, from the fourth century onwards, the church achieved her end also by increasingly grasping at the reins of political power was not in every way a bad thing, whatever is sometimes said. The settlement with the Roman and Byzantine empires is now attacked on all sides. It is attacked by secularists because it supposedly led to the imposition of religion by force, to the murder of Jews, to the persecution of early scientists like Galileo – one of the church's own devout members – to the infliction of savage penalties by secular law and to the prosecution of wars against Muslims and others. It is increasingly attacked from within the church also as a dilution of the gospel, in direct conflict with the behaviour of Jesus himself, who had refused to use force to save himself from death.

In this case also, however, the truth, to quote Oscar Wilde, is rarely pure and never simple. There are many things to be placed in the other pan of the scales. On the one hand, much of the West's incomparable culture, including science, works of art and music of unequalled beauty, quite apart from hospitals and educational institutions, owes its origins more or less directly to the influence of the Christian faith. On the other hand, it cannot be said too often that the wholesale murder of millions of people by self-consciously atheist regimes and the personal, social and ecological damage inflicted on the world by our secular culture alike suggest that, however damaging this religion can be, its rejection has produced frightful evil. Despite all this, however, no author should embark on the topic of the church without being chastened by history, and without seeking to avoid above all the idealizing of any human institution, especially any self-consciously Christian institution.

The principles on which things will now be taken forward must then be made clear. The first takes us back to the doctrine of the Spirit which has

---

[1]   Alfred Loisy, *L'Evangile et L'Eglise* (Paris, 1902), p. 153, cited by Robert W. Jenson, *Systematic Theology*, vol. 2, *The Works of God* (New York and Oxford: Oxford University Press, 1999), p. 170.

been with us from the beginning. In view of what has been said of the Spirit's perfecting and particular activity we should not be surprised to find that his work is centred on the church. It is not, as has often been suggested, if not actually taught, that the Spirit is in some way at the disposal of the church, so that what the church does the Spirit is doing. It is rather that the Spirit's first function is to realize in the life of particular human beings and groups of human beings the reality of what God in Christ achieved on the cross. By calling its members out of darkness into the glory of God reflected on the face of the man from Nazareth, the Spirit gathers around the risen Jesus a people whose *sole* calling is to praise the one who made them. That 'sole' should not be understood in any way narrowly. It involves both the praise of conscious and explicit worship and that worship carried over into forms of communal life and individual action.

The second principle is concerned with the form of social life that flows from the Spirit's calling. Because, as we have seen, human life takes essentially social form, and because the place where human beings work out their fallenness is also social, because of all this the place of rebuilding must also be social. Israel ever reminds us of this, but there are also important differences to note. The church is different from Israel in not being identifiable with any single national or political entity. Where attempts have been made to make it so, the relation between the individual and social dimensions of the faith has regularly been distorted. Prominent in western history are two dangerous tendencies: to see the church as an expression of national life and consequently to narrow its universal calling and responsibility; and to see it as a given institution into which individuals come, rather than as a society whose distinctive reality is shaped – in its 'horizontal' dimensions – by the particular people within it. In western Christianity we often witness the two distortions coalescing in a system in which individualism and collectivism exist side by side. Under such an arrangement, individuals live in more or less complaisant relation to a collective body, often identified with the clergy, rather than together being a society which is reciprocally shaped by and shapes the people who make it what it is. Justifiably, therefore, the right social form of the church has been a major concern of recent theology.

The third principle, also essential if we are to maintain a right orientation, is that the doctrine of the ascension must continue to remind us that we are concerned with the absent Jesus, and one whose presence to both church and world is essentially problematic. The church can no more claim automatically to be the body of Christ than it can claim to possess the Spirit. The risen Lord is made present only by the Father's Spirit, and any institution claiming either in some sense automatically to mediate – let alone to be – the presence of Christ or automatically to be in possession of the Spirit is in danger of subverting its own constitution. Here, as so often in theology, we meet perils on both sides. On the one hand, we neglect the promise of God that the church is called and empowered to represent his love in the world in a particular way, one shaped by the career of Jesus; on the other, we forget that this becomes real only by the Spirit's free giving. The conception of the church as the body of Christ can in this regard cause as much harm as good, as we shall see.

The three principles are all eschatological in force. The Spirit's work is to make real, from time to time and as divine gift gives rise to human freedom, anticipations of the true community of the last days. In this regard, the church's mistake is too often to claim that these conditions are too directly and by her own inner strength realized in her life and institutions, rather than being anticipated in them only by the gracious and free action of the Lord the Spirit. Many of the worst disasters of that partly sorry story known as church history derive from too confident a claim to realize, now, what can be fully realized only in the kingdom of heaven. The church may be the servant of the kingdom, but once she begins to think that she is the kingdom she displaces the work of the Spirit with her own rather than receiving her true being as gift.

Despite all these warnings, the eschatology with which we are concerned is none the less one which bears upon and interprets positively a firmly historical and social reality. Let us recall chapter 3, where it was suggested that the one truly sacramental reality, the one created being which was created *of itself* to point to the divine was man, created male and female in the image of God. This creature, however, we have also seen to be at the heart of the fall, so that the one meant to be like God has sought sustenance from other sources, and so has experienced a fall through worship of the creature rather than the creator. It has sought to point to itself rather than to its creator, to be god rather than to be like God. That is the reason for the fact that, for the most part, the New Testament restricts the attribution of the image of God to Jesus Christ, whose resurrection attests that here only is to be found human life as it was created to be. He it is who is 'the image of the invisible God, the first born of all creation' (Col. 1. 15). That he was raised from the dead is testimony – in Barth's expression, 'the verdict of the Father'[2] – that here is the one just, truthful and free human being. For others to realize the image and likeness of God now involves being brought into reconciled relation with God the Father through him; indeed, in Paul's expression, being conformed to him. What insight does this starting point offer us for a theology of the Christian community?

§25. The Words of Proclamation and of Scripture

In as much as the life of the incarnate Son of God was lived in free dependence on God the Father and empowered by the Spirit, it was free from the idolatry and self-seeking which is the root of sin and evil. Concretely, as we have seen, Jesus' life took shape as the concentration of those offices through which Israel's life was maintained in relation to her God. It is on this basis that we can essay a definition of the kind of social institution that the church is. The church is the place – the living space – where the kingship, priesthood and prophetic work of Jesus is appropriated – taken on board, we might say. It is therefore a particular form of social existence ordered by the Spirit to God the Father by virtue of its relation to this one and only life lived truly as the image of God.

How, then, is the orientation to God by which this man lived realized in the social order gathered around his memory? The early history of the church and the message of its greatest apostle are agreed: it is first of all by word of mouth, precisely as was Jesus' message before it. Paul's assertion that without a preacher the gospel will not be communicated (Rom. 10.14–15) is illustrated in the way the church first came to be. The account of the giving of the Spirit in Acts 2 shows that the community was called into renewed relation to God by a preaching of repentance.[3] The appeal was grounded in the narrative of the life, death and resurrection of Jesus, understood as the action of God. This proclamation becomes what is called the gospel, the good news that God has acted in this particular way decisively for human well-being. The earliest preaching – as recorded, for example, in

---

[2] Karl Barth, *Church Dogmatics*, translation edited by G. W. Bromiley and T. F. Torrance (Edinburgh: T. & T. Clark, 1957–75), vol. 4/1, pp. 283–357.

[3] The narrative is highly symbolically charged, and neglect of this aspect has led to attention being paid more to the apparently ecstatic phenomena than to the creation of a community of worship, teaching, prayer and life which is its centre.

1 Corinthians 15.3–8 – declares some of the themes expounded in chapter 4 above. The gospel events are such that their telling becomes the means by which the achievement of Jesus as a divine and human saving action is made, so to speak, transferable. Accordingly, the proclaimed gospel contained in the first preaching *instituted* the church: that is, made it an institution, a form of human being together ordered around Jesus and taking settled if changing form in time and space.[4]

The Pauline and other summaries of the gospel were extended in the New Testament letters, which often take the form of classifications, elaborations, applications and defences of particular aspects of it. In turn, these mostly early expositions were supported by the books called Gospels, writings which fill out the narrative details of the divine and human life which is the focus of faith in God. Some of the early writings became 'scripture', by which is meant in this case works judged suitable to be used in the church's worship for ever. In the first part of this book something was said about scripture as a cultural artefact, unique in what it has to say, but yet recognizable none the less as one among a myriad of human cultural productions. We now begin to see more clearly the reasons why such uniqueness is claimed for it, central among them being that the early church saw itself as dependent on scripture for its understanding of the gospel. The scriptures of the first Christians were given to them.[5] Israel's scriptures, now known in the church as the Old Testament, are what are referred to when Paul says of Christ that what happened with him was 'according to the scriptures' (1 Cor. 15.3–4). Luke's report of the words of Jesus on the road to Emmaus makes the point summarily and explicitly: 'and beginning with Moses and all the prophets, he explained to them what was said *concerning himself* in *all* the scriptures' (Lk. 24.27, italics added). These were the only scriptures that the first generations had, and it was only under a number of pressures that the situation changed, and further writings were accepted. These additional books were written on two assumptions: first that the Old Testament scriptures were the key to an understanding of Jesus; and second

---

[4] By 'institution' is meant something far broader than is found in expressions like 'I do not believe in institutional religion', which usually reject the form which the institution has taken. Those who speak like this often, though not always, seek other institutional forms through which to develop their religiousness.

[5] Even if there is a case for claiming that the church is in some respect the creator of scripture, that can hold only for the New Testament writings.

that, reciprocally, he was also the key to their meaning. The one through whom the world was created and who was the Word of God to Israel had now become personally present to the world in such a way that clarification and reinterpretation of the ancient witness to him was necessarily involved. The decision during the early centuries to recognize another set of writings to be called the New Testament alongside the Old was a response to a number of pressures: among them (1) heresy; (2) the fact that the unique personal speech of God was fixed at a particular time in history, now past; and (3) the need to decide which works were appropriate to order the worship and life of the increasingly far-flung community.

Since some time early in the life of the church, therefore, there has been a recognized canon or measuring rod against which the worship, life, faith and thought of the community could be measured. It is the Bible, a single book containing two sets of books. The 'Old' Testament, by which nothing disparaging is or ought to be implied, is the record of foundations, of that which God did 'of old' in creating the world and preparing it for the appearance in due time of his only-begotten Son. The New Testament consolidates the realization, at the appointed time, of what had been prepared for. The relation between the two collections, mutually inter-pretative, as has already been suggested, is to be found in the use of the term 'covenant'. By that is meant the one-sided initiative whereby God bound himself to particular forms of relationship with those made in his image and likeness. The 'old' covenant, manifold in content, was with Adam, Noah, Abraham, Moses, and, through him, with Israel as a whole. Its own prophets had themselves promised a 'new' covenant, and therefore the new is but the outcome of the old. An exposition of Jeremiah's promise of a new covenant, written on the heart rather than tablets of stone, lies at the heart of the Letter to the Hebrews' argument that the priestly sacrifice of Jesus at once fulfils and transcends the institutions of the old order (Jer. 31.31–4; Heb. 8 and 10). In their accounts of the Last Supper, to which we shall return, Paul and Luke explicitly refer to a 'new' covenant. It is in what happens at that Supper and its aftermath that both the new and the old come together. Jesus is the key to the Old Testament, but cannot be understood without it. That asymmetrical reciprocity is the focus of the unity in duality of the Bible.

Scripture is the essential medium of the transmission of the gospel by virtue first of God's historical action in both Israel and Jesus Christ and second of Jesus' ascension and absence. Unless the Word is communicated by these words and the interpretation of those words by the ones to whom the gospel has been entrusted, it will not be heard. (That is not to rule out other forms of communication, but to make them secondary to it.) In that respect – in being dependent on a process of tradition, of handing on the core of its beliefs and practices to later generations – the church is identical with any other community of belief, teaching and action. Where it is different is in the content of that which it seeks to propagate and transmit. The gospel – the news that is conveyed – is that God has acted in Jesus Christ personally, decisively and universally in such a way that response to his proclaimed story is definitive for the shape of life on earth and beyond. It is that proclamation which brought about the foundation of the church, whose life must also be determined by it, because it presents in summary the words which prepared for and arose out of the life, death, resurrection and ascension of the one Word of God.

§26.   The Elect Community

And so we come to the doctrine of the church. The inextricable relations of old and new are as evident in the theology of Israel and the church as they are in the doctrine of scripture. That the church is often described in terms used of Israel in the Old Testament does not imply that the church has superseded Israel, as has often been taught, but that she is Israel expanded to embrace the Gentiles, in precise fulfilment of the covenant with Abraham. All this is God's act, gift, covenant, promise, forgiveness: the gift by God of his Son which needs only to be accepted. Those who accept the gospel, at first Jews only, but later, as the logic of resurrection comes to work itself out in time, Gentiles also, are a kind of reconstituted Israel, not displacing her but – in Paul's agonized thinking through of the relation – called as a living challenge to Israel to be truly the people of God. 'You are a chosen people, a royal priesthood, a holy nation, a people belonging to God,' says the first letter of Peter (2.9), and it is with these words that we should begin, because they involve also the offices of Christ as they take shape in the present.

The reference to Israel and to the calling of the church reminds us that only in a very restricted sense is the church a voluntary organization in the modern sense of the term. It is indeed a voluntary organization, but only in the sense that those who join it respond willingly to the invitation of the gospel. This implies from the outset a difference between the church and the 'worldly' order into which we are born, or join by immigration. The Acts of the Apostles shows that there are many who hear and refuse the invitation to membership of the holy people of God. The invitation comes from God. Just as nothing can be itself without being enabled to be so by God, so the rebuilding of ruined humanity is and can be only first of all the act of the creator God through his two hands. Like Israel, the church can come to be only by divine choice and call. We have seen that God's intention for his creation is universal: it is, in the words of the New Testament epistle most eloquent about the blessings of election, 'to bring all things in heaven and on earth under the headship of Christ' (Eph. 1.3–10). To achieve this universal end, rooted in his eternity, however, God uses, as is appropriate for a world structured in space and through time, particular groups and people. The centrality of the calling of Abraham and Israel has been stressed earlier in the book. This is now broadened out into the church, which is, none the less, still a particular people called out from the whole for the sake of the whole. That is why the reconciliation of Jews and Gentiles, worshipping and living together as one community, is for the writer to the Ephesians the central mark of salvation, almost salvation itself.

This is a rather different form of the doctrine of election from that which has prevailed for much of our history. There, often called predestination, it has often served, first, to narrow rather than broaden the purposes of God and, second, to appear to take away human freedom rather than to confer it. As was reported in chapter 4, there has always been a tendency to see predestination as meaning that God's design is to bring a limited few souls to heaven and consign the remainder to the rubbish heap. The biblical doctrine of election is far more this-worldly than that. Abraham is chosen to be a blessing to the nations, Israel to be their light, Jeremiah to be the vehicle of God's word to Israel; and instances could be multiplied. For the New Testament, these callings are not abrogated but fulfilled in the calling of Jesus and the election of the church. We have seen something of what Jesus' election to messiahship involved: a life of relentless pressure leading to the cross. What is the focus of the election of the church?

It is first of all a calling to praise and worship. The church is the society whose distinctive way of being in the world – distinctive polity, we might say – is oriented to God primarily in terms of thanksgiving and worship. As we have seen, this is not to be understood narrowly but as an offering of all life, so that the question of the nature of the church is best approached by means of a discussion of the kind of social order that it represents.[6] And it is as follows. The church's way of being in the world is one that corresponds to Israel's way of being while allowing for the changes that are consequent upon the movement from particular nation to a community incorporating all peoples. We have seen, however, that there are different ways of being universal, so that we must raise again the question of what kind of particular social order the church is. It is, accordingly, particular like Israel in being called out and so distinguished from the rest of humankind; it is unlike Israel in that representatives of all peoples and nations are explicitly included within it. This inclusion is, further, unambiguous because the nations are included without a requirement that they cease to be the particular peoples they are. All the particularity, therefore, converges in the fact that this society is distinguished by one feature: its relation to the Jesus proclaimed in the message of the gospel.

The relation to God through Jesus is maintained by two distinctive but interrelated cultural forms, words and actions. To be sure, the distinction is not an absolute one, despite what we sometimes think. Words are a form of action, certainly for the Bible's God, whose word 'accomplishes that which it sets out to achieve' (Is. 55.11). Words can, indeed, be deceptive and slippery, and are often used to seduce, deceive and betray, but then so are actions, notoriously by Judas Iscariot. But because Jesus is the Word who both spoke and acted in particular ways, the words and actions which maintain the church in relation to him are those which seek to embody in its structures the form or pattern of his career. In that light, the church is a way of being socially whose life is ordered to God by means of words and actions which are evoked by the Spirit's action. Because what the Spirit gives is the presence of the community of worship to God the Father through Jesus the incarnate Word, the worship in which the relationship is centred contains, as we might expect, both divine and human actions and words, in a complex interaction of word and response – the latter including especially prayer and music – in which genuine human response is elicited by the Spirit's action.

---

[6] An alternative approach to this question would be through a discussion of biblical images, for example of the church as the body of Christ. The inadequacy of this approach is that it lacks a criterion by which a choice of one concept rather than another – for example, the bride of Christ or people of God – is to be preferred and ordered in relation to others.

What is the point of all this? All particular human societies have bound-aries which determine their criteria of membership. Calvin, for example, held that the two marks by which a true church can be recognized are the preaching of the gospel and the right administration of the sacraments.[7] These are the means by which the life of a community is oriented to and held within the structure of Jesus' life in the flesh. Proclamation and the exposition of scripture are prior to the rites of baptism and the Lord's Supper because, unexplained, the application of water and the ingesting of food and drink can mean a variety of things, from any religion or none. The indis-pensability of what we call the sacraments, however, derives from the incarnation and its outcome. The Son's involvement in the created order which is the object of his redemptive love requires a broader conception of the word than simply that which is spoken. Because the Word became flesh – involved himself within the structures of createdness – the church must, if she is to be truly the church, give corresponding expression to this aspect also in her worship.

The customary way of summarizing the two indispensable features of the church's worship is as word and sacrament, but the latter term is problem-atic, partly because it is historically a contested term, dividing the churches and affecting their lives deeply. The heart of the underlying problem is revealed in the traditional definition of a sacrament as an outward and visible sign of an inward and spiritual grace, with its implicit dualism between inner and outer. On the one hand, this encourages a broadening of what counts as a sacrament, effectively diluting the importance of what can, for want of a better expression, be called the gospel sacraments of baptism and the Lord's Supper. The inflation of the list of sacraments from the two reaffirmed in the Reformation to the seven of the mediaeval development effectively under-mines baptism and the Lord's Supper by diluting their significance.[8] On the other hand, the dualism also tends to call attention away from the outward and material dimensions, whose reference rather should be primarily not to something going on *within* the believer but to concrete material and histor-ical realities. Jesus' life and death are not the outward sign of something

---

[7] John Calvin, *Institutes of the Christian Religion*, edited by J. T. McNeill, translated and indexed by F. L. Battles (Philadelphia: Westminster Press, 1960), 2 vols., Library of Christian Classics 20 and 21, IV. 1. 7–12.

[8] It also led to the clericalizing of the sacraments in which they are made the focus of ecclesiastical control and aggrandizement.

invisible, but the invisible become visible, God in action not only inwardly but also outwardly.

In his words and actions, and especially in his making through the whole of his life and by the eternal Spirit a perfect offering of worship and obedience to God the Father, Jesus realizes the mandate of Genesis 1 to exercise dominion of the creation as God's representative on earth. He is therefore the sole sacrament, in so far as 'sacrament' denotes a created reality that is unambiguously also God's presence and action in the world. The things that we call sacraments, therefore, are only rightly so described so long as they are held to be strictly derivative from this: as being the definitive forms of speech and action which bring and hold us in relation to God through Jesus. It follows that the Reformers were right to build on Augustine's teaching that, as visible words, the 'sacraments' depend upon the word which Jesus is and which is required to set him forth. The basis of the rites is therefore to be found in two factors: the historical and temporal career of Jesus, especially as that comes to a climax and crisis in his death; and the life of the people of God in the world which is consequent upon his embodied life. They are what they are because they are directly to do with membership of the holy people of God. We shall come to baptism in chapter 8, and here I shall concentrate attention on the Lord's Supper in all the complexity of its relation between Jesus' past presence in the world, present absence and future return. Aspects of Paul's First Letter to Corinth will here be our guide, because that is where the theological, incarnational, ritual, social and ethical dimensions of the Supper belong so inextricably together.

The letter is dominated by questions about the way in which members of a young Christian congregation live together and live in the world. The assumption which shapes Paul's letter is that different ways of living alongside other people embody different relations to God and 'the gods'. For example he argues that to share meals in pagan temples may appear to be harmless because the gods they serve do not really exist, but none the less runs the risk of submitting to powers which determine human life outside its loyalty to Christ.[9] To eat with idols is to enter a social and political realm which is in competition with that of Israel's God; it is to sleep with the

---

[9] At the very least, it implies approval of the activities of the temples, just as offence was recently caused by the presence of the Archbishop of Canterbury at a dinner in honour of the President of China.

enemy. The same holds for those who resort to pagan law courts to settle disputes between church members. The church is a different form of social order from that of the world around. It is holy in a way analogous to the way in which God is holy. Like God, it is different. That does not imply that it has no involvement in the world and there is no suggestion of an 'alternative' political order which rejects the whole of the old one. The Christians remained citizens of Corinth and subjects of the Roman empire. Yet acquiescence in certain forms of activity, for example the sacrifices to the emperor as to a divinity which were later demanded of some Christians, was ruled out because it subverted the higher and primary loyalty. The church is accordingly a way of being *within* the wider social and political world which yet rejects the latter's religious, social, political and legal institutions *in so far as* they claim absolute devotion.

Alongside the concern for the integrity of the community is one for that of the particular people who make it up. Because – as we have seen – people are inseparable from their bodies, the use of the body also reflects (literally, embodies) ultimate and other loyalties. Because it is the body which is promised resurrection, what is done in and with it is of paramount importance. Bodies are those dimensions of our persons by and through which we relate to other human beings and the world. What we do in and with the body forms and anticipates what we shall be. It is in this context that Paul's recapitulation of the Ten Commandments, the charter of the holy people of God, has its place (1 Cor. 6.9–10; compare 1 Tim. 1.8–11). Like sharing meals in the context of divided loyalty, improper or adulterous forms of sexual union displace the union with Christ which is the basis of the life of the church. Paul's reasons for saying this are wholly positive. Unrepentant perpetrators of practices which destroy community – in one instance, a case of incest – must be, at least temporarily, excluded from the life of the community for both its and their sakes. That, however, is the only case in which expulsion is recommended, and the main emphasis is on the formation of relationships which derive from the freedom of those who are set free by the gospel. The end in view is right social embodiment of the gospel.

Now at last we are ready to return to the sacraments, or at least to the one centrally concerned with membership of the church in and over time. Without wanting to moralize the Last Supper, we must yet insist that the two focuses of right relation to God and right relations between embodied human beings are at the centre of Paul's discussion. The Supper he describes is a social event by virtue of the fact that it is something that people do together. Its due ordering is disrupted by greed, insensitivity and the importing from the outside world of social divisions which are forbidden in the new order in Jesus Christ. The failure Paul identifies has nothing at all to do with what happens to the bread and wine at consecration – that is a completely anachronistic consideration – but everything to do with what happens in and with the community of worship. The Supper falls when the members of the community fail to adopt a due orientation to God's redeeming action in Christ, and especially his death, as that is mediated by the Word and the Spirit in the life of the community.

There are two poles to the discussion, and they may appear on first acquaintance to be not so much poles as contraries. First, there is a near identification of the community with Christ himself, clearly implying that those who are 'in Christ' are, because they are brought to God the Father through him, in a realistic though still metaphorical sense, his body.[10] That is not, however, to imply that it is a mere metaphor which makes no claim to be true. Because the church is the body of Christ, it is a distinctive way of being in the world whose form can be understood to have several varying dimensions all of which enrich a theology of the community: In 1 Corinthians 12.12–27 he [Paul] is concerned with the multiplicity of functions required within an organic unity, in Romans 12.4–5 with the mutual dependence of Christians, in Colossians 1.18 with the common dependence of Christians on their head, and in Colossians 1.24 with an extension of Christ's life and character.[11] Several aspects of those passages, and especially the notion of Christ as head of the body, take us to the second pole of the topic. For all the nearness of identification of Christ with the body, there is an equally strong movement to distinguish him from the members of the church and the members of the church from one another. In 1 Corinthians 12 Paul is concerned with the oneness of Christians in relation to Christ *in and through* their diversity of gifts and graces. What we find throughout is a straining to show that the way the members of the church are and act to one another is at the same time the way in which they live before God and in Christ.

---

[10] Despite what is sometimes argued, to speak of the church as the body of Christ is to speak metaphorically; if it were literally the case, it would be possible, as George Caird used to remark, to identify which member was a fingernail, which a left ear, and so on.

[11] G. B. Caird, *New Testament Theology*, edited by L. D. Hurst (Oxford: Clarendon Press, 1994), p. 205.

As in the doctrine of the person of Christ, the levels of divine and human action are inextricably related and can be understood only at both levels of what remains a relation in tension.

To be sure, it is the former level, that of divine action, which determines the latter: 'You are not your own; you were bought at a price' (1 Cor. 6.19–20). The relation of the Corinthians with God, and so with one another, is determined first by the proclamation of the cross as the power of salvation (1 Cor. 1–2) and only second by the resulting form of life which embodies that salvation. It is in this light that we must understand the treatment of the Lord's Supper in Paul, which takes place *in one respect* in the absence of Christ. 'In memory of him, until he comes' (1 Cor. 11.24–6) implies that he is not there, and therefore a real absence.[12] The crucial action is accordingly that which brings the church into real relation with the ascended and bodily absent Lord whose presence this side of the end is mediated by the Spirit. To eat bread and to drink wine in the context of the proclamation of the cross and in anticipation of the resurrection places the congregation in a salutary relation to God so long as they do not turn the relation into a destructive one by importing into it ways of behaving which deny their oneness with Christ. The problem is not of failing to believe theoretically that the bread and wine are the body and blood of Christ; it is their behaviour to one another ('One remains hungry, another gets drunk', 1 Cor. 11.21). The meaning of the words Paul uses to describe the event must also be understood in that context. While 'body' ('This is my body') refers both to the bread and to the community that is the body of Christ, 'the cup' (note, not 'the wine'), is clearly a reference to Christ's death under judgement. And just as the body refers at once to the community and to the bread, the cup refers to the judgement (as cleansing) which the cross brings. That judgement turns into judgement (as death) by misuse in a community which is unreconciled within itself. Those who eat and drink (offending in whatever way is intended) eat and drink judgement (*krima*) on themselves. Notice how in the following passage Paul plays on the various meanings of words derived from the root meaning of 'judgement' in a way not always visible in translation.

That is why many of you are weak and sick, and a number of you have fallen asleep. But if we judged [die*krin*omen] ourselves, we would not come under

---

[12] See Richard B. Hays, *First Corinthians* (Louisville, KY: John Knox, 1997), p. 199.

judgement [ekrinometha]. When we are judged [krinomenoi] by the Lord, we
are being disciplined [paideuometha], so that we will not be condemned
[katakrithômen] with the world (1 Cor. 11.29–32).

To accept the salutary judgement involved in identifying ourselves with
Christ's death under judgement is one thing; it is to accept godly discipline,
as children of the one Father. To play fast and loose with that calling is to
risk condemnation.

The Lord's Supper is accordingly the rite according to which membership of the community is rooted in a conscious orientation to the atoning
death of Christ as it releases praise of God and the living out of that praise
in forms of life in community. Throughout, the bread and wine both
represent the bodily incarnation of the Son of God and carry through
its significance for the whole of created being. As we have seen, the
celebration is bracketed behind by the proclamation of the saving death of
Jesus. It is likewise bracketed before by the return of this same Jesus in
which the perfecting of all things will be completed. By exploring
something of that eschatological dimension – 'until he comes' – we
shall be able to expand our understanding of the implications of the
incarnation of the Son of God. First, the eating and drinking together
of the elect community anticipates the true human community of the
end time and this is expressed by images of the eschatological banquet at
which all God's children will be reconciled to him and to one another.
That is to say, universal human fellowship under God is representatively
anticipated in the congregation's eating together. Similarly, second, the
wider created world is also representatively incorporated, for the
bread and wine, as the prayers often used at the Supper imply, are at once
the fruit of the earth and the product of human manufacture. Just as
Jesus' body was formed from the dust of the earth, so these physical
creatures become the means whereby the whole created world is taken
up, by anticipation, into the praise of the creator. It is there that is to be
found the basis not only of an ethic of community but also an ecological
ethic which does not deny the need for active intervention in the structures
of nature ('which human hands have made', to cite a familiar prayer) but
presupposes that this should take place only to the glory of God and the
good of the creature, especially the human creature. And that takes us to
some very brief remarks about the place of the church in the world in which
it is set.

§27. The Church and the Social Order

The church's distinctive way of being in the world follows, like its inner life, from the embodiment of the Son of God in Jesus of Nazareth and his involvement by the Spirit in the life of his people. Just as Jesus is the invisible God become visible for the sake of the world, so the church is called and from time to time also enabled to express her relation to him by her visible social structure in the heart of the world. This requires us to reject deeply entrenched ways of thinking of the church. In an era of official Christianity when it was assumed that all members of society were Christian, there developed a doctrine of the invisible church to distinguish the 'real' Christians from the so-called hypocrites. The church was a 'mixed' body of believers and hangers-on, with the believers distinguished from the rest as the 'invisible church' known only to God. This had serious effects on the church's conception of her mission or sending. 'Mission' effectively disappeared, or – more recently – it was either applied to cultures other than the Christian or took the form of revivals in which the lapsed were called back into the fold. We can say, without wishing in any way to deny the importance of both of the latter, that this involves a narrowing of the church's mission, which, in a broad sense, is a sending to be and act for and on behalf of the world as Israel and Jesus Christ were and are sent. As Jesus came to save a perishing world, so the church's mission is to proclaim and embody the significance of his death and resurrection for all realms of the world's life.

We thus return to the matter of the church's visible social structure. The church is visibly like other human institutions in having a structure in many ways similar to theirs, subject to sociological and historical laws. But it is unlike them in operating differently in certain essential respects. It is like other 'voluntary' organizations in being joined freely; it is unlike them in attributing that joining to the work of God the Spirit and in orienting its life to worship and learning the ways of love, rather than, say, to making music or eating together, though it may also do both of those things. It is like the broader social order of which it is a part in being oriented to human welfare; but unlike it in the understanding that it is given of that welfare and the means by which it is achieved.

One example will illustrate and develop the point. All civil societies maintain order by coercion and the imposition of penalty, often violent penalty, on those conceived to threaten them. Although the church has often colluded with the secular authorities in the use of coercive power,[13] it is now almost universally agreed that this is theologically, and therefore morally, intolerable. Churches may rightly exclude from their societies those who are judged to subvert them by false teaching or breach of divine law – if they are quite certain that that is the case – but may not exceed that. Does it follow that because the church lives, or seeks to live, non-coercively, while the civil order necessarily uses coercion, that the church should reject the civil order and all its ways? Not at all. Let us consider the case of punishment, which, as we have already seen, is theologically significant for all kinds of reasons.

It is widely believed to be part of the order of things that breach of the law should be recompensed by an appropriate penalty, though there will be wide disagreement on what is appropriate in a particular case, say a murder or a brutal rape. It is also almost certainly the case that no social order could survive without a system of judicial punishment; in that respect, the church is, like all other intermediate human communities, set in a larger whole and therefore requiring the broader social context without which it could not exist. However, at the heart of the Christian faith is the conviction that by virtue of the 'blessed exchange' of the just for the unjust, a new order obtains. In this order, evil is overcome not by the infliction of further evil, but by good. It is the way of things, therefore, that in the relations of Christians with other human beings, and especially in their relations with one another, such vengeance as there is should be left to God and the enemy reconciled by being loved (classically, at Romans 12.17–21, where, it should be noted, the Old Testament is quoted in support). Here is a society which is *required* to order its own life differently from the way of the world.

The complication comes when it is realized that what is being taught is, indeed, a way of doing things for a particular community but one which also claims universal validity. It is a universal truth that evil can be overcome only by good. Does this, again, mean that the church must reject civil authority and its way of coercion altogether? Rather, it is necessary to acknowledge the inescapability of punishment, of violent restraint, and possibly even of war as a provisional mandate; but only provisional, only in order to hold the fort, so to speak. If the way of forgiveness is the only

---

[13] Perhaps among the most fateful political acts ever performed by a bishop was when Augustine sought the assistance of the state in the forcible restraint of heretics.

way to change things, it has to be acknowledged that coercive punishment, and the same goes for war, will, except in certain contexts, at best maintain only an equilibrium and is more likely to exacerbate the evil. Has it not been argued that the difference in outcome of the First and Second World Wars has something to do with the difference between a vengeful and a more conciliatory attitude of victors to vanquished? It is also the case that a system of punishment organized both to embody just recompense and to facilitate repentance and amendment of life is more likely to make punishment's repetition unnecessary. In that regard, therefore, the church lives by a way of doing things which she both recommends to the civil order and yet recognizes to be in certain – but not all – respects beyond that order's capacities and resources.

The basis for an account of the church and the social order which allows for the complexities of the human condition and the entrenched nature of evil is provided by a theology of creation upon which have supervened both the fall and the promise of redemption. The doctrine of a providentially ordered creation holds that even the social and political order, dominated as it tends to be by the rich, powerful and self-interested, is upheld in Christ and by the Spirit. Unlike, however, the church, which consciously orients itself to the life of the one who became poor, the secular order is more likely – though only that – to close its ears to the word of God. A theology of the 'principalities and powers' is here essential. To refer to the powers is to speak of the way in which political power gains its own momentum beyond and above the individual acts of those who make up any social order. They have two sides. First, as part of the good order of things they are necessary for human good, expressing one dimension of what is sometimes called the social contract. Human beings require structures within which to order their lives, and the political order is there to serve that need. Second, however, by setting themselves up as rivals to God – by placing the emperor's image in the temple (2 Th. 2.4) – the powers, like the sorcerer's apprentice, let loose forces which they cannot control. We have in the last century seen all too well how that happens in our world. Yet, as Revelation 6 indicates, even these forces, the four horsemen representing invasion, rebellion, famine and pestilence, are not outside the overall providential control of God, being actually let loose by the crucified lamb who is the real ruler of history.

The powers become demonic have their way, however, only for a while. They have been conquered on the cross, for they could not keep Jesus in the tomb, and therefore their doom is sealed. All the great empires, even those claiming and seeking to be Christian, go the way of Nineveh and Tyre, on to the scrap heap of history. However, while, eschatologically speaking, their days are numbered, they also have a task to perform, as it is from time to time enabled by the perfecting Spirit. For the theology developed in this chapter is designed to show that the Spirit is the one who forges communion and community, first in the elect people of God but then also, and sometimes with the active assistance of that people, more broadly in the human social order. The difference between the church and the civil order is that the Spirit's activity in the former but not the latter derives from the church's explicit ordering of her life to the Word of God, incarnate and proclaimed. That rules out neither the church's failing to heed the Word nor the Spirit's action enabling the civil order to be what it ought to be, but it does make obedience to the divine will less likely in the latter case. Yet we must insist that both forms of human living together are the gift of God, essential for our humanity which is a social humanity.

How the Spirit's action can be understood in relation to the particular people of which the church is formed will provide the burden of the next chapter. Only after that shall we broaden out again into a consideration of the Spirit's work in the whole created order.

Chapter 8

The Shape of the Christian Life

§28.   Justification: Living by Faith Alone

The apparent polarity of life and death has been with us for much of the book. As we have seen, it is only an apparent polarity, for, according to scripture, life and death are by no means equal and opposite. God is the God of life, not of death, even though the domain of death is not outside his providential control. We must once again distinguish death from mortality. Mortality simply refers to the end of this life on the earth as it is, and may or may not be a blessing. In the second sense, death means experiencing both life and death in a world which moves to dissolution rather than to perfection. Death means life lived apart from God, and is truly deadly because it is life attempting to maintain itself in separation from its true source. The death of Jesus was so deadly because it involved his being consigned to the realm of that which is sundered from God; his resurrection, therefore, is a victory over death not because it is a *restoration* to life but because it is the gift of life beyond and so out of range of the realm of death.

That much is clear from Paul's classic treatment of the meaning of the resurrection in 1 Corinthians 15. We shall come to the resurrection in due time, but in this section of the chapter will consider first the link Paul makes towards the end of it between the law and death ('The sting of death is sin, and the power of sin is the law', 1 Cor. 15.56). The parallel link between sin and death, made there and elsewhere, is easy enough to understand. Sin means a false relation to God, and therefore living a lie. Simply speaking in terms of the natural consequences of actions, those who live a lie – who worship the creature rather than the creator – render themselves liable to death, for they walk out of the realm of life. A link between sin and the law, however, is less clear. We need to be very careful about what this should and should not be taken to mean. On the surface it is easy to understand, because as Paul himself shows, perhaps especially in the argument of the Letter to the Galatians, the law prescribes the death penalty for those who break it. But this is not a matter of surface meanings, as the endless history of church-dividing controversy all too well indicates.

We need to bear in mind two aspects of the situation. (1) The link between the law and sin does not entail that the law, simply as law, is a bad thing. On the contrary, it is the good gift of God: a framework within which people and societies may structure their lives. Further, as God's good provision for life in the world, the law is 'holy and just and good' (Rom. 7.12). Torah is grace and revelation. (2) Nevertheless, the Torah became necessary only because there was sin. That is the teaching of Genesis and Paul alike, to name but two important authorities. Because fallen man no longer lives in the relation to God for which he was created, a framework is needed within which the worst effects of human fallenness can be obviated. The law is good because it enables life on earth and under God to be continued with minimal disruption, but its limits are indicated by the negative form it takes: 'Thou shalt not . . .'. It is, as Jesus said of the divorce law, given for the hardness of human hearts (Mk. 10.5). It needs, said Jeremiah, to be replaced with something better, because it does not, as it stands, deal with the central problem, which is the human heart. Notice, however, that even under the 'new covenant' the heart is not to displace the law, but to submit to the law in a different form: 'I will put my law in their minds and write it on their hearts' (Jer. 31.33). It will be an internal qualification of the human person, not an external imposition.

In our rationalistic culture we have tended to understand the essence of the person to be the mind, as, for example, in the oft-repeated query whether a computer able to think would be a person. The absurdity of the suggestion is shown by the counterquery of whether a computer could love, and what that could mean. It would mean at least that it needed an organic body, which it does not and cannot have; in other words, it would need a heart. The advantage of privileging heart over mind is that the heart is bodily; it is, we might say, that which makes us tick in more senses than one. (I believe that it was Wittgenstein who said that when we speak of the heart in the way we do we are not speaking merely metaphorically.)

The mental, emotional and bodily dimensions of our being all converge in the heart, so that what our hearts are, that we are. In that regard, the story of our salvation is summed up in two verses in Genesis, ante- and postdiluvian. The flood happened because, 'the Lord saw how great man's wickedness on the earth had become, and that every inclination of the thoughts of his heart was only wicked all the time. The Lord was grieved that he had made man, and his heart [sic!] was filled with pain' (Gen. 6.5–6). Then, after the flood and Noah's thanksgiving sacrifice, God promises: 'Never again will I curse the ground because of man, even though every inclination of his heart is evil from childhood. And never again will I destroy all living creatures...' (Gen 8.21).

Why does the law bring death? There are two subsidiary reasons, which will lead us to an answer. The first is that the law must, being law, sentence those who break its requirements, as all do. The second is that in so far as men and women believe that they can find their way back to God by its means, can claw their way back up to God by moral effort, they simply exacerbate the problem. In this refusal to accept our createdness, in the fact that we are what we are only in dependence on God's grace, we replicate and entrench the very attitude which first caused the problem. In linking law and sin, Paul is making this point and this point alone. The law which is good is corrupted into a religious principle outside the relation to God which it is designed to realize. Many of Jesus' charges against his opponents also fit into this pattern. By their use of the law they harden their hearts, and so bring themselves and others into the realm of death. They use the law in such a way as to invalidate it.

Why does the law bring death? We come to our chief answer, that not the law but only a personal act of mercy by God himself in the person of his Son is able to set back on the path of life those who are on the way to death. That is the message of Jeremiah as he is interpreted by the New Testament authors, and is the heart (again) of the gospel. It is not that the Old Testament dispensation has been superseded; it is rather that it has been concentrated on the life of the incarnate Son of God. Only there can be broken the slavery of the moral agent to the self that would live out its destiny apart from God. Not the law itself, not the sacrificial system, not the rebirth of prophecy in John the Baptist – none of them can cleanse the conscience from dead works to serve the living God gladly and joyfully. That is why the Reformers were right – despite the fact that recent scholarship about Paul's thought makes it necessary to qualify some of their particular emphases – to argue that justification is the *articulus stantis et cadentis ecclesiae*, the article by which the church stands or falls. The reason is that the wish ourselves to be God is the desire most entrenched in the human heart, and so the most difficult to eradicate, especially for those who are most deeply serious religiously, whether Pharisee or Christian. Only a heart-changing initiative from God can achieve what is necessary.

'[Jesus] was delivered over to death for our sins, and was raised to life for our justification' (Rom. 4.25). In earlier chapters we have seen something of the meaning of the first clause of that lapidary juxtaposition. We now engage with the second. Justification has to do with the way in which the death of Jesus bears upon the life and death of the human being. Justification is the human status and condition which derive from the just act of God. Here Luther's discovery is definitive: God's just act is the one by which he does not punish the sinner, but makes the godless to be just. Justification is giving to the human being the status of being a child of God. Another way of putting it would be to say – as Paul does – that it is a way by which those who are lost in hardness of heart are adopted as children of the household of God. (Notice the use of the household image in John 8.34–8 also, where the contrast is this time between the slave and the child of the household.) It is, as Paul makes clear, through the Spirit that adoption takes place (Rom. 8.12–17). By relating the godless to the Father through Jesus Christ the Spirit achieves what nothing else can achieve.

Much ink and worse has been spilled in the effort to decide whether justification takes place by a *declarative* act on God's part – on the grounds that if God says that you are just by virtue of Christ's death and resurrection, then just you are – or whether it is *ontological* by virtue of the fact that it in some way alters the actual being of the justified person. The apparent implication of the first, as its opponents have not been slow to point out, is that it makes justification into a kind of legal fiction; that the justified are not truly just, but merely declared to be so. The objection to the second, which we shall discuss first, is that it makes claims which are falsified in fact. Is not the claim that the faithful are *made* just disproved by the evident fact that no one becomes just overnight, or even by the end of life on earth? Many are indeed partially transformed by conversion from a life of crime or alcoholism, for example, but it remains the case that all remain sinners in need of repeated forgiveness and of final transformation in the resurrection. Luther described this situation by the words, 'at once justified and a sinner', which is one of those slogans that happen to get things right (so long, that is, as other things are also said, things to which we shall come in the next section). Nothing can be theologically right if it is empirically false, at least in so far as that means falsified by the way human life under God actually takes form. Hearts are indeed warmed, lives are changed, but are not in this life perfected. If that were demanded or expected of us, it would indeed be a dispensation of death, for justification is liberation from the need to make or remake ourselves, and we are remade only through time, and then only partially.

An attempt might be made to evade this conclusion by drawing a radical distinction between inner and outer, to the effect that the inner person is made new while the outer remains a sinner. That is suggested by those versions of the doctrine of baptismal regeneration which teach that by virtue of the grace of baptism an inherited stain is washed away and its subject is inwardly transformed. This doctrine has done immense harm over the ages, being sometimes used to suggest that baptism is to keep people out of hell rather than to institute them into membership of God's holy people. We cannot, to be sure, entirely avoid a contrast of inner and outer, as in Paul's use in 2 Corinthians 5 of the metaphor of the earthly tent that is wearing out while 'our heavenly dwelling' is being prepared. Paul's point, however, is a different one, for it is conditioned by an understanding according to which something is begun in the baptized which is only completed at the resurrection. He makes more or less clear that what is being renewed is not some non-bodily or merely inner self but the whole person. The context is eschatological and implies not an instant transformation of one dimension of a duality, but the anticipatory participation in a perfection that will be completed only at the resurrection. Whatever else we say, therefore, of the life of the justified, we must include the fact that it is lived out in a body that must make its way to its perfection through the realm of death.

Are we therefore restricted to a merely declaratory, 'fictional', justice? Not at all, for the very eschatological perspective which Paul's discussion presupposes enables us to combine the truth of the declaratory and ontological theologies of justification. If we bear in mind that justification is inseparable from adoption as children of God, we shall realize that the *being* of the justified is indeed changed, for they are, like an adopted child, brought into a new set of relationships. The first, which we can call – metaphorically – the vertical dimension, is with God. As we saw in chapter 4, God has in his Son moved into a new position with respect to the human race whose situation is therefore changed universally and for ever. The cross must therefore be the bedrock on which any doctrine of justification is built. Indeed, as Anselm said, so all-encompassing is this act of atoning love that it serves also for those outside its direct influence: for those alike, that is, who came before it and those who are prevented in other ways from hearing its liberating message.[1] For liberating it is, as an act of sheer grace and love, in which, when one party to the relation had incarcerated itself in a prison from which there was no escape, God sent his Son, in the likeness of sinful flesh, to bear the consequences of the self-incarceration. The Reformers were right: it is only by an act of sheer grace that the entrenched hardness of the human heart is overcome. The situation requires that the only righteousness or goodness that is possible is one that is given: the righteousness of Christ conferred on those who otherwise would remain unreconciled. That is a declarative act which changes the being of its recipients, because they now stand in a different place, just as the words 'I declare you man and wife' actually bring about a change in the situation, and therefore the being, of those married by them.

Thus far, we have mainly reiterated the implications for life in the present of the first half of Romans 4.25, that Christ died for our sins. The second, that he was raised for our justification, affirms that the resurrection releases into the world that which was won on the cross. The resurrection of Jesus from the dead makes both possible and actual, that is to say, the only possible response to such an act of love, that of faith. Despite what has sometimes been suggested, faith does not mean the acceptance of credal propositions but a human response which consists of both trust in God and sheer gratitude that past rejection of God's love is no longer definitive for the status and person of the sinner. That is the meaning of the Reformation slogan, 'by faith alone', and implies that faith is a responsive movement of the heart, responsive to God's awaking movement into the world in reconciliation. This human response, like all authentic human action, is the gift of the Spirit who enables people to become what they will be by relating them *to* God the Father through Christ. Another Reformation principle follows directly, that justification is by grace alone, by God's act in liberating those imprisoned in deadly forms of life. 'Grace', accordingly, refers to God's gracious action that liberates rather than compels right human response, while faith is a way of characterizing the human response as trust. Faith, we might say, is the *subjective* response to God's *objectively* gracious action. It is subjective in being the response of a human subject, but not something merely subjective, for it is a response that is itself also an act

---

[1] Anselm of Canterbury, *Why the God-Man*, II, 16.

of God in being brought about by the Spirit. Both the objective and subjective dimensions of the one act take place through Christ and in the Spirit. There is thus a single divine act which has both objective and subjective dimensions by virtue of the fact that it is the work of God the Father through Christ and the Spirit which takes shape in a human response.

§29.   Baptism

The interrelation of divine act and human response is focused in baptism, the rite in which justification is appropriated. Just as the Lord's Supper is the churchly action by which continuing membership of the church is maintained, so baptism realises its beginning. Just as the former is the action of the community to which every particular member of the body makes a distinctive and necessary contribution, so baptism is the churchly rite which initiates particular people into the life of the people of God. Both rites are centred on Jesus' death under the judgement of God: the cup which it was necessary for him to drink to achieve all righteousness (justification) for himself and for others. We saw in chapter 6 that by accepting the baptism of John, Jesus accepted solidarity with Israel, and ultimately all humankind, under God's judgement. To be baptized is to accept that judgement, just as in the Supper, but this time more radically, to be *killed*. Water is indeed that which washes, but the inescapable link of Jesus' baptism with his death on the cross brings into the centre the notion that water is the stuff which drowns, as the waters of the flood destroyed all but Noah and his family, and that of the Red Sea drowned the Egyptian army. Baptism therefore symbolizes the death of the 'old Adam' – self-divinizing man – in order that new human beings, men and women living through faith in God, should be enabled to be godlike in the way they were created to be.

To be justified is to be made right with God by the acceptance of God's judgement and the consequences of its being borne in our place by Jesus. Baptism, then, is not only a matter of symbolism, for, as with adoption, which it appropriates publicly, it brings about a change in being also by setting human lives in a new set of relationships, both 'vertical' and 'horizontal', the second by means of the first. To be baptized is, first, to be placed savingly under the judgement of God, just as eating and drinking bread and wine under promise means a continuation of the acceptance of judgement. It is the seal of the free acceptance by God of the sinner apart from any merit or desert. It is a sign of the sheer grace of God whose Son accepted death on behalf and instead of the sinner as that is realized in a community of praise and love. Baptism thus, second, gives social embodiment and expression to that different place in which justification sets the sinner, the place where the Word is heard and the Supper celebrated. To live under the discipline of the Word and the Table *is* to be one whose way of being is altered, just as is the way of being of one adopted into a new family who henceforward shares a new set of relationships, with all that they imply.

The difference between those who would baptize babies and those who insist that it is only for those who have reached the maturity to decide for themselves to follow the crucified and risen Lord largely hangs on the degree to which they stress, respectively, the objective and subjective strands of the doctrine of justification. In favour of the position that only those who are consciously believers should be baptized is the apparently almost universal New Testament practice of baptism in response to a request from the believer. Further support is given by the historical misuse of the practice of universal baptism in the era of official Christianity as a social as much as a churchly rite. In favour of what is called the paedobaptist position is the parallel between Israel and the church, for the former of whom it would be inconceivable not to include the child in the promises of the covenant. What seems to me to be the deciding, though by no means decisive, argument in a debate bound to be inconclusive is that it would be a strange church that did not include within its membership the whole families of participants in its life. That is to say, the baptism of infants is a function of the catholicity of the church, its all-embracingness.

The position does involve some not entirely confident theological argument. Its strength comes from its development of a conception, designed to avoid the individualism of much of the tradition, of what is meant by the remission of sins for which baptism is administered. Baptism is indeed the rite by which justification is appropriated by the particular person. It is, however, a churchly rite and not simply something done to or for an individual. Justification is appropriated by an act in which the baptized is made a member of the community of the justified. To be baptized is to enter the sphere of death, the water which drowns, or, in the case of those unable to decide to do so, to be brought into it by those responsible for the infant or the handicapped. Contrast this with the tendency to view baptism as the washing away of a stain inherited by an individual, without which the baptized will go to hell, or at best to limbo, and it will be evident that here we have a theology of baptism as initiation into the life of the people of God, according to which it is easier to understand how those who are bound up with the life of the community or with that of members of the community may be conceived to share alike in the undergoing of judgement and the life of the justified. The community of the church is the place where human beings are together instituted into a form of life in communion. Recall again the fact that with one exception Paul is not interested in subjecting the variously remiss members of the Corinthian church to disciplinary sanctions. However disorderly he judges their life to be, he still regards it as the firmly founded life of the people of God, for whose building in the gospel, and that alone, he is prescribing. It is surely significant that in this same letter the unbelieving spouse of a member of the church and their children are included within the promises of the gospel (1 Cor. 7.14), and it can be argued that that is the case even more truly for those who by virtue of their insertion into the life of the community share at once its acceptance of judgement and the forgiveness of its sins.

A final point to be made in this section is that, in the light of the practice of baptism, justification is an eschatological conception. Sinful human beings will only be made fully just when they are perfected in the resurrection of the dead. To be justified is therefore to be given in anticipation but really the status as children of God whose full reality will be realized only at the end. God does not justify in advance of this by a legal fiction, but by making men, women and children just in Christ, by virtue of his atoning death. Their justification is therefore an 'alien' righteousness in the respect that it is Christ's righteousness and not theirs; but it is truly theirs because it is one conferred upon them by the Spirit who brings them to the Father through Christ in the communion of the life of his elect people. To be justified, in sum, is to be given a new status and to be set on a road in a forward direction in reversal of the slide backwards on which the human race was doomed before Jesus' recapitulation of the human story and its appropriation in baptism. It is a change of status which makes possible a change of heart, from a bondage to the self to the glad service of God, and so is at the same time a change of being.

§30. Sanctification: Living in the Realm of the Holy

Faith embodies a change of relation to God, and therefore a change of relation to the world also. As justification is being set in a new position, a new movement, so sanctification is an acceptance of the status and responsibilities which it implies. While justification denotes the status of the faithful, their adoption through the work of the Spirit, sanctification denotes the way upon which they are set. Sanctification means being made holy, and it is the purpose for which justification is conferred. The holiness of the community is not primarily the holiness of the individuals within it – though that is a part of it – but that of a people bound together because they share in the life of worship, proclamation, teaching, sharing and good works. However, despite what may appear to be the case, it is not at all obvious what to be holy means and involves. We must begin to explain it by a return to the treatment of the doctrine of God's holiness as it is founded in the Old Testament. God is holy by virtue of his difference from all that is created, and this gives rise to a difference in his ways from those of both the gods of the Gentiles and of fallen humanity. We have seen how from the beginning this is manifest in a gracious refusal to allow human transgression to suffer the full weight of its consequences. Cain the murderer is protected from the vengeance of the vendetta, with its endless chain of multiplying ill effects. The human race is protected from the further inundation which their continuing intransigence in sin would naturally merit; instead, Jesus enters the deadly waters of judgement on their behalf. God's holiness is like his justice in being directed to redemption rather than to vengeance, as a much loved verse from the prophet Hosea emphasizes: 'I am God and not man, the Holy One in your midst. I will not come in wrath' (Hos. 11.9).

God's holiness is expressed historically in the election from among all the peoples of a nation which is called to be, like him, different. In many ways it *is* different, decisively different in the institutions which shape its life. There are, to be sure, parallels with other nations and cultures in the way Israel is ruled, shapes her cult, gives rise to prophets and teachers of wisdom and understands her law. As we have seen, there are also parallels in the way her creation belief is expressed. Yet, as it was there, so it is here: the differences are more significant than the likenesses, because all are in some way decisively shaped by Israel's historical beginnings and the way her institutions are repeatedly referred back to them and to their promised fulfilment through time. Israel is set apart to be different, and is different, however variously deficient her prophets regularly reminded her that she was. She was above all different in her calling as that was to be realized in a distinctive way of being human in community.

The shape of Israel's way of being human in the world was determined above all by the law. As we have also seen, by law is meant far more than the codes of behaviour we call ethics. The law had 'two tables' respectively concerning what we can call the 'vertical' – to God – and 'horizontal' – to and in the world – relationships that were distinguished in the previous section. Justification was concerned primarily with the former of these, though with the latter always in view. Sanctification is, we might say, concerned with the way in which the former gives rise to and shapes the latter. The danger of a stress on justification out of the context of sanctification has often been noted by the religiously and morally earnest. If we are set free, simply by divine act, to a status which we can do nothing to earn, does that not encourage a frivolous indifference to morality? If past sin was answered by God's free and loving forgiveness, why not continue to sin in order to obtain more grace? There are two main answers to this charge. The first is that it is a risk well worth taking if the religious, who are liable enough to it in any case, are not to be turned back in on themselves to an anxious and self-defeating preoccupation with the health of their souls. (It would be only partly frivolous to remark here that the citizens of the modern world are obsessed enough with the health of their bodies not to be in need of further self-preoccupation.) The second answer, however, goes more to the – literal and metaphorical – heart of the matter. Paul's counter to the kind of objection with which we are concerned is to stress the changed situation of the justified (Rom. 6.1–14). This is not a legal fiction, but being placed in a new relationship with God and in the life of his holy people. Being in a new place necessarily gives rise to different ways of behaving, even though its implications often need to be spelled out. The new vertical relationship is bodied out in a new horizontal set of relations and their consequent responsibilities.

The law provides a framework for the life of those who are on the way to the resurrection, but are not yet raised. If it is indeed the case, as is often suggested, that the weakness of the life of the Corinthian community derived from the fact that some of its members thought their resurrection had taken place already, the point of Paul's reaffirmation of the law becomes clear. Something decisive has indeed happened to them: they have been bought at a price, and given the Holy Spirit to shape the life of their congregation (1 Cor. 6.19–20). Yet rather than evoking indifference to what they do in the body, their new status as liberated from sin should rather elicit a new moral seriousness. It is possible even for the justified to disqualify themselves from the life of the kingdom, and that is why earlier in the same chapter Paul produces a summary of the Ten Commandments (1 Cor. 6.9–10). He has to remind this no doubt mostly Gentile church that the law given to Israel is still their law. Yet its basis is now different, being secured in the cleansing, sanctifying and justifying death of Jesus which they have appropriated ('You were washed, you were sanctified, you were justified in the name of the Lord Jesus Christ and by the Spirit of our God', 1 Cor. 6.11). The New Testament's chief theologian of justification is also a major proponent of life within the framework of the law. The law he proclaims is no more a new law than was that taught by Jesus, though it contains a new way of understanding that law as the result of Jesus' death and resurrection.

The holiness of the church is thus a conferred holiness, but it is also one which has to be lived out. Like Israel's it is the holiness of a people before it is that of individuals within the community. Only in the case of those whose offences threaten to subvert the life of the holy community is Paul concerned to speak to or about individuals, and the same can be said for the ethics of John's Gospel. This is not to diminish the freedom and responsibility of individual members of the church, but to say that they only become themselves in communion with others. It is in the discussion of the relation between the one and the many, the community and its members, that Paul's discussion of the body of Christ takes its chief orientation. The humblest member of the community is as essential to its life as the apparently superior. Again, the reference in 1 Corinthians 12 is to baptism and the Spirit. All the variety of the congregation's particular contributions to the life of the whole are the gift of the Spirit, 'For we were all baptized by one Spirit into one body...' (1 Cor. 12.13). The part does not exist for the sake of the whole, nor the whole for the part. The holiness of the community and that of its members coincide precisely.

Sanctification, then, is that calling to be different which is both given to and demanded of the church. Its source is not the law, though the law provides its frame. Its source is Christ, so that in another letter Paul tells his readers not to shape their lives by that of 'the world', but to situate themselves where they will be transformed by the Spirit (Rom. 12.1–2). Christian ethics does in certain respects consist in the imitation of Christ and of God, but to rest there is to encourage just that anxious striving which involves a return to the law. The content of sanctification is a freedom to be what one is created to be, a child of God living confidently and unafraid in the creator's world, even when surrounded and threatened by death. Freedom is the gift of God's free Spirit, and this freedom forbids a return to any form of idolatry, including that turning in upon oneself which is the source of the ill. Holiness is formation through conformation: allowing life to be shaped after the pattern and manner of the life of Jesus. It is in a word to live by faith in the God who has changed the human situation for ever and in expectation that what he began in the justified he will complete. Only thus is the love of the other made possible. Those who live by the faith in Christ and hope in the resurrection that are given by the Spirit are shaped in the ways of love; trained to be like the God who gave his own Son so that their achieved reconciliation with God might finally be perfected.

As that last sentence suggests, the concept of love being used here is derived from the pattern of the love of Father, Son and Spirit by which they mutually give to and receive from one another that which they are. Love in a fallen world inevitably involves the renunciation of the self for the sake of the other, and the cost that that may involve. That is why the word 'sacrifice' still appears in so many secular contexts, of a life or benefit given up for others. Love in the community of redemption, however, is given in promise that because that cost has been already borne, it can be given in confidence. The discipline of the Christian community follows from that, generating a willingness to give without a desire to receive in return, yet in a confidence that those who give will also receive. The same community's mission to love the world, including the enemy, again in grateful response to the self-giving of the Son of God, is a more risky endeavour, for there is no guarantee that the enemy will not recompense love with hatred. But that is what being like God – being holy – involves.

The linking of love with holiness reminds us that the love of which the gospel speaks is not primarily a matter of moral striving, though moral effort is indeed involved, as is shown in Paul's analogy of athletic training (1 Cor. 9.24–7). In the Gospel accounts, Jesus' relation to his Father in the Spirit is realized through prayer. It follows that for us prayer is both an attitude and an action, both a churchly and an individual activity, because it maintains the orientation of the faithful on the source of their faith. Just as, however, we cannot justify ourselves, neither can we pray without the enabling of the Spirit. Barth characterized the whole Christian life as invocation, or a calling on God, and this is illustrated above all in the Lord's Prayer, whose various petitions maintain the primacy of divine action, consisting as they do largely in a request for it.[2] Those requests, however, begin with the assumption that those who pray the words of this prayer do so as those who have been incorporated into the relationship that Jesus had with his Father. They take the form of prayers first for God's rule on earth, then for the ones who pray them. The latter petitions indicate that prayers for the self are the reverse of being selfish, for they express an acknowledgement of glad dependence on God in everything. Prayers for the world, similarly, should not be understood either as alternatives to or merely motivating impulses for faithful action within the world, but as a request that God will grant his people the opportunity to share in his gracious government of the world. Because his is the kingdom and the power and the glory, where his writ runs all other manner of things also will be well.

§31. Resurrection

The resurrection is God's transforming completion, through his Spirit, of human life in the body. A satisfactory account involves the following features. First, it must be distinguished from doctrines of the immortality of the soul, though it may share some features with them. There are two reasons for the distinction. First, the doctrine of an immortal soul encourages the belief that the soul is in some way automatically godlike, or even continuous with God; but second, and more important, it overlooks what has been stressed in this book from the beginning, that it is the whole created person whom God has created and promises to perfect. The doctrine of the resurrection is not first of all about immortality, but about God's purposes for his creation, and especially his human creation. We shall come to the meaning of the qualification 'especially' below, but at this stage wish to stress the notion of continuity: that whatever happens 'after death' it is continuous both with what happened before – life in the body – and with the life of the whole material creation.

Second, the continuity, however, is not a direct one, as is the case where one supposes a person to be transported to heaven without alteration. The resurrection is different from all notions of the transmigration of souls, which at best minimize the significance of life in the body. The promise

---

[2] Karl Barth, *The Christian Life. Church Dogmatics, Volume 4/4, Lecture Fragments*, translated by G. W. Bromiley (Grand Rapids, MI: Eerdmans, 1981).

of the creation is a perfecting of that which was begun; and the case of Jesus of Nazareth suggests that this perfection can come about only through transformation. As we are, we are shaped and destined for death. The understanding of human being suggested by 2 Corinthians 5, referred to above, suggests that even the life of the justified takes its course through the realm of death. The end to the creation's 'bondage to decay' can come about only by a radical remaking, which indeed completes that which is begun in Christ, but only by lifting it up to a new level. Paul claims that, 'flesh and blood cannot inherit the Kingdom' – possibly here conceding half of the point to his opponents; and the reason is that 'the perishable must clothe itself with the imperishable, and the mortal with immortality' (1 Cor. 15.50,53). That statement, however, must be interpreted with great care, because it is clear that in making it Paul does not wish to suggest an escape from embodiment but rather its transformation and perfecting under radically different conditions. Everywhere he seems to have in mind the form of the risen Jesus, who remained bodily – eating and drinking – but in other respects appears to have transcended some of the limits of temporal and spatial existence. He transcended them, however, without forsaking them.

The key is to be found in Paul's much discussed claim that 'If there is a natural body there is also a spiritual body' (1 Cor. 15.44). This could in theory – never a good theological guide – be taken to refer to a disembodied body, although only if it is taken out of its context in 1 Corinthians 15 and the New Testament witness to Jesus as a whole. Eastern Orthodox interpreters will often say that it refers to a body filled by the Spirit, and that takes us some of the way. We are taken further if we ask what is meant by 'spiritual', and hear the answer that it means everything which pertains to the activity of God the Holy Spirit. The so-called third person of the Trinity, as we have had cause to remark at many places, does not interest himself only in those things we call spiritual. The message of Ezekiel 37 is that the Spirit's function is to transform dry bones into a living army. The spiritual body is therefore the body transformed from being a body of death to one which lives for, to and with God. And that takes us to our third feature.

The resurrection is not a taking of the human soul out of the world, but the perfecting of the whole human being along with it. As has been suggested elsewhere, the use of bread and wine, nature manufactured, in the Lord's Supper shows that Christian worship is in some way bound up with the life of the whole world. Jesus is the first-fruits of the resurrection of the dead, which means that he is the first of those who will also be raised.

But his resurrection, as Paul in Romans 8 makes clear, in some way involves other created reality with it, but in subordinate fashion. In these days of heightened ecological consciousness we are in danger of overstressing the first clause of Romans 8.21 at the expense of the second. We need to say of the creation that it will be *both* 'liberated from its bondage to decay' *and* 'brought into the glorious freedom of the children of God'. The resurrection of the flesh, of the whole person, is the completion of the promise inherent in Genesis 1.26–7, because those created in the image of God are to be perfected in the context in which they were created.

Likewise, the promise of Revelation 21.1–4 is that there will be a new heaven and a new earth, so that God will truly be praised in the completion and perfection of all his works. Far from being chiefly about 'life after death', as it has often been made to be, the point of the resurrection in this context is rather its impact on this life, as another reference to its place in Paul's First Letter to Corinth will indicate. The resurrection throws its light backwards, illuminating life lived in expectation of it. It gives in particular an eschatological orientation to ethics rather different from the one which has popularly been held to be the case. The latter is best illustrated by the well-known Victorian dispute in the course of which the theologian F. D. Maurice was dismissed from his professorial chair for casting doubt on the eternal punishment of hell. The reasons for the desire to maintain this doctrine are instructive, for they centre on a belief that, without the deterrence it supposedly offered, the floodgates would be opened and all kinds of immoral behaviour encouraged. Whether or not the prophecies of doom have been fulfilled is not here to the point, which is that for the Apostle Paul this was not at all the reason for teaching the resurrection, but quite the reverse. The resurrection provides grounds for a confident keeping of the hand to the plough, 'because you know that your labour in the Lord is not in vain' (1 Cor. 15. 58, the concluding words of the chapter). In that respect, the resurrection is a truly this-worldly doctrine.

Finally, the promised resurrection of the dead indicates thus the third way in which the Spirit shapes the life of the Christian. The first is in the past: that full and free remission of sins has been achieved on the cross, and that God restores to fellowship with himself, through the community that is the body of Christ, all who put their trust in that achievement rather than any of their own. The second is in the present, that those who allow their lives to be shaped by the worship and fellowship of the church are those who are becoming like God in the way purposed in the creation, shaped by and conformed to the manner of Christ's life and death. They are being made holy as God is holy: free to serve God and the neighbour by being different. And the third is in the future – our future – that through the same Spirit God will complete at the end the holiness that is in process, so that the justified will finally become the perfectly just.

In the meantime, they are both justified and sinners, accepted children of God while still living in large part by and in the world of death. The promise of the resurrection is that just as life and death are not polar opposites because the one overcomes the other, so it is with justification and continuing to sin. Sin does indeed remain, just as death does, but is no longer definitive of the being of the faithful because they are set on the way to something other. The image used in the Letter to the Hebrews is better able than Luther's slogan, for all its truth, to express the eschatological orientation of the baptized. Sin is something that holds back the runner in a race, something therefore to be thrown off like some encumbering garment in order to live the life of freedom (Heb. 12.1, in another employment of the athletic metaphor).

§32.   Spirit of Freedom

In sum the Spirit is the one by whose agency God the Father justifies, sanctifies, and, at the last, raises from the dead through and with his Son. As what we may call the eschatological member of the Trinity, as the one who brings about in advance the perfection of particular created actions and things, the Spirit brings the freedom of God especially to attention. Freedom, however, is not arbitrariness, the absolute freedom to do what happens to enter the head or appear desirable at the time. (As Calvin well remarked, even God is not absolutely free, in the respect that he can do nothing but good.[3]) The freedom *of* the Spirit is expressed first of all in the creation of the world that did not have to be, but was created because God willed there to be another reality alongside himself and able to enter into relationship with himself. But, second, it is expressed in God's sovereign dealing with his creation, his involvement in its structures in Israel, Jesus Christ and beyond,

---

[3] John Calvin, *Institutes of the Christian Religion*, edited by J. T. McNeill, translated and indexed by F. L. Battles (Philadelphia: Westminster Press, 1960), 2 vols., Library of Christian Classics 20 and 21, II. iii. 5.

a freedom also realized by and in the Spirit who is the Father's power and energy. But third, as we have seen, the freedom of the Spirit is revealed in the way in which God achieves the end for which his world was created, preventing it from taking its 'natural' course to dissolution, and perfecting it by calling, justifying and sanctifying to his praise and through that same Jesus a community whose sole basis for what they are and do is the free grace of God. To bring together the conclusion of the previous chapter and this one, we can therefore conclude by saying that the Spirit is the one who gives freedom through community: through the gift of the other. Corresponding to this, freedom *in* the Spirit is the God-given freedom to be like God in learning to love even the unlovely. Freedom thus takes shape in community, and centrally in the church, which lives from the communion that God is and gives. That, surely, and not some individual endowment with spectacular capacities, is the meaning of baptism 'in the Spirit': it is the gift of life with others. Because the Spirit is the one who perfects all the creation, his work is centred on enabling the ordinary, and especially ordinary life in the human body, to be what it is made to be.

Chapter 9

The Last Enemy

§33. Death

If you read a standard dictionary definition of eschatology, you will probably find it defined as 'the science of the four last things: death, judgement, heaven and hell'. In so far as that represents traditional teaching, it shows only how far traditional teaching has gone astray. It has so many faults that it would take up much space to do justice to them all. Let me make the three points which will help to advance the positive thesis. First, it supposes a merely otherworldly account of eschatology: first we die, then we are judged, then we go to either heaven or hell. These things may well be the case, but the inadequacy of so limiting an eschatology becomes apparent in the other two weaknesses. They will take somewhat longer to unfold, and lead us into the positive things that have to be said.

Second, the standard definition supposes a merely linear account of the way things are. Now the line is important. Time is the vehicle of the outworking of God's purposes, and there is a line to be drawn from the creation which was reviewed in the first part of this book, through the centre in which God decisively renews the creation – Part 2 – to the end for which the whole creation strains. Yet it does not follow from this, as much of the tradition seems to have supposed, that eschatology pertains only to the end of time. Eschatology has a primarily future orientation, just as creation's is to the past, but these things are primary, not the whole. Everything depends upon how we see the tenses to be open to one another – interwoven, so to speak – through the Spirit's action. There are occasions in which, as we have seen to take place in the ministry of Jesus, the 'end' is anticipated in the middle of time, especially when the suffering are set free from their affliction. Another way of putting this would be to say that the eschatological and the future are not precisely equivalent. Eschatology has a future orientation, but it cannot be reduced to that. In so far as, common-sensically, we understand the future as that which comes after the present, we have to distinguish the eschatological from it. The 'end' is *also* that which breaks into the present, by anticipation. This can be illustrated from both Old and New Testaments. In the former, the 'Day of the Lord', especially in the prophets' usages, is realized in events that happen in history: it is to come, and yet imminent in a way that bears directly on the present. (See, for example, Joel's use of the prophecy of the locusts, Joel 2.1–11.) In the New Testament the same is the case with both Jesus' teaching of the kingdom and his resurrection from the dead in anticipation of the general resurrection of the end-time. There are truly eschatological events which take place in time.

Third, death but not resurrection is mentioned in the traditional defin-ition. This is the most astonishing omission of all, and suggests that the accusation is justified that the tradition has effectively taught the immortality of an immaterial soul rather than the resurrection of an embodied person. The important point here is that the items with which eschatology is to be occupied are not symmetrical. Death is the enemy to be overcome, resur-rection is the gospel of its overcoming. The subordination of resurrection to the other themes of eschatology accounts also for the otherworldliness which characterizes so much of the tradition, an otherworldliness which has rightly been the object of much modern criticism. There is, to be sure, a respect in which eschatology is otherworldly, to do with the end of our time and space. Yet, as we have seen from the beginning, the end is understood biblically in terms of the perfecting, not the abolition, of the created order. There may indeed be a 'new' heaven and a new earth, but they remain heaven and earth, not some utterly timeless and spaceless realm, and they already bear graciously on this one.

Belief in eschatology is one of the features of Christian belief that has suffered most grievously at the hands of its modern critics. In the era of the mechanistic universe it tended to be reduced to 'immortality', the 'survival' of a soul, perhaps for reward or punishment. The world was not quite conceived to be timeless – for machines grind their way relentlessly through time – but none the less was something whose being through time – whose history – was not significant for what it was and where it was going. Machines are at least in theory reversible, so that time is irrelevant to what they essentially are. Upon this ideology of mechanism there later supervened a tendency to dismiss eschatology as in some way simply a function of a refusal to be content with this life, and therefore the product of wish-fulfilment ('pie in the sky when you die'). Yet contentment with life is precisely what the culture produced by these tendencies has failed to engender. Eschatology has instead been brought down to earth in various versions of the doctrine of progress, notable among them the economic (salvation through development) and the medical, with its horrifying – and essentially godless – visions of life endlessly prolonged through scientific techniques. We live in an era not of the loss of eschatology, but of its displacement into ever greater unreality, because this-worldly eschatologies are not truly eschatological but merely projections from an unsatisfied and unsatisfying present.

Therefore, in order to expunge as many traces as possible of this essentially nineteenth century optimism, we must begin a theological response on a strongly negative note: 'The day of the Lord is coming. It is close at hand – a day of darkness and gloom' (Joel 2.1f). Similarly, Mark 13 and the chapters of Revelation which precede the visions of the heavenly city that we prefer to read, remind us, along with many other biblical eschatologies of catastrophe, that there can be no cheap hope any more than there can be cheap grace. There is no hope without repentance in face of imminent divine judgement ('The time is fulfilled, and the Kingdom of God has drawn near; repent and believe the gospel', Mk. 1.15). It is often today asserted that late modern culture is pervaded by hopelessness and despair, but the answer to that is not to adopt an easy optimism. Cheap hope is no hope at all. Biblical eschatology is inseparable from what we can call a negative apocalyptic, from the direst disasters and prophecies, for which the great flood in Genesis is the beginning and the continuing symbol, at least as important for New Testament eschatology as the Exodus, that fashionable vehicle of too easy a hope. It may indeed be the case that, as in Luke's parallel with Mark 13, 'When these things begin to take place, stand up and lift up your heads, because your redemption is drawing near' (Lk. 21.28), but 'these things' are a catena of historical and cosmic disasters. There is no resurrection without death, which is also of eschatological significance because it represents the end of life, of relation to God and the other, and therefore the extinction of hope. If we recall once again the essentially embodied nature of our being human, we shall continue to bear in mind that our bodies come from and will return to the dust of the earth, and can be rescued thence only by a wholly eschatological act. Death is for that reason the first eschatological reality with which this chapter must deal.

The problem, as we have seen from time to time, is that of death, meaning not simply mortality, which might be bearable, but death as representing the meaninglessness and failure that dogs all human life: 'Do not be afraid of those who kill the body but cannot kill the soul. Rather, be afraid of the One who can destroy both soul and body in hell' (Mt. 10.28). It is sometimes observed, particularly in the obituaries of political figures, that there are respects in which every life ends in failure. Certainly, every life is highly particular, bearing its achievements and failures in different ways. If eschatology is to bear upon the way in which we envisage our human particularity, it is especially relevant at this place, where we face not only the question of the relative failure of those who die full of years and sometimes of honour, but also the lives of those who die apparently before their time, especially perhaps children and young people. In that sense, it is death that defines the limits and so the eschatological reality of each human life.

We are, moreover, increasingly aware that death defines the future of our universe also. Predictions that the universe will end with a cosmic freeze or burnout suggest to at least some cosmologists that the whole thing is pointless. And, nearer in both time and space, there are predictions of the destruction of our earth's ecosystem which are often called 'apocalyptic'. To be sure, many of the predictions may be exaggerated, and may indeed be characteristic of an era which, no longer having the last judgement to fear, as it thinks, invents a secular equivalent to keep it awake at night. But they make it possible to say two things. The first is that whether or not their short-term pessimism is justified, they are right in pointing to the fact that our earth will, like everything in it, suffer death. It will 'wear out like a garment' (Is. 51.6). The second is that the modern apocalypses lack serious-ness simply because they are secular. For the Bible's apocalypses, the train of disaster is the prelude to God's final salvation, and as such serves to explain the times in which their readers were living. Modern apocalypses, for all their useful function in reminding us of the disasters we bring upon our world, are almost wholly pessimistic, and are designed to elicit action in a quite different way. They have their point, which is to reveal the truth that apart from salvation of some kind, the only way we can go is down, but they cannot themselves save.

§34. Judgement

'Shall not the judge of all the earth do right?' (Gen. 18.25) There are three things to be said in response to that question. The first is that it comes from Abraham's plea on behalf of the wicked city of Sodom. The assumption underlying it is that it would be wrong for God to destroy the city if even a small and representative number of just people could be found within it. What an astonishing assumption that is. God has failed if he has to impose retributive punishment. As it turns out, it appears that he has in that case failed; but that is not the point here, which is the implied meaning of divine judgement. To do justice is not to punish offenders but in some way to allow them to be treated mercifully through the good offices of the just. Compare that with the Greek gods, who for the most part are bound to visit iniquity with recompense, as is indeed our commonsense view of the matter, to let the punishment fit the crime. That is the first problem of divine justice. Who is this God whose justice is apparently dependent on his success in bringing about justice on earth – whose justice is aimed at the overcoming of evil rather than its punishment by the infliction of further evil?

Yet alongside this – and it is our second point – the Bible also assumes that the oppressed and afflicted, especially those persecuted for the truth, have the right to ask God to avenge them. 'How long, O Lord, how long?' is the cry, endlessly repeated in the Psalms, of those who fear that the wicked will never cease to hold the upper hand. The writer of Revelation knows what it is like to be a small and persecuted minority in the apparent power of a ruthless empire which mercilessly martyrs the people of God, lest they threaten its power. 'How long, sovereign Lord, holy and true, until you judge the inhabitants of the earth and avenge our blood?' cry the souls of those who had been slain for their faith (Rev. 6.10). There is, we must note, a distinction between a cry for mere vengeance and a cry for justice, although it is to be noted that both notions appear in that verse. Interestingly, the writer does not necessarily approve the cry for vengeance: the martyrs are told 'to wait a little longer', thus, we might say, to share the patience of God. However, that does not deal with the real problem of justice. If, finally, the oppressed and martyred are not in any way given justice, whatever that might involve, can it finally be said to be a just universe? That is the second problem of the divine justice.

The third point is this. For the New Testament, the one who exercises God's judgement is Jesus Christ, who dispenses justice as he mediates all of his Father's works. For Calvin, that is one of the great consolations of the faith: 'No mean assurance, this – that we shall be brought before no other judgement seat than that of our Redeemer, to whom we must look for salvation!'[1] To discern what that judgement involves, however, is not a straightforward matter. At least two sides must be taken into consideration. As we have seen throughout this book, the Son is the one who mediates the Father's work, so that what the Father does, he does; and what he does is the work of the Father. What is the Father's judgement that he mediates? The oft-quoted statement that judgement begins with the household of God (1 Pet. 4.17) suggests that it is first of all the judgement of Israel and the church, and therefore refers to that process of cleansing and correction by which they are made what they are called to be. There is no prospect of favouritism, because much is expected of those to whom much is given. Jesus' parables of judgement make precisely that point in his polemics against his opponents. Being the elect people of God is indeed a privilege, but one that imposes responsibility.

The other side of the matter, however, involves a measure of distinction between the judgement of the Father and that of the Son, in respect of the fact that on the cross, Jesus bears God's judgement on sin in order not that sinners should not be judged (condemned), but that they should endure judgement in a different form, as discipline. The point is indicated in Barth's observation that Jesus' bearing of God's judgement for us does not mean that we are not judged ourselves.[2] We return here to Paul's teaching that in the Lord's Supper the congregation is judged salutarily, we might say, in order that it should not be judged, by the judgement of death in its fullest sense (1 Cor. 11.31–2). Christ, we might say, bears anticipatorily the eschatological judgement of death – he goes to *hell* – in order that those who trust in God through him should be able to bear the judgement that cleanses rather than annihilates. An important but not always much noticed observation of Paul's is here illustrative: that someone's inadequate *work* may

---

[1] John Calvin, *Institutes of the Christian Religion*, edited by J. T. McNeill, translated and indexed by F. L. Battles (Philadelphia: Westminster Press, 1960), 2 vols., Library of Christian Classics 20 and 21, III. xvi. 18.

[2] Karl Barth, *Church Dogmatics*, translation edited by G. W. Bromiley and T. F. Torrance (Edinburgh: T. & T. Clark, 1957–75), vol. 4/1, pp. 294–5.

be destroyed in the fire which tests it, but 'he himself will be saved, but only as one escaping through the flames' (1 Cor. 3.15). The work is judged, perhaps rejected, but not the worker.

We return to the place where this section began. Ten just people would representatively have saved Sodom from its fate. The divine purpose is for universal salvation. Abraham, the one who begs for mercy on the wicked city, is called to be the one in whom all the nations of the earth will be blessed. Israel is called to be a light to the nations of the world, so that all may finally bring their tribute to the holy city. This implicit universality leads us into two more questions. The first is this. If Jesus embodies in his person and work the fulfilment of the promise to Abraham, and if on the cross he bears the judgement of God on the sins of the world, in what sense is his achievement universal? On a strongly realized eschatology such as Barth's it is the case that all have *de jure* been brought within the covenant. This is consistent with the universal thrust of Barth's doctrine of election which holds that in Christ the whole human race is, so to speak, already elect, just as according to the traditional doctrine of original sin all human beings are already in the loins of Adam and so sinful even before they actually sin. According to Barth, there remains a possibility that some may walk away from their election, but the point remains: Christ has already borne God's eschatological judgement on all flesh, so that all are already in some respect reconciled.

The weakness of this position lies in its overrealized eschatology. Not only is reconciliation an eschatological reality, and so something that has not yet been completed; but it is also an interpersonal one. That is to say, to teach that reconciliation has already happened may appear to imply that relations between two estranged parties have been healed in such a way that they are expressly at one. In other words, to give an unqualified account of universal reconciliation is to risk abstraction from actual reconciled relations, for while it may be said of those who have accepted baptism, or have been brought into the sphere of proclaimed and lived reconciliation, that they are reconciled to God, the same cannot be so easily said of those who have not. This, however, in no way excludes a theology of the universality of the saving significance of the cross. Paul's statement that 'God was in Christ reconciling the world to himself' (2 Cor. 5.19) implies universality, but not that universal reconciliation has already taken place. Only from the kind of doctrine of election which was rejected in earlier chapters – that God from eternity elects some but not others – does that follow. On the view adopted here, Jesus does indeed do something for the whole human race; but the *perfecting* of that *complete* work continues to depend on its realization in time by the work of the Spirit who brings particular people into the community of the reconciled. Reconciliation is thus universal in intent, but not yet fully realized.

Like, however, the hypothetical Sodom 10, the elect may stand in for the others, as their representatives. As we have seen, God does not simply elect one group rather than another; he elects one group for the sake of and on behalf of the others. And that leads us to our second question. Will all in the end be saved? To answer that, another two considerations have to be brought to bear. The first concerns how we reconcile the two conceptions we have met of God's justice. (1) The destruction of the sinner, in so far as the case of Sodom is our model, represents a divine failure, in the sense that it presents a world in which God's purposes of perfection have not finally and universally been realized. Yet (2) we must take seriously the possibility of a blasphemy against the Holy Spirit, not in the sense of saying disparaging things, though that may be a symptom, but in the sense implied by its context in the Gospels, that one can come to be so hardened in evil that one can look good in the face and call it evil (Mk. 3.23–9). Can the heart be so hardened as no longer to be capable of repentance, as appears to have happened in the case of those who could weep at the music played by the Jewish musicians whom they were imminently to herd into gas ovens? At least one refugee from Hitler's regime has argued that annihilation is the only possible fate for the utterly wicked.[3] (I think that we should take it that images of eternal fire in scripture do not refer to everlasting torment so much as to the notion of simply being discarded on the rubbish tip of history.) We cannot rule out the possibility that some may finally exclude themselves from the kingdom.

That does not, however, answer the main question, which is whether the justice of God can in such manner be seen to be realized. Is God *justified* so long as one of those made in his image is cast away unperfected, one sheep remains lost on the mountainside? What is to be included in God's sovereign completion of that which he began at the creation of the world? Here the eschatology of the book sometimes dismissed as containing a sub-Christian glorying in vengeance is worth a glance. Not only does Revelation end – or nearly end – with a vision of the new heaven and the new

---

[3] Ulrich Simon, *A Theology of Auschwitz* (London: Gollancz, 1967).

earth, but it is prefaced by a vision of the lake of fire, whose only named victims are death and Hades. The author proceeds: 'If anyone's name was not found written in the book of life, he was thrown into the lake of fire' (Rev. 20.11–15).[4] It is not expressly stated that there will be any not so written, but it is noteworthy that our author does retain, to the very end, the possibility that some may wilfully exclude themselves.

That naturally takes us to our second consideration, the nature of human freedom. The chief objection to the teaching that all will ultimately be brought within the kingdom is that it appears to be contrary to human freedom to compel into heaven those who wish to go to hell. Underlying that is a tangled web of topics indeed. Is it conceivable that ultimately all will be brought, kicking and screaming, so to speak (or would they be?) into the fold? Here we must put out of our minds the idea that naturally occurs, of a simple time line, at the end of which one might or might not receive another chance to make amends (etc.). There are two objections to this, and to the doctrine of purgatory which it has encouraged. The first is that it undermines the sufficiency of the work of the cross. That does not rule out judgement of the kind we have met Paul expounding in 1 Corinthians – the testing of works – but surely must exclude anything more by virtue of the fact that Jesus has paid the price, so that, whatever eschatological judgement there is, it cannot include further disciplining or punishment beyond the final judgement, however reformatory, simply because it is final: the final verdict on human lives now come to an end. We shall be judged, as Irenaeus says, by what we have done in the body,[5] and it is the time span that we are given in this life that is decisive. The second point reinforces the first. Eschatology is not about movement unchanged into another world where judgement takes place; it is about transformation. As Jesus' body is miraculously transformed not into another body but into another kind of body, so the promise of the resurrection is that 'we shall all be changed – in a moment, in the twinkling of an eye . . .' (1 Cor. 15.51–2). In needing this transformation, all are in similar need, believer and unbeliever, good and evil alike. The faithful may have accepted the call to discipleship and the training that involves, but they too live in the body of death until the last day. It seems to be scripture's teaching that all will be judged for what they make of what they are and have received;

[4] Similarly, for John 16. 11, judgement means the judgement of 'the ruler of this world', the devil.
[5] Irenaeus, *Against the Heresies*, 2. 29. 2.

whether any will receive final condemnation must be left to the merciful justice of God. We must here recall another and disturbing feature of the parable of the sheep and the goats, which is that both are surprised to find themselves in the categories in which they are placed, a warning against complacency as much as anything (Mt. 25.37,44).

The question of universalism therefore hangs at once on our conception of God's justice and on what is made of the representative function of Israel and the church. Those communities are clearly meant to stand in for, as priestly representatives, all the nations of the earth. Is, then, the representative faithfulness of Israel and the church a sufficient as well as a necessary condition for the salvation of all the world? Could it be that so long as all the nations contain at least 'ten' of the justified, their fellow citizens will in some way along with them all be brought perfected before the throne of grace? There is a case for arguing that the urgency of the church's early mission, certainly as it is represented by Paul, was driven not by the fact that those unreached might go to hell – though to be sure, the hell of lives apart from God in the present should be cause enough – but in order that, once representative samples of all nations could be brought into the people of God, God could bring time and history to an end in the eschatological kingdom, to universal blessing. But what might that – and in particular the defeat of the 'last enemy' – involve?

§35.   Redemption

The resurrection, the eschatological fulfilment of the only relatively 'successful' ministry of Jesus and the death which was its logical outcome, alone offers the promise that the death of ourselves and our universe is not the final reality. It is as such a *promise*: that the final judgement on a life and a world may be the divine Yes, according to which human successes and failures alike are permitted variously to play their part in the summing up of all things, things in heaven and things on earth, by God in Christ (Eph. 1.10). Accordingly, the third eschatological reality with which we have to engage, following death and judgement, is redemption: the promise that in God's good time 'the whole creation will be liberated from its bondage to decay and brought into the glorious freedom of the children of God' (Rom. 8.21).

Those realities which are subject to fallenness and so in need of redemption can be placed in three classes: (1) the created order as a whole; (2) what the Bible calls the 'nations' or 'peoples' – which are not coterminous with our modern nation states, and certainly not our notion of races, but refer generally, it would appear, to peoples named after a supposed founder or ancestor and occupying an identifiable geographical area; and (3) particular 'individual' people. There is a definite order of priority: the non-personal world is to be redeemed only in, with and for the personal. And so we begin with the personal, and specifically with the fact that scripture appears to understand particular people largely in terms of their relationship with other people in nations and groups: Edom, Israel, the church. It is sometimes pointed out that those who are judged in what is traditionally called the parable of the sheep and the goats are not in the first instance individuals, but the peoples. Similarly, as we have seen, the assumption seems to be that Sodom could have been spared had there been a sufficient and representative number to leaven the whole.

The theological reality indicated by these examples is that there are no individuals in the modern sense, for all are in some sense bound up with the life and fate of those others with whom they are in closest relation. In some sense, our groupings are of eschatological significance. Here we must return to the matter of the principalities and powers which were introduced in an earlier chapter. While not limited to them, these only apparently mythical figures are in particularly close relation to the political powers of the day. Kings and emperors in some way represent or realize these powers which are in some respect more than the sum of the human agents who make them up. Both in Pauline theology and in that of the last book of the Bible, what they do is understood eschatologically. More than individual actions theirs bear eschatological significance, anticipating final rebellion and judgement. Paul's expression, 'the rulers *of this age*' (1 Cor. 2.8) – those who crucified Jesus – hints at both their supraindividual reality and eschatological significance, while for the author of Revelation the Roman empire's persecution of the faithful indicates a battle being fought at a higher than merely human level. It is therefore in the political sphere that we best identify the specific character of biblical eschatology. In it there is almost always a combination of concrete historical events and divine action which is in some way of final significance because it represents something ultimate happening *within* time and history. So it is with the 'day of the Lord' in the prophets, with Jesus' eschatological pronouncements and with the presentation of history in the apocalypse. Joel's plague of locusts *is* God's final judgement taking place in time, as is the fall of Jerusalem which Jesus appears to have prophesied.

'When these things happen, flee...' shows that these are recognizable historical events which are also in their way, anticipatorily, final. They are at the same time God's judgement and precursors of final redemption, 'When these things happen, rejoice...'. The doorstep preachers who ask us to consider a world full of wars and disasters may naively take them to be indications that the end may come tomorrow or the day after (they may, of course, be right), but they are justified in seeing in them indications, anticipations, of the very end.

Human political acts can, on this understanding, serve as symptoms of the idolatrous worship of the creature so extreme that they represent the creature's attempting to displace God from his throne and so become the worship of the beast from the abyss. For the New Testament, the Roman emperor's placing of his image in the Holy of Holies in the temple is the concrete expression of this human rebellion (2 Th. 2.4). That is why the 'Antichrist' is sometimes used to refer to someone guilty of acts of over-weening human arrogance. There has been much speculation about the identify of such a figure, from the Roman emperor to Adolf Hitler and beyond, but that is to ask the question in the wrong way. Anyone may stand in for the Antichrist, serve as a model for his portrait; any truly wicked and idolatrous human act may be of eschatological significance by virtue of its demonic arrogance.

Here we must pause to qualify the use of the words 'final', 'ultimate', 'eschatological' and so on in the characterization of historical events. It is more accurate to say that these acts and events are – from another perspective, so to speak – of penultimate significance, for there is so far only one eschatologically ultimate event in the historical–political sphere, and that is the resurrection of Jesus from the dead, and as such it relativizes, and so, in the light of eternity, disempowers, all those sitting for the portrait of the Antichrist. It also reveals why they are the Antichrist, for they attempt to displace the true mediator of the Father's rule. To say that the cross and resurrection 'disempower' the enemy does not imply, to be sure, that acts of rebellion do not do grievous harm, as we know that they do. It rather implies two things which must be held in tension. The first is the utter seriousness of the calling of those who follow Christ. The eschatological significance of the political order derives from the fact that the kind of things that happen in it are more than simply the sum of their parts. Evil takes on a momentum that exceeds the combined actions of individuals, so that whole nations can be catapulted into evil. The struggle, therefore, really is 'not against flesh and blood, but against the authorities, against the powers of this dark world . . .' (Eph. 6.12). No one who knows the history of the twentieth century should fail to see the truth of this conception. It follows that the life of the people of God, in all its everyday moral struggle and seriousness, is at the same time part of the rule of Christ this side of the end. The book of Revelation presents Christ as the crucified one – 'the lamb bearing the marks of slaughter' – who, as such, rules the nations with a rod of iron, his Word (Rev. 5.6, 2.27). All the chaos let loose by the lie that is the politics of power and arrogance happens only by his permission, and the witness of the church has that for its context.

That leads to the second point, which is that history is allowed to take its course and actions are allowed to generate their logical consequences; but only so far. There is one who restrains (2 Th. 2.7), and whose providential action has restricted the possibilities of evil since the days of Adam and Cain, and continues to do so until the end. And who is that? 'Since by man came death, by man also comes the resurrection of the dead' (1 Cor. 15.21). If the Lord of history is the crucified lamb, ascended to the right hand of the Father while still bearing the marks of his immolation, then the end of history, however it is signified and anticipated by the catastrophic and redemptive acts and events which take place in it, will be realized by his return in glory. Just as his resurrection is the only fully eschatological event taking place within the realm of time, so his return will complete the recapitulation of Adam's story begun in his conception in the womb of the virgin. We should not speculate further about the form this return will take. Millenarianism in its various forms is an improper attempt to plan the details of the heavenly city (and we know the effect that town planning too often achieves) beyond the simple promise contained in Jesus' resurrection and ascension.

It is, accordingly, not so much the details but the implications of Jesus' return in glory that we must consider. (1) As we have seen, the point of the concept of the Antichrist is that it indicates the heart of eschatological rebellion: to take to oneself the pretension to rule history in place of the one who rules only as the crucified. (I am tempted to say that it includes aspects of modern politics in almost every form, democratic and absolutist alike.) (2) History is the first object of eschatology, which means that we are concerned in it not primarily with leaving time and space to be in some way taken into God's eternity, but with the eternal God's perfecting and trans-forming of time and history. The vision and promise is of a new heaven and a new earth. Just as the eternal Son moves into the midst of time to become incarnate, so he will move into it to perfect his finished work.[6] (3) But history, the living out through time of human lives in their various churchly, social and political orders, takes place in a more than merely historical context, for the theatre of history and of God's glory is the whole created world, the material world on which we feed, which we inhabit, and to which on death we return, in expectation of the universal resurrection of the dead. The human flesh of Jesus, his resurrection, the fact that water, bread and wine are intrinsic features of the church's worship, together show that God's redemptive and eschatological action by the Spirit through Jesus involves all the structures of created reality. Romans 8 is the somewhat overused charter of ecologically conscious theology, but we must remember that it is the chapter of his letter in which Paul spells out the Spirit's place in the realization of God's justifying action. Let us follow through aspects of the pneumatological logic of this chapter.

The promise God made to Abraham, on which the meaning of history depends, has been fulfilled. God's justice, his justifying action, is that by the life, death and resurrection of Jesus, all significant human groupings, Jews first and then Gentiles, have been together brought into the community of praise. The Spirit of the one who raised Jesus from the dead is truly present to the community to achieve the faith and hope that now characterize their lives, so that they must henceforward bear themselves in a manner appropriate to those who live in the realm of life and freedom, and not of fear, slavery and death. The suffering and endurance this entails is worthwhile because of the expectation of universal salvation: that 'the creation itself will be liberated from its bondage to decay and brought into the glorious freedom of the children of God' (Rom. 8.21). The suffering, therefore, that is the mark of all the created order, is not, eschatologically understood, a foretaste of death, but, rather like the suffering of a woman about to give birth, a promise and foretaste of life. Through the Spirit the travails of the world are enabling it to become truly the theatre of God's glory.

I believe that we should interpret this by saying that the end – the *telos* to which it moves – of the history of the creation is life and not death. The Spirit who hovered over the face of the waters of creation and raised Jesus from the tomb is indeed the bearer of eschatological life. In other words, the final word on the creation as a whole, human and nonhuman alike, is that

---

[6] Notice the combination of incarnational and eschatological language in Rev. 21. 1–4: God *has* his 'dwelling among men' and *will* 'wipe away all tears from their eyes'.

which will be spoken by the crucified Lord on his return. Both the human historical and political story and that of the world, the stage on which the drama is played out, will take their final meaning from the one who entered history by taking to himself the dust of the earth from which the whole human race is constituted by the creator Spirit. The incarnate Lord is the one in whom is bound up the destiny of man and nature alike by virtue of the fact that he assumed flesh, the human being that is at once material and spiritual in its constitution. The end, therefore, is life, whatever form of life that entails.

> Then the end will come, when he hands over the kingdom to God the Father after he has destroyed all dominion and authority and power. For he must reign until he has put all his enemies under his feet. The last enemy to be destroyed is death. (1 Cor. 15.24–6)

Does the 'logic' of the drama – the fact that some of its characters apparently choose that their stories end in rebellion and evil – mean that some may finally exclude themselves? Here, there is one dogmatic certainty, and that is the one eschatological event of which we can be confident, the return of Christ in glory. Whether his universally representative death necessarily hurries every human being to redemption is something that is endlessly debated and cannot be decided; so that this one reality is what we must hold to, and work out its bearing on life in the present. One celebrated book of over half a century ago ended with the subsequently much quoted words, 'Hold to Christ, and for the rest be totally uncommitted', and that is especially the case with eschatology.[7] All speculation beyond that takes attention away from the point that it is its bearing on the present that is a primary interest of biblical eschatology: its capacity to ground the faith, hope and love that are the imperatives that follow from the promise.

In tension with that, therefore, and as part of its implication, we must place a second definitive reality, and it is one also supplied by the doctrine of the Spirit: 'I, John . . . was on the island of Patmos because of the word of God and the testimony of Jesus. On the Lord's Day I was in the Spirit . . .' (Rev. 1.9–10). Being in the Spirit means, perhaps most obviously but also most dangerously, being in an inspired state – dangerously, because we are always in danger of mistaking the Spirit of God for a force or an experience

---

[7] Herbert Butterfield, *Christianity and History* (London: Bell, 1949), p. 146.

of some kind. But I think that John means much more than that. It is the reference to the Lord's Day that is significant, for it refers to worship, and it is through sharing mysteriously in the worship of his separated fellow-Christians that John is enabled also to share the worship of heaven and the vision of what is both happening now and is going to happen at the end. The Holy Spirit reveals to the seer at once the present and the future as it shapes the present, but only as a function of the communion of the church in which he is enabled to share. This experience of worship may scarcely appear to be identical with what goes on in such local churches as we may know. And yet there is something in it to teach us about the fact that worship is an eschatological reality, a way of sharing divine eternity. John's book is, to be sure, the most extraordinary in the Bible; and yet it is also a consciously literary work, drawing on a stock of language which the author had received in large part from the Old Testament scriptures.[8] Just as was the case with the language of Genesis, with which this book began, so here: an inherited stock of words is used, this time to characterize not a primal so much as an eschatological reality.

In this light, the observation with which to conclude our treatment of the Spirit's eschatological action is that he teaches us to find perfection in the ordinary and power in weakness. That is the way things are transformed this side of the end. The churches to which John wrote were numerically and politically far less significant than the churches we know, and yet it is their worship and faithful witness which, he believed, challenged the dominion of the demonic powers. These, rather than the great political events whose protagonists believe are the real motors of history, are the means by which the end is anticipated. That is as difficult to believe as it is to believe that a crucified man will one day return to sum up all things, things in heaven and things on earth. But, as history shows again and again, the truth of a claim is by no means to be assessed in the light of its apparent credibility. Only time – and the end! – will tell. In the meantime, much depends also upon the backing a claim may have, the reasons given for believing it. In this case, they depend on the doctrine of the triune God, to which we now turn.

---

[8] The suppositions that this book is both a consummate literary product which draws on a long tradition of language and imagery and the product of some kind of ecstatic experience are by no means in conflict with one another. The processes of deep learning and inspiration involved are wonderfully illustrated by J. Livingston Lowes, *The Road to Xanadu* (Boston and New York: Houghton Mifflin, 1927).

Conclusion

Chapter 10

The Triune God of Christian Confession

§36. Experience Redeemed

In 1830, Friedrich Schleiermacher published the final edition of *The Christian Faith*, and set the scene for most Protestant, and some Catholic, theology ever since.[1] The form of the book was somewhat similar to this one: one part devoted to foundations, another to christology, and another to the Spirit and the church. Schleiermacher's approach was from experience: from a felt experience of God which he held to be above reason, suprarational, to the rational expression of the experience, which was theology. The weakness, as I would like to suggest, lay largely in the conception of experience as being above reason and therefore essentially opaque rather than in an appeal to experience as such. Barth was thus right to reject the approach, as he famously did, setting the scene for his century's revolt against its predecessor. He rejected both the overgeneral concept of experience and Schleiermacher's refusal of the rationality of theology. For him, by contrast, theology is a rational art, because 'where the Creed is uttered and confessed, knowledge should be, is meant to be, created'.[2] Theology's object is not irrational or suprarational but rational in the sense that its basis is to be found in the truth of God both in himself and in his making himself known in the world.

[1] F. D. E. Schleiermacher, *The Christian Faith*, translated by H. R. Mackintosh and J. S. Stewart (Edinburgh: T. & T. Clark, 1928).
[2] Karl Barth, *Dogmatics in Outline*, translated by G. T. Thomson (London: SCM Press, 1949), p. 23.

Things look rather different, therefore, if we consider not experience in general but experience of things in their particularity. That is to say, there is not experience *simpliciter*, or even that indefinable oddity called religious experience, but experience of – let us say – the song of a bird, the pain of an injury or the love of another human being. The pit into which Schleiermacher fell was to accept the dogma canonized by Immanuel Kant that we do not experience things; rather, we shape the appearances of things into rational patterns which may or may not be true to reality. Even more insistent was Kant that there is nothing that can be called the knowledge of God, only an oblique positing of his existence on the basis of certain moral realities. The result was that the concept of experience that Schleiermacher developed in order to climb out of the pit dug by his enlightened predecessor was internal rather than external, a kind of inward human dynamic through which God was given, rather than the objective self-giving of God to and within the world.

Christianly speaking, God was for Schleiermacher given in a basically threefold way. He followed tradition in shaping his thought to the pattern of the three articles of the creed, as has been the way of this book. The creed affirms belief in God the Father, maker of heaven and earth, Jesus Christ, the Son of God, the saviour, and God the Spirit, the Lord and giver of life, who, among other things, also inspires the prophets and empowers the church. The three phases of *The Christian Faith* were understood by Schleiermacher to represent versions of this traditional pattern, and in the famous conclusion to his great work[3] he set out to draw such implications as he could for his doctrine of God from the threefold pattern of the previous developments. But because his God was a God *filtered through* experience rather than *given to* experience, he could go no further than to conclude that although God appears to us in three masks, it is impossible to say any more. He acknowledges, then, that his concept of God is Sabellian, by which is meant generally and for our purposes three manifestations of an underlying God who may or may not be the same in his inner being as he is in experience. Schleiermacher thus rejected the traditional teaching of the church that God is triune both in his action and in his eternal divine or 'inner' being.

We shall return later to the question of why it is important to say more than Schleiermacher was able to, but let us first complete the discussion of experience. There is much to be said for the Kantian view. We know that

---

[3] Conclusion, not appendix, as is often charged.

we often fail to see things rightly, and that indeed, we know things and people only through the concepts and language which our minds supply for the purpose of describing or characterizing our experience of the world. However, there are theological objections to such a position if it is made into the whole story, and effectively to deny that our experience in any way gives us access to the real world. The first objection is that it underplays the doctrine of creation, which assures us that at least the basis of our experience is reliable, because God has set the world on a sure foundation. Second – and this is the same point from a different perspective – Schleiermacher's is essentially a theology of the fallen intellect; or rather, it supposes that human thinkers are so stuck within their heads that the world – or God – is unable to break through them to shape and change the way they see things. A theology of experience more centred on particularities would want to say against this that although we are fallen creatures, and certainly often do fail to know things as they are, our experience can yet be and is from time to time redeemed.

Nowhere is this almost Manichaean restrictiveness more evident than in Schleiermacher's theology of the Spirit. It is not much of an exaggeration to say that for him the Holy Spirit is conceived to be little more than the *esprit de corps* of the church. To limit the action of the Spirit to the church is one of the most dangerous steps a theology can take, for it both falsely increases expectations of the institution and underplays the part the Spirit is conceived to play in the created world as a whole. Now it is indeed the case that it is in relation to the believer and the church that we understand the Spirit's primary role, as converting, gathering and sanctifying those who constitute the community of worship and faith. The biblical promise is that through the Spirit we who have cut ourselves off from our maker may come to know him as, in Calvin's term, an indulgent Father. That is to say, the Spirit's most recognizable function is to create reconciliation between alienated parties and at the same time to give knowledge of God to fallen human beings. That knowledge, it must be emphasized, is not primarily propositional or factual knowledge, but personal knowledge, like the knowledge we have of someone we love. The Spirit creates access to the Father through Jesus Christ (Eph. 2.18), and in its turn this takes shape in a new apprehension of what it is to be a human being in God's world.

The Spirit is in this regard the Spirit of *the* truth which is Jesus Christ, 'in whom are hidden all the treasures of wisdom and knowledge' (Col. 2.3). But that is precisely why we may not limit the Spirit's action to those who acknowledge it. Christ is, it will be remembered, the mediator of the whole creation, and we must spell out some of the implications of this for a broader conception of the Spirit than one restricted to the believer and the church. It is here that we again encounter the weakness of the Kantian theory of experience on which Schleiermacher depended. Wherever there is truth, goodness and beauty; wherever things turn out to be what they are created to be, there is to be experienced the work of the perfecting Spirit, giving access to the created world. If the Spirit is indeed the one who, through Christ, enables things truly to be themselves, then there is no justification in limiting the sphere of his action. Even fallen agents in a fallen world will be enabled to experience what is truly there, despite all the sin and error which impedes knowledge, and even after making all due allowance for the limitations of created human capacity. Otherwise, we are plunged into a Manichaean vision according to which the created world is not merely fallen but intrinsically incapable of truth and goodness.[4]

There is, as the great Bishop Berkeley realized, a direct link between scepticism in general and theological scepticism, the two feeding and reinforcing one another. Historically speaking, it was the doctrine of creation which enabled the emergence of science, which requires for its very possibility a conviction that the material world is real and meaningful: *experienceable*, at least within certain limits, as it truly is. The way in which the philosophical theorists of early modern science developed their account, however, generated a narrowness which effectively undermined the very foundation on which science rests. In time, this gave rise to the reaction known as postmodernism, which in its extreme form denies to even the once impregnably respectable sciences the right to claim knowledge. This is further evidence that loss of the theological underpinning of human thought and culture leads it finally into a spiral of scepticism. Much postmodernism is a Manichaean doctrine of the meaninglessness of the creation rather than a realistic view of a fallen creation which is yet not immune to the Spirit's inbreaking.

The theology of the Spirit, therefore, gives us reason to believe that there can be true knowledge both of the way things really are and of the being of the God who made them. This is not simply, however, to throw theology at the world's problems but to argue that in its light we simply are able to make better sense of the richness of our experience and the reality of its basis,

---

[4] In that regard, we should not expect Christian faith and scientific truth – and that does not mean all the statements made by scientists – to be finally in conflict with one another.

despite all the doubts and problems, than the reductionist and sceptical theories that have dominated the history of recent centuries. We require, therefore, a rehabilitated concept of experience, one according to which we are not simply presented with a show of appearances, but live within the realities that encompass our being in such a way that we may know them and their creator, partially and according to the limits of our faculties and their being, but really none the less. The fundamental Christian claim in this regard is that God in Christ gives himself to be experienced in such a way that knowledge not simply of a human figure is granted, but through him knowledge of God as he is in himself.

This can be put more theologically. In the Christian faith we are concerned with the gospel, which is God's transforming historical act in Christ, realized in the present through the Spirit. In it God comes alongside the human race in mercy and judgement, bringing reconciliation and the godly repentance that shapes human being away from the realm of death and to the promise of life renewed in hope of final perfection. If this is truly the action of God, then we are bound to ask: what is its basis? Is it simply an experience about which we can ask nothing more? If Schleiermacher is right, God in his inner being may be, for all that we know, radically different from the God we meet in experience. In that case, we cannot rely on the gospel, for our experience may be finally deceptive. And this is not simply a case of our specifically Christian experience, for we can have no confidence either in the structures of our world or the course of our history. Only if God is unconditionally the Lord of the world, life and history are we able to engage in the day to day tasks of life in the confidence that they are worthwhile. To put it at its extreme, if there is no final basis for things in the being of God, we are in the position of the character in Dostoyevsky for whom the choice between life and suicide was a matter of absolute indifference. More restrainedly, we can say that only if our particular experiences are grounded in the universal doctrine of God's good creation are we likely to be able to escape the perils of relativism and subjectivism.

§37. 'Economic' and 'Immanent' Trinities

One of the reasons for the indifference, if not outright hostility, of many moderns to the doctrine of the Trinity is that it has often appeared not to work like this at all: it has appeared to have no point other than a fruitless attempt to reconcile apparently contradictory numbers. The nine foregoing chapters of this book have been designed to refute this practically in an account of divine action in the world conceived in thoroughgoing trinitarian terms. First, attention centred on the work of God the Father, who in his love wills that there be both for its own sake and for his glory a reality other than he. Creation is the action of God the Father, through the Son and in the Spirit: made through the Son and directed to its perfection by the Holy Spirit who refers it back to the Father through the Son.

A similar pattern was discerned in the second main part of the book, its treatment of salvation. Here, in the centre is the act of God the Son becoming incarnate and living, suffering, dying, being raised, and finally ascending to the Father in promise of final return to sum up all things in himself. This also, however, was conceived to be the act of the Father, who sends – sacrificially 'gives up' – his Son and to whose work the incarnate Lord freely devotes himself. He is the divine Son, eternally one with the Father and yet also become human, being enabled to become so and remain truly so by the action of the Spirit through whom Jesus refers his being and action to their source in God his Father.

In the third part of the book we were concerned with human acceptance and appropriation of the work of Jesus Christ and finally with its eschatological completion. Here the light falls especially on the work of the Spirit who shapes the church and the life of its members. Once again, however, the central agent cannot be abstracted from the work of the other two persons. The Spirit never works independently of the Son, for it is the latter to whom he is sent to bear witness. 'By the Spirit through the Son' is the necessary specification of all his action. But, as we have seen, the Son's work *is* that of the Father, so that in referring things through the Son the Spirit is, by that very action, referring them to the Father, from whom and to whom are all things.

In this development as a whole a theology of what is called the economic Trinity, the Trinity in act, has been formulated. The word 'economy' was a theological coining long before it came to be reduced to the dreary concern with money, although sometimes also politics, of our modern world. The underlying Greek suggests the running of a household and metaphorically refers to the way in which God directs his world, from its creation to its final consummation. The theology of the economic Trinity sketched in chapters 1–9 provides an account of the trinitarian way in which God creates, shapes and perfects his creation in and through time.

The definitive difference between the account so far developed and that of Schleiermacher is in its concept of mediation: of the way in which God acts and is recognized as acting. For the latter mediation was through experience, and what emerged was an essentially unitary and unknown God whose action happened – so far as it can be experienced – to be differentiated in a threefold way. The account of mediation developed in chapters 1–9 similarly speaks of one God, the Father, but one this time whose action is mediated in a twofold way, by his Son and Spirit, not *through* experience but *as they are* experienced. This might appear to be what the tradition calls subordinationist, and is one of the two dangers to which trinitarian theology is liable: suggesting that only the Father is truly God, and the Son and the Spirit are in some way less divine than he, subordinate realities. In the account, there is clearly an element of what can be called economic subordination, for in the economy the Son and the Spirit are sent to do the Father's work. But does it follow that there must be an essential subordination*ism* – a subordination in the eternal being of God; that because in the patterns of divine action one does the will of another, it follows that he is less truly God than the Father?

Two considerations will show that a negative answer must be given. The first is that because the Son and the Spirit are God in action; because they do the work of God in the world, then they are truly and fully God, as truly so as is God the Father. Irenaeus' analogy is with the hands: when our hands do something, we ourselves do it. So, when the Son and the Spirit act in time and history, their acts are the acts of God the Father performed through them. The contribution of the Fourth Gospel to this topic is that John sets out this complicated matter so clearly. Jesus acts, truly and autonomously of himself: yet what he does is the work of the Father, so that those who see him have seen the Father. There is a unity of action and of revelation: what he does, the Father does; and what he does is the revelation, the making known, of his Father, in such a way that through him human beings may themselves share something of his filial relation to God. The position of the Letter to the Ephesians is similar, and provides a model characterization of action trinitarianly conceived: 'Through him [Christ] we both [Jew and Gentile] have access in one Spirit to the Father' (Eph. 2.18).

The second consideration can also be illustrated from John's Gospel, and can be summarized in Barth's observation, already used in an earlier chapter, that it is as truly godlike to be humble as it is to be exalted.[5] When Jesus does

---

[5] See above, p.116.

the work of his Father and when he performs the apparently menial task of washing his disciples' feet he is not only setting a model for human action,[6] but showing what kind of divine being he is: one who is divine in not grasping at divinity. That is why christology is so important, for by insisting that it is the eternal Son of God who became man, it reveals to us something of the heart of the godhead, that, again in Barth's way of putting it, there is in God both superordination and subordination, both command and obedience.[7] It is in his very difference from God the Father that the Son is divine: God in a distinct way of being God.

Once the christology is in place, an equivalent argument for the divinity of the Spirit provides less difficulty. If the Son is subordinate in being to the Father, it is indeed likely to follow that the Spirit is somewhat lower still in the chain of being, as a number of theologians were driven to think in the early centuries. If, however, his equal but different way of being God is accepted, it becomes easy to argue that the Spirit, by virtue of the kinds of things that he does, is also plainly divine. The basis for this is again most clearly seen in John's Gospel. The promise of 'another paraclete' ranges the action of the Spirit alongside that of Jesus: of the same divine status, but different in mode of activity, for he mediates – the physically absent because ascended – Jesus and thus brings men and women to the Father.[8] The early case for the equal divinity of the Spirit depended heavily on the claim that because he makes holy, and because only God can make holy, it must be the case that he too is divine. The case made in this book is for a broader conception, beginning with the mediation of creation – certainly something found in the tradition, in, for example Calvin – but stressing also the eschatological action of perfecting through the Son the created order in all the dimensions of its being, the human first and then the non-human along with it.

What is significant about the New Testament way of putting these matters is that the writers clearly imply the divine status of both the Son and the Spirit and yet there is no sense of crisis. They were in no doubt that

[6] And would that those in positions of 'leadership' in the church had better taken that to heart over the ages.

[7] Karl Barth, Church Dogmatics, translation edited by G. W. Bromiley and T. F. Torrance (Edinburgh: T. & T. Clark, 1957–75), vol. 4/1, pp. 202–3.

[8] Jn. 14.25–6, 16.7–11. Notice the point made in the latter passage: it is to 'the advantage' of the disciples that Jesus go away in order that the Spirit should come.

their God was the God of Old Testament confession, with its strong assertion of divine unity, 'The Lord your God is one God...' (Dt. 6.4). Of this, two things must be said. The first is that the Old Testament writers' insistence on the unity of God was in no way inconsistent with their attribution to him of a wide range of differentiation in his action. God is not a blank unity, but a richly diverse personal agent whose works in the created world are mediated by his word, his wisdom, his glory, his name, his Spirit. The second is that Deuteronomy's insistence on divine unity is in one of the earliest developments in the New Testament glossed and interpreted christologically. As we saw in chapter 5 above, Paul quotes Deuteronomy 6.4 in 1 Corinthians 8.4, and then glosses it in verse 6: 'yet for us there is but one God, the Father, from whom all things came and for whom we live; and there is but one Lord, Jesus Christ, through whom all things came, and through whom we live.' All things are from and to the Father and through the Son. Similarly, and again with somewhat less difficulty, it is impossible to read the Bible without gaining a sense that when the Spirit does something, it is being done by God. The Spirit is the personal power and energy of God in action.

The real problems are not biblical but philosophical, and emerged when all this moved into the Greek world with its far more abstract and restrictive conception of divine unity and its insistence that the church clarify what it means to worship a God so conceived. The New Testament did not have a doctrine of the Trinity as such, though, as we have seen, it has a trinitarian conception of mediation. The challenge to the first centuries of Christian theology – and it is no different from the challenge we face, except that we have the advantage of centuries of debate and exposition – was to answer the question about the identity of the God who made his presence felt in the threefold way we have described. *Who* is the God whom the church worshipped through the Son and in the Spirit? And here one central consideration differentiates the biblical faith from that of the Greek world in which it hammered out its concepts. Disillusioned with the mythological dress in which their theology had come down to them, with competing and quarrelsome deities little more than projections of human characteristics and natural forces, the Greek philosophers had sought for an impersonal cosmic principle as the basis of their world. Corresponding to their question of *what* divine principle, the Christian question was rather *who*? Who is the personal deity who creates, reconciles and sanctifies in the way in which their experience assured them that he did? The doctrine of the Trinity proper is an attempt to answer that question, but it is at the same time an answer to the quite proper Greek question of *what kind of God* it is with whom we have to do.

We are now in a position to answer the question with which this section began. Is there any point in asking about an eternal or immanent Trinity, in some way distinct from the God made known in the economy? The qualification, 'in some way' distinct is important, because there have been in history treatments of the immanent Trinity which appear to float free from the God who becomes present to history in his Son and Spirit. The complaints about this approach are so well known that I shall not discuss them here, except to say that they have generated a number of books, from Catholic and Protestant perspectives alike, which effectively or explicitly deny the need to move beyond the economy.[9] We shall come to the question of 'need' later, but begin with reasons why we should think it possible to do so at all.

The answer lies in the nature of the doctrine of the economic Trinity which has been presented from the beginning of the book. If the Son and the Spirit *are*, as his two hands, God the Father in action, then they are the *eternal* God present to the world. The reason is that they are not manifestations of a possibly different deity filtered through human experience; they are rather God in his action given, by God himself, to the communally mediated experience, centred on worship, of those whom he has called. This is the eternal God in action, and, because that is so, we are bound to distinguish between the action and the agent, at least to the extent of answering the question of who it is who so acts in our time. To say, in effect, that he just is the one who acts in our time is to evade the implications of the word 'eternal', simply because we need to be responsible for the implications of our claims, especially the claim of the doctrine of creation that it is one thing to be God, another to be the world. If we can give no answer to the question of the identity of this supposedly eternal God, are we right to make the kind of claims that we do in the first place for his action?

---

[9] For recent unsatisfactory attempts, Catholic and Protestant respectively, to minimize or abolish the doctrine of the immanent Trinity, see Catherine Mowry LaCugna, *God for Us. The Trinity and Christian Life* (New York, HarperCollins, 1991) and Ted Peters, *God as Trinity. Relationality and Temporality in Divine Life* (Louisville, KY: Westminster/John Knox Press, 1993).

That is not to say that we should speculate about the 'inner being' of God in any way that takes us away from the implications of his action. The point of the doctrine of the immanent Trinity is to provide a ground for the theology of the economy, but to go no further than is licensed by his revelation. Once it becomes a game of, for example, seeking in some way or other to demonstrate, apart from the unity of action of the one God, how one and three may be reconciled, there lies irrelevance. It is not a matter of mathematics, but of the particular personal being of the one God who makes himself known in the way that he does.

In this regard the Eastern Fathers were surprisingly agnostic, and we should begin by following their example. The fact that Jesus' historical identity, from beginning to end, is determined by his relation to his Father gives reason to conclude that he is eternally the Son of an eternal Father, sent in time to recreate the fallen world, but coming from, returning to and remaining intrinsic to the being of the eternal God. The way this was expressed conceptually was that the Son was 'eternally begotten' by the Father, the 'eternally' making it clear that the relationship is analogous to the relation between a human father and son in only the most limited way. It is not a projection from human biology but comes from the personal relation between Jesus of Nazareth and his Father manifested in the course of the incarnation. Similarly, seeking to find a way of characterizing the relation of the Spirit to the Father which accounted for the difference of economic patterning – and did not make the Spirit into a second Son – the Fathers took from the fourth Gospel the notion of 'proceeding'. To say that the Spirit 'proceeds from' the Father implies that his relation to the Father is distinctly, yet mysteriously, different from the Son's. Together, these two concepts provide a way of distinguishing conceptually two ways of being in eternal relation to God the Father, the source and principle of deity. The Son is eternally begotten; the Spirit proceeds, and is therefore in God in a different way.

In the case of the Spirit, however, the early theologians might profitably have gone a little further. We have seen throughout this book that there is reason to suggest that the Spirit's work is best considered to be eschatological: as perfecting that which was created in the beginning, in the many and various particular ways in which that can take place, both ordinary and extraordinary. Suppose that we were to infer from this the suggestion that in eternity the Spirit is the one who similarly perfects the being of God, so as first to enable the relation between the Father and the Son to be properly

described as one of love; and second to provide the basis for God's movement out into the world in his Son to create and to redeem. This would be
in some way similar to Augustine's characterization of the Spirit as the bond
of love between the Father and the Son, but with a correction of its
tendency to turn the deity into an eternal inward turning circle rather
than a being from eternity directed outwards to the other.

To give such an account of the being of God is to show that the Son and
the Spirit are as essential as the Father to the being of God. The economic or
functional subordination suggested by the two hands imagery – the inescapable implication of the biblical story that the Son obeys and the Spirit is sent
– does not entail a correspondingly subordinationist theology, because Son
and Spirit are, as obedient and sent, truly God. The Father may be, in the
traditional language, the fount of the Trinity, but the Son and the Spirit are
equally constitutive of the eternal being of the one God. This further implies
that God is not a monad – God is not lonely, as some of the early
theologians said – because communion is intrinsic to his being. If we ask
how three can be one, the answer is that *this* God is one only by virtue of
the way in which Father, Son and Spirit mutually and reciprocally give to
and receive from each other everything that they are. The Cappadocian
Fathers coined the concept of *perichoresis* to characterize this unique form of
being. God *is* 'a sort of continuous and indivisible community' says the letter
usually attributed to Basil of Caesarea. The writer realizes that he is here
trying to describe a new concept of what it is to be. It is, he says, 'a new and
paradoxical conception of united separation and separated unity'.[10] God is
only what he is as three persons whose being is so closely bound up with
one another that they together constitute one God.

On this account, the being of God is describable as love, but love of a
particular kind. To say that God is love means, first, that God is constituted,
made up without remainder, of a personal structure of giving and receiving.
Internally, God is a fellowship of *persons* whose orientation is entirely to the
other. The notion of there being three persons in God is problematic for us,
because we think that person means individual in the modern sense of one
whose being is defined *over against*, even in opposition to, other individuals.
(Hence, of course, the essentially competitive ideology of much modern
social order.) The trinitarian notion of person does incorporate one aspect of
the notion of individuality, because it holds that each person is unique and

---

[10] Basil of Caesarea, *Letters* 38, 4.

irreplaceable. The Father is not the Son, the Son is not the Spirit, and all three of them are essential to God's being as God. On the other hand, these three are, while distinct from one another, not in competition, as in modern individualism, but entirely for and from one another. There is accordingly an orientation to the other within the eternal structure of God's being. That is our first account of what it means to say that God is love.

The second is that the orientation of this God, his inner drive, we might say, is not to remain content with his eternal ordering as eternal love, but to move outwards to create a world which he loves and wishes to bring into relation with himself. The 'immanent' eternal orientation to the other is the basis of God's creation, reconciliation and redemption of the other reality that is his world. At this point we come to one of the chief reasons for developing a doctrine of the immanent Trinity. To say that God is already, and eternally, an order of love prevents us from having to say that it is in some way necessary for God to create a world, to have another being alongside himself without which he is not truly himself. We need to be able to say that God could remain content with his eternal being, and did not have to create a world. Hypotheticals, as we have seen, are generally to be avoided in theology, because we are in it concerned with what God has done, is doing, and will do. Yet sometimes they are necessary if we are to understand the consequences of denying a central doctrine. There are two reasons for affirming that God did not need to create the world. The first concerns God's integrity as God. A doctrine of divine sovereignty and glory maintains the utter self-sufficiency of God's being, without which he could not be worshipped as truly God. A God who has to have a world around him is a miserable godlet, a pagan projection, and not the omnipotent God of Christian confession.

The second reason is equal and opposite. The independence of God's being, his aseity – his being of and from himself – is also necessary for the integrity of the world, 'It is only the heathen gods envy man.'[11] A sovereign God is able to allow the world to be itself, and not simply a function of his being, a 'clone' or 'puppet' as it is fashionably expressed. Indeed, as we have seen, that is precisely the function of the doctrine of the two hands of God, the first establishing God's creative and saving relation to that which is not God and the second representing his concern to enable it to be truly itself. It is a terrible burden for the world to be needed by God, to have to look, so

[11] Barth, *Church Dogmatics*, 3/2, p. 87.

to speak, over its shoulder all the time rather than simply being itself. This does not at all contradict the fact that the world is only truly itself when it seeks to give glory to God, for that is what gives it its final integrity. It is rather that the glory should be given gladly and gratefully simply because God is good.

§38. The Difference the Trinity Makes

During the course of this book, especially in the first three chapters, a number of what are called the attributes of God, the ways in which God is God, have been introduced. One way of seeing the point of the doctrine of the immanent Trinity is to realize that understanding the attributes trinitarianly leads to a uniquely different way of conceiving God's being. The Trinity founds the development of a unique doctrine of God. How do the attributes fare under the new regime? The outcome can be characterized in a number of ways.

The first thing that happens is that different attributes come to the fore from what might be our normal expectations. Prominent among the attributes we have encountered has been that of the divine mercy, which would rarely appear high up the list of the attributes in a 'natural' account of the divine, whether that of Greek and Roman antiquity or the philosophical theology which succeeded it and continues to form the basis of much modern discussion of the philosophy of religion. At the heart of the difference is God's personality or personal character, something else with which philosophical theology, with its preference for abstract description of the deity, is uncomfortable. If, however, God's being is, as we have seen, without remainder personal, because to be God is to be three persons in communion, then the personal attributes must be the prior, the abstract and philosophical secondary.[12] For the triune God, mercy is not an occasional but an intrinsic quality, because it is the outworking of the way in which God is eternally love. Mercy is the outworking in fallen time and history of the action of a God for whom love of the other is central to his being.

---

[12] For a fine discussion of this question, see Christoph Schwöbel, *God, Action and Revelation* (Kampen, The Netherlands: Kok Pharos, 1992), chapter 2. A classical treatment of God's being and attributes is to be found in Barth, *Church Dogmatics* 2/1, pp. 257–677.

The second feature of the change is that the more abstract and philosophical attributes have their meaning shaped by personal trinitarian categories. An interesting test case here are those twin negatives, immutability and impassibility. As we have seen, we do need to be able to affirm that God is immutable, in the respect that his being is ontologically secure, so that his promises can be relied on. But the tradition has sometimes turned this into something more abstract and impersonal. What is immutability trinitarianly construed? Immanently speaking, God cannot but be love; economically speaking, he will not but see to it that his purposes for the perfection of the creation come to be fulfilled. Impassibility, as we have seen, is more problematic, for at the heart of the economic action of the triune God is the Father's sending of the eternal Son to suffer and die on the cross. As we have also seen, however, it does not follow that the suffering of the cross can be used to generate a doctrine of general divine passibility. Rather, we must say that God's historical action in the Son's suffering demonstrates that he is not 'passive' in face of history. Rather the cross is the Father's relentless action in shaping history to his reconciling will.

And what of the 'omni-s'? In what sense is God all-powerful, all-knowing and all-present? The same kind of arguments apply. One who can direct history through an incarnation leading to a cross is one to whose power no limits can be set. This, however, is omnipotence not abstractly conceived, but personal and ordered to the needs of its object. Again, however, not all of the cases are so easily described. The question of divine knowledge cannot be decided in a sentence or two, but only its form can be stated here. Many are the disputes which have been aroused by worries about whether, and in what respect, God, being outside and the creator of time, can know what we call the future. They do not admit satisfactory and final answers. Trinitarianly we can but concentrate on what we are shown, and that is that Jesus Christ, being the incarnate wisdom of God the Father, personally embodies the Father's 'foreknowledge' of and provision for the redemption of all things. Omnipresence is less of a problem, for the one who can so differentiate his action as to be present to the world in Jesus Christ must also be able to be present more generally to everything that he has created and upholds, to be everywhere while retaining his difference from created things. (Recall here the discussion of providence in chapter 2 above.)

The third thing that happens to the attributes is that a long-reigning distinction is called into question, or at least modified. This is that which distinguished between two classes of attributes, those which are absolute or intrinsic – those which characterize God's being absolutely, which God must have if he is to be God – and the relative attributes, those which God has by virtue of there being a creation to relate to. On a trinitarian account, this distinction must be qualified, for in one respect there are no absolute attributes, in so far as the term suggests attributes that are non-relational. All God's characteristics are what they are because they are functions of the relations of Father, Son and Spirit in eternity. They are what they are because God is eternally personal love, the love that gives to and receives from the other. It follows that the characteristics that God displays in relation to the world are rooted in, are indeed expressions 'outward', of what the Father, Son and Spirit are immanently in their relations to one another. That is why Barth is right in arguing that God's eternity cannot be mere timelessness nor his infinity the mere negation of space.[13] In some way or other – and here we must be agnostic about the precise connotations of the concepts – God's eternity and infinity are revealed in his capacity to become temporal and finite in Jesus of Nazareth; indeed, in his capacity to create the world of time and space which is the object of his providential love.

This third feature can be illustrated by reference to another attribute which is prominent in scripture and which undoubtedly does characterize God's immanent being and economic action alike. If Rudolf Otto's famous contention is right – and it is a big 'if' – that at the centre of human religiousness is a sense of the holiness of God, then all religions are in some way concerned with the holy. However, the holiness of the triune God is not that of Otto's famous description of the holy as the fearful and fascinating mystery. It is rather oriented to otherness, the otherness which is intrinsic to the being of God as Father, Son and Holy Spirit in all their relatedness-in-distinction. This ontology of otherness gives rise in its turn, as we have seen in earlier chapters, to a theology of a created order that is other than God, and an account of human being centred on the otherness in relation of man and woman. In the economy of salvation it also founds the election of Israel and the church as the holy people of God, called to be other than the nations for the sake of the nations. Just as God is different both from the world and from the other gods, so his concern is to make holy those whom he creates in his image.

[13] Barth, *Church Dogmatics*, 2/1, respectively pp. 608–20, 464–70.

Similar points can be made about the glory of God. God's inner and eternal glory overflows into creation and redemption, in order that his glory should be made known in all the world. God glorifies himself in Jesus, so that his people may glorify him now and for ever. In what sense is glory conceived trinitarianly? For the Fourth Gospel, God glorifies his name in what happens to and with Jesus in the whole movement from incarnation to ascension. The heart of the economy of redemption is the historical series of events in which God the Father glorifies his Son by and through his Spirit. The incarnation of the eternal Word of God – 'and we beheld his glory' (Jn. 1.14) – flows from the eternal triune love of God in response to the sin and evil which would futilely arrest the movement of creation to its perfection. At the centre of human history is the place where God's eternal triune glory is made known in one particular human being, so that it may on the last day fill the whole world.

Glory be to the Father, and to the Son, and to the Holy Spirit.
As it was in the beginning, is now, and ever shall be, world without end, Amen.

General Index

Index of Biblical References

INTERNATIONAL JOURNAL OF SYSTEMATIC THEOLOGY

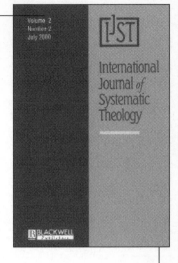

Edited by
COLIN GUNTON, JOHN WEBSTER & RALPH DEL COLLE

Systematic theology is at the leading edge of contemporary academic theology, both in North America and Britain. The discipline, which is concerned with the constructive articulation of the meaning, coherence and implications of Christian claims, has undergone a remarkable transformation in the last two decades, and is now firmly established as a central area of teaching and research.

Until now, no English-language journal has focused on making available high-calibre constructive Christian theology. The *International Journal of Systematic Theology* will be devoted to publishing the best new work in the discipline, and to reviewing major new works of scholarship.

INTERNATIONAL JOURNAL OF SYSTEMATIC THEOLOGY ISSN: 1463-1652. VOLUME 3 (2001) CONTAINS 3 ISSUES.

COWLEY ROAD, OXFORD OX4 1JF, UK
MAIN STREET, MALDEN, MA 02148, USA
INFO@BLACKWELLPUBLISHERS.CO.UK

BLACKWELL *Publishers*

VISIT OUR WEBSITE FOR CONTENTS LISTINGS, ABSTRACTS, SAMPLES, AND TO SUBSCRIBE

W W W . B L A C K W E L L P U B . C O M